The Road to Vietnam

The Road to Vietnam

America, France, Britain, and the First Vietnam War

Pablo de Orellana

I.B. TAURIS

LONDON • NEW YORK • OXFORD • NEW DELHI • SYDNEY

I.B. TAURIS
Bloomsbury Publishing Plc
50 Bedford Square, London, WC1B 3DP, UK
1385 Broadway, New York, NY 10018, USA

BLOOMSBURY, I.B. TAURIS and the I.B. Tauris logo are trademarks of
Bloomsbury Publishing Plc

First published in Great Britain 2020

Cover design by Charlotte James
Cover image: French parachutists, Dien Bien Phu, Vietnam, 1953.
(© Keystone/Hulton Archive/Getty Images)

A catalogue record for this book is available from the British Library.

A catalogue record for this book is available from the Library of Congress.

ISBN: HB: 978-1-7845-3897-2
       ePDF: 978-1-7883-1727-6
       eBook: 978-1-7883-1728-3

Typeset by RefineCatch Limited, Bungay, Suffolk

To find out more about our authors and books visit www.bloomsbury.com
and sign up for our newsletters.

Để dành tặng cho những đứa con chưa chào đời
của tôi và để xua tan mọi mối hận thù.

To my unborn children, against hatred.

He had no more of a notion than any of you what the whole affair's about, and you gave him money and York Harding's books on the East and said, 'Go ahead. Win the East for democracy.' He never saw anything he hadn't heard in a lecture hall, and his writers and lecturers made a fool of him. When he saw a dead body he couldn't even see the wounds. A Red menace, a soldier of democracy.

Graham Greene, *The Quiet American*

Contents

Acknowledgements

The author of this book has incurred enormous intellectual, material, ideational and emotional debts to so many. This project, with research in archives in Paris, Aix-en-Provence, London and Washington, has benefitted from the help of kind academic, intellectual and friendly fellow-travellers, friends, colleagues and mentors without whom it would not have been possible. I am grateful to:

Professor Vivienne Jabri of King's College London, my doctoral supervisor and mentor, who led me in the ways and means of Poststructuralist philosophy, corrected my numerous mistakes and guided me with patience. Perhaps just as importantly, her great conceptual, political and disciplined mind and friendship indulged and furthered my many intellectual fishing trips: from my love for poetry and the arts to the tragedy of identity politics which determine that the Other can be killed. Her intellectual power and rigour have been an inspiration.

Dr Peter Busch, the most patient historian whose critical and practical advice gave legs to this project on the diplomacy of the First Vietnam War. I thank him for the many occasions when he allowed me to bounce ideas off his historical wisdom and imparted advice for archival research. His constructive insistence and expertise of the Vietnam Wars was key to this project and its inclusion of Britain's role in the diplomacy that led to US involvement in Vietnam.

My family has been crucial to making this project possible. My sister Tally de Orellana helped me with her friendship, patience and mirth in this long journey of philosophical and historical research. As sisterly assistant she is responsible for the diagrams and charts in this book. My parents, Gaston Orellana (Dad) and Isabel de Calles (Mum), are responsible for a lifetime of inspiration in the intellectual, artistic and political world. Their intellectual courage as art practitioners, their limitless patience as parents of a son living far from home, their indulgence of my curiosity and endless conversations are in no small way responsible for my work. When I was drafting this book, they hosted me, gave me love, calm space and a view of the sea.

In their kindness, the heavens lent me the help of loving friends that held me when I fell and listened to me rant. Beloved Oxonians, you saved me with dry humour, regular friendship, and far too few unforgotten moments: Jeff, Dwiar, Jojo, Conan, Jean, Brian, Rach, Flora, Dutton, and so many more Catz! After long days at archives Zach cheered Washington summer evenings with whiskey, conversation and hospitality. Moon (蔡敏婕, Cai Minjie in our inadequately tonal tongue) helped with translations from Chinese in Part II, patiently critiqued drafts of my earliest research on Vietnam, gave me years of kindness, 爱, never-ending and enthusiastically stimulating curiosity, and insights in history and culture I never thought I could grasp. Tom, who once with a pencil reinvented a Légionnaire fighting in Vietnam: your friendship and affection are a rock I would despair without. Kiran, I stand in awe of you; with you I travelled in Spanish words to lands unknown. Fey, ratoncita y leoncita, you met me at the archives in Aix and revolutionized the summer of this book's first draft. Diem-Hang guided my very first steps in Vietnam's epic history and showed me the role of poetry, philosophy and intellectualism in that ancient culture. She once told me that just as a lotus flower is so strong that it can grow on mud, Vietnam could grow out of war, hatred and pain.

I must thank all the scholars that I have encountered over the years and with whom I have discussed this project, diplomacy, theory, analysis, sociology and the Vietnam Wars. Profs Richard Parish and Manuele Gragnolati of the University of Oxford guided my first tentative steps in the world of literature during my undergraduate, forever impressing upon me the power of words, letters, constructions, texts across time immemorial and the great challenges of analysing them and doing them justice. As Manuele would say, I learnt to 'focus on the text!'. In my later scholarly life, many great intellectuals corrected my mistakes, encouraged my research, challenged my thinking, and helped me recover when I fell down. I owe them all, across countless workshops and conferences, from Michael Shapiro's exhortation to retrieve the power of text at a workshop in Hawaii to Mark A. Lawrence who many years ago encouraged me to pursue this Vietnam project. My colleagues at King's College London's Department of War Studies, at *StrifeBlog* and *Strife Journal*, kept me thinking, discussed ideas with me and provided so many instances of critical insight, support, practical help and countless long conversations during my doctoral and my postdoctoral life there. I am ashamed not to properly celebrate their great minds and friendship, but their names will always ring true as friends: Jill, Filippo, Joana, Flavia, Thomas, Claire, Bobby and oh so many more: thank you.

Sometimes, encouragement and help also came from unexpected quarters. From beyond the grave Graham Greene excited my curiosity years ago. As I researched this war I found that he was not writing fiction as much as disingenuously disguising and decorating history such that Phuong, Thé, Pyle and Tunning all eventually came back in the pages of this book. My students at

King's, particularly those in my *History of nations, nationalism and theories of the state* course, gave me endless cheer, hope and challenged me with their unrelenting desire to learn and understand. My housemates at the Hornet's Nest, particularly Oliver and Alex, kept me company and conversed with me at ungodly hours. Alex's music and his musical recommendations will forever sound like theory, diplomacy and tragedy in the rice fields of Vietnam. My landlady Geraldine, the only and very last honest landlord in London. Crucially, I must also thank archivists in Paris, Aix-en-Provence, London and Washington who indulged, tolerated or were bent to my unquenchable thirst for more documents to analyse.

This project was made possible, during my doctoral research, by a full grant from the UK Economics and Social Sciences Research Council. Later, during the summer when this book was written, my parents set me free for three months so that I could pursue this project.

Finally, I am grateful to the editors at I.B. Tauris in London, especially Sarvat Hasin and Tomasz Hoskins, who shepherded this project from a proposed historical spin-off from my diplomatic research, through drafts, revisions, reviews, to the volume in your hands.

To all, I sign off as if I were one of our diplomats; not just in form but with sincere gratefulness.

I have the honour to be,

With the highest respect

Madam/Sir,

Your most obedient, humble Servant

Pablo de Orellana

Abbreviations

CCP	Communist Party of China
CIA	Central Intelligence Agency
COMINDO	Comité Interministériel pour les affaires d'Indochine, Interministerial Committee for Indochinese Affairs
DRV	Democratic Republic of Vietnam
ICP	Indochinese Communist Party
KMT	Kuomintang, Nationalist Party of China
OSS	Office of Strategic Services
PRC	People's Republic of China
SEA	Southeast Asia (refers to Departments in the Foreign Office and State Department)
SEAC	Allied Southeast Asia Command (also SACSEA in British archival sources)
Vietminh	Việt Nam Độc Lập Đồng Minh Hội, League for the Independence of Vietnam

Figures

Prelude

Why did the United States become involved in Vietnam? To combat communism, evidently. But just how did a Southeast Asian French colony already devastated by two wars become an existential threat? Films, scholarship, conspiracy theorists, artists and even religious figures have long sought to provide answers to this question, one of the most studied diplomatic and security conundrums of Cold War international history, political science, international relations and statecraft. Students of this nightmarish conflict are quickly introduced to some of its most spectacular figures such as the volume of ordnance dropped on North Vietnam, greater than in all of the Second World War, or the three million Vietnamese and 58,000 Americans that were killed; all for an American defeat that concluded in 1975 with the reunification of Vietnam by the North, a goal Vietnamese rebels had sought since 1944. Students of the conflict quickly reach the realization that the Second Indochina War, or the American War, as it is known in Vietnam, was the continuation of a French colonial conflict, the First Vietnam War, in which the United States was persuaded to stake its diplomatic and economic might in the late 1940s. That is, before France withdrew in 1954 and it became an American burden, leading to the 1965 deployment of US forces to stop Communist advance in Asia. The idea that this was a Cold War conflict rather than an anticolonial one is so powerful that we still don't think of this war as the Vietnamese War of Independence. If this is how the United States was already involved in Vietnam by the 1960s, how did the US come to invest in a late 1940s French war to retain Indochina as a French colony? How were American policymakers persuaded to assist France?

My own introduction to this question was an unconventional one. Studying postwar French literature and philosophy for my undergraduate degree, I came across references to *La Guerre d'Indochine* during readings about the end of French colonialism. They included ideas about Vietnam unfamiliar to the anglophone scholar: the theft of the most civilized outpost of France, memories of *la belle colonie*, pride in a colonial civilizing mission wrecked by American capitalist greed or by Communist conspiracies in France and abroad, all riveted with accusations of Anglo-Saxon connivance, Vietnamese treachery and even references to Asian Fascism. These were further confused by the seemingly obsessive inferiority complex of humiliated postwar French *grandeur*, not to mention the hindsight of later colonial struggles, particularly the Algerian War. This, I would later find, was the product of conflicting trends in French historiography reflected and distorted through the prisms of contemporary and present-day politics, literature, and, of course, vast problems in assessing the legacy of French colonialism and its extremely violent outcomes in Indochina, Madagascar and Algeria. During these first forays into the problem of the First Indochina War, I had fallen into a common mistake that has long plagued the historiography of that conflict: there are only partial answers to be had in the history of each of the participants. This book does not repeat that mistake.

Researching diplomacy and diplomatic communication as an International Relations student several years later, Vietnam came back to my mind. At this point, the only clarity in understanding the American involvement in the First Vietnam War that raged 1945–54 came from a well-informed novel by British author, journalist and spy Graham Greene. The book's protagonist, Alden Pyle, sees Vietminh, the Vietnamese rebels fighting French colonialism, as part of a global Communist conspiracy.[1] Pyle's conviction seemed like a tantalizing explanation for America's shift in policy from opposition to French colonialism to acquiescence and support of the French military effort from 1948, and thereafter for its direct involvement in the Second Vietnam War. Regardless of Greene's fiction, persuading the United States to pay for most of the French colonial military effort in Indochina represented an incredible feat of diplomacy. Quickly discarding the alliance-building role of Ferrero Rochers, the question emerged: how did French diplomacy manage this feat? How were American diplomats and policymakers persuaded?

The answer that emerged from the historical, International Relations and policy analysis scholarship pointed to a barely tangible object of research: perception of the conflict and of the Viet Minh, the Vietnamese rebels that fought France to a standstill 1945–54. The Pentagon Papers, a US Department of Defense investigation into the origins of the Vietnam debacle, similarly concluded that perception was a key factor. This was not the only factor responsible for US involvement in the war, clearly, but scholarship is coalescing around the view that, in the context of the beginning of the Cold War, this was a decisive factor. That is, inclusion of Vietminh as part of the Red Menace unleashed the global strategic thinking of the era and its responses. In addressing the question of perception in Vietnam this book posits that it was far more complex than perception of Vietnam alone. Researching it requires analysing mutual and quickly evolving perceptions of French progressivism and postwar colonialism, British postwar colonialism and post-colonialism, Vietminh nationalism and communism, and US anticolonialism and anticommunism.[2] Consequently, this book does not seek to ascertain the "real" identity of Vietminh, how communist they really were. Rather, it works from the assumption that what influenced policy decisions was what policymakers thought of Vietminh at the time. Thus the endeavour of this book is to analyse, firstly, how the diplomats of these international actors constituted understanding of each other and, secondly, determining whether, when and how through diplomacy they influenced each other's understanding of the conflict.

The broader question of how diplomacy describes, identifies, reports and advises drove a far wider research project. During and following from my doctorate at King's College London, I studied how diplomacy's production of knowledge constitutes representations of the political identity of subjects and their spatial, temporal and normative contexts. Representations are different from perceptions: representations lie at the basis of perceptions – which are, conversely, *personal* understanding and interpretation of representations. Since political scientists and historians are not qualified to enter the heads of policymakers – when we try only questionable speculation ensues– we are left to study the representations, descriptions in text, analysis and reports, which inform policymakers. In other words, this project determined how diplomatic information gathering, reporting and analysis systems dealt with the thorny question of working out and describing whom we are talking to.

The identity and politics of a political group or an international actor in diplomatic reports, analysis, presentations and briefs is rarely determined by easily identified "real" material factors. When it is, it can be disastrously misleading – for instance, in the diplomacy of the First Vietnam War we often find the Vietnamese qualified as politically 'feckless' and 'corrupt', which is explained as the material physical consequences of the torrid tropical climate on Asian races. This is because ideational motivations like ideology, security concerns, racism or nationalism, respond to wider and more complex dynamics, not always material but most often ideational. We are talking therefore about the dynamics that shape the history of an idea. To rigorously and empirically research the construction, interactive dynamics and the evolution of ideas like the representations carried in diplomatic dispatches required serious theoretical work. This was resolved through Poststructuralist International Relations theory, the approach to international relations that emerged from the work of French philosopher, Michel Foucault. This approach privileges the role of language, discourses, text and groups of texts in the quest to understand how knowledge about something is constructed. On the basis of these theories I developed a method to determine how representations of international actors emerge from diplomatic practice.

This book's international history is an outcome of this project.[3] In its quest to understand how diplomacy led to US involvement in Vietnam, it applies these Poststructuralist theoretical insights and analytical tools to explore how diplomacy represented the countries and peoples involved in the First Vietnam War. This book therefore represents a novel, philosophically driven and unconventional effort to understanding the origins of the Vietnam Wars. It is the first analysis of the crucial diplomacy that led to US involvement in the First Vietnam War to draw on new critical approaches to identity-formation and to bring this understanding of political subjectivity to bear on the debates surrounding this conflict. In an effort not to torture the reader with too much theory, it is confined to two sections in Chapter 2, where it is expounded and treated from a practical perspective: how theory addresses specific research requirements and the empirical analytical method that emerged.

This book is therefore the result of this theory-powered analytics of representational discourses. Rather than a theoretical exposition, it offers, firstly, an in-depth analysis of how the very texts of diplomatic – communication, reporting, analysis – constituted the representations of the political actors and contexts that informed policymakers. Secondly, the book presents a history of the development of these representations. In so doing, it maps how they changed within diplomatic practice from the reports of diplomats on the ground to policy briefings, charting representational developments and changes. Thirdly and most importantly, this method reveals the crucial instances when one actor persuaded another of a specific representation – or, indeed, when it failed to. This is because such an approach to the history of ideas like representations makes it possible to identify when a country's diplomats first start reporting the exact subjective representation that we previously found in another actor's diplomatic knowledge production. That is, it pinpoints when a specific representation crossed from the diplomatic knowledge production processes of one state to another's that then made it its own, that has been persuaded.

This book, therefore, focuses on the documentary evidence of the diplomacy of the early years of the First Vietnam War. It is written as an international history, a multi-archival project drawing on French, British, Vietnamese and

American documents. This book takes the reader into the minute detail of those diplomatic texts, word by word in some instances, the representations of actors that were so powerful in shaping policymaking. It is an epic documentary journey through over 7,000 diplomatic texts from Saigon to Washington, from shakily handwritten reports drafted under French siege artillery fire in Hanoi to the briefings handed to advise President Truman. This is an international and diplomatic history powered by advanced theory with a Nietzschean élan, a history that takes Friedrich's advice to the letter and writes genealogical analysis backwards in a rigorous search for the roots of the understanding that Vietnam, France, Britain and the US had about one another. This book is above all the history of the struggles over identity that determined the understanding of Indochina and its context that in 1948 led to American involvement in a colonial war waged by a faltering European empire.

The book reaches an analytical conclusion of historical relevance. Firstly, it demonstrates that diplomacy had a key role in constituting the understanding as to whom, where, when and why did what in Indochina. While this seems instinctive, this book provides a minutely detailed understanding as to how this occurred in the run-up to US involvement in the First Vietnam War and therefore in the Vietnam Wars more broadly. The most powerful ideas in informing policymakers were race-driven conceptualizations of the political agency of colonial peoples, paternalistic developmental ideas about decolonization, and an understanding of communism as a monolithic Moscow-driven conspiracy for global dominance.

Secondly, this project's most novel contribution is showing *how* these key ideational factors interacted in the economy of – often contradictory – representations that informed policy. This subtler and detailed understanding includes representations of colonialism as an exploitative, paternalistic and even enlightened enterprise that drove comparisons between exploitative French against the enlightened and paternalistically framed American colonization of the Philippines and Puerto Rico. These were key to how US policymakers made sense of the late 1940s developments in British colonialism that negotiated the independence of British India in contrast to stubborn French colonialism in Indochina. Representation of French colonialism as gradually transforming towards one resembling British and American practices was key to US acceptance of French representation of the conflict and paved the way for US assistance in 1948. Another key factor that worked well with US and British ideas of the postcolonial condition was a racist representation of the Vietnamese as unready for self-rule, which in that logic additionally represented Vietnam as particularly vulnerable to communist penetration. Most important of all, we find that representation of Vietminh as communist up until 1949 worked almost entirely by approximation; by rhetorical accusation in other words.

Thirdly, it is worth highlighting two historiographical contributions made in this book. While the role of the UK in the early French reconquest of Indochina in 1945 is well understood, this book explores in detail its role in enabling the French drive to involve the US in Indochina in 1947. British diplomacy, it is found, was the first to be persuaded by French representations of Vietminh as part of a Moscow-directed global communist offensive and, crucially, also to accept the gestating French 'Bao Dai solution' initiative as a British-like progressive development of French colonialism in late 1947. It is shown that in late 1947–early 1948 this British understanding of Vietminh and the Bao Dai solution contributed to this representation being the one that, finally after many failed French attempts, successfully crossed into US understanding of the situation in Indochina. This book's analysis of the role of representations in diplomacy highlights the previously underestimated crucial role of the UK in persuading US policymakers of both Vietminh's Soviet communism and the progressiveness of French plans for Vietnam.

Fourthly and as a consequence of the above, this means that this book is in a position to offer a historical reassessment of the point at which US involvement had become possible and almost unavoidable: late 1947. In November of that year all the conditions fell into place for the possibility of US policy shifting from disapproving acquiescence to involvement. These conditions, created by dominant representations in diplomacy, made it possible to represent Vietminh as part of a global communist offensive when the Cold War political context was changed in 1948 by the Malaya Emergency, the Berlin blockade, and Mao's staggering turnaround of the Chinese Civil War in the Liaoshen Campaign. This book posits that this would not have been possible without the diplomacy of 1947. Without it, a different US understanding of the Indochinese context, and thus different policy, might have been possible: perhaps understanding Ho Chi Minh as an Asian Tito (US diplomats use those very words and weigh this option well into 1947) or a response to Vietminh's violent anticolonial challenge akin to the determinately anticolonial US response to the Suez Crisis or the French war in Algeria. 1947 is the year that French representation of the conflict successfully crossed over into American reporting, the year of the Stalinist domino.

Finally, this book also reaches a number of conclusions of significance to the practice, dynamics and analysis of contemporary diplomacy in our own time. Demonstrating the crucial role of diplomacy's representations of political subjects and their contexts is an important lesson for contemporary diplomacy. It is evident, for instance, that understanding of the various political actors involved drives key aspects of the ongoing Syrian Civil War, particularly Western support. Among the problems of representation that feed into policy in that conflict I would cite difficulty in identifying and irreconcilable disagreements in defining which rebel groups are 'moderate'. The analysis of the conflict's various actors that informed Secretary Clinton's early 2010s support for the constitution of the Saudi-led Friends of Syria Group to support anti-regime rebels in the Syrian Civil War appeared to absorb Saudi and Turkish assessment of militant Islamic groups. This appears particularly relevant in relation to assessment of groups such as Jaish al-Islam as 'moderates' despite their strategic and tactical collaboration with Al-Qaeda affiliate, Jabhat al-Nusra. Considering there is more evidence for this collaboration than there was in 1947 of Vietminh's part in a Stalinist conspiracy of global conquest, I would ask how this occurred in diplomacy.

The diplomatic conundrums of our time would benefit from the analytical method deployed in this book. Its analytics can, in fact, be applied to many instances of diplomatic intercourse for which there is abundant evidence, as other research avenues pursued with this method have shown.[4] Such an analysis would focus, as this book does, firstly on the constitution of the most policy-relevant representations in the text of diplomatic intercourse to understand how they are constructed. Secondly it would identify the exact instances when these representations are persuasive, when they cross over from the diplomatic machinery of a state or actor to that of another. Taking a step back to contemplate the relevance of this book and its mode and tools of research, its relevance is perhaps best reckoned as the power of the detail of texts that bear and convey the knowledge produced by diplomacy. It ought to serve as an exhortation to seriously examine who we are talking to, how we determine whom they are, and how assessment of whom they are is affected by our policy. The First Vietnam War should serve as the most powerful warning of the power of diplomacy to define to policy what the world looks like.

The structure of this book responds to the analytical needs of this endeavour. The following pages proceed as follows. Part I sets the stage for the analysis offered in this book and expounds its ways, means and the sources it draws on. Its first chapter discusses the scholarship of this conflict, highlighting the need for this specific study and how it responds and adds to existing debates surrounding the role of diplomacy in the First Vietnam War. Chapter 2 briefly recounts the theoretical developments this book draws on for its analytics before explaining its methodology and detailing the rationale for the selection of archival documents this book analyses. Chapter 3 describes the avenues taken by the diplomatic communication and information reporting of each of the international actors involved, the diplomatic pathways in other words, from the reports authored on the ground abroad to the briefs handed to leaders and policymakers.

Part II takes the reader deep into the detail of how diplomacy constitutes representation in individual diplomatic documents. It is divided into eight short chapters, each analysing a single diplomatic document, two for each the Vietminh, France, Britain and the US. Each of these detailed studies determines in minute detail the very words, articulations, and principal discourses that formed the core of how each actor represented itself and other actors in the conflict. In this way, this project shows how exactly the devil in the textual detail constituted representation of the actors involved in the conflict.

Part III takes this detailed understanding of representation of Self and Other to the highways of diplomacy, analysing how these representations changed over the period 1948–45. This part of the book takes the form of a Nietzschean genealogy, that is, it begins at the point in 1948 when internal State Department documents show the finalization of the shift in policy towards Indochina to one of full support of French military and political efforts in Vietnam. From there it works its way backwards 1948–45, seeking the previous incarnation of each idea of representation of various actors and their contexts. This is, as is explained in Part I, Chapter 2, because it provides historical and methodological transparency and, most importantly, because it allows the discourses studied to themselves drive analysis. In these three chapters the genealogical history of ideas of representation fulfils two objectives: it accounts for the development and context of changes in representation and determines when specific representations crossed from one international actor's diplomacy to another's, and thus how and why some representations were persuasive. Crucially for understanding the diplomatic road to the Vietnam Wars, we are looking to determine when and how France's representation of Vietminh finally made its way to Washington after numerous failed attempts.

Part I

Ouvertures

'what the East needed was a Third Force.'

*Perhaps I should have seen that fanatical gleam, the quick response to a
phrase, the magic sound of figures: Fifth Column, Third Force.*

Graham Greene, *The Quiet American*

1

The Road to Vietnam: historical debates and the question of representation

Historical debates

During a 1951 visit to Vietnam, Congressman John F. Kennedy noted that '[i]n Indochina we have allied ourselves to the desperate efforts of the French regime to hang on to the remnants of an empire'.[1] For Kennedy and many US policymakers, American support had been granted on the conviction that Vietminh, Vietnam's anticolonial rebel alliance, was part of a global Communist offensive directed from Moscow. In the second half of 1948 Vietminh's bid to end French colonialism blurred into events that appeared to show a coordinated global Communist offensive. Most salient among these was the Communist insurgency in British Malaya, the emergence of a Communist movement in recently independent India, and the Berlin blockade. The most worrisome development in Asia, however, was the spectacular advance of Mao Tse-tung's Chinese Communist Party (CCP) against Chiang Kai-shek's Kuomintang (KMT) during the Liaoshen Campaign in late 1948. KMT had received American military and economic support, but this CCP campaign, together with the Pingjin and Huaihai offensives, marked the reversal of the balance of the Chinese Civil War and sealed the Communist takeover of Northern China. It looked as though communism was on the march and Vietminh was a small part of it.

Association with French colonial imperialism in Indochina was clearly not part of the American policy equation. By 1951 it appeared to observers rather like an extremely unfortunate and counterproductive coincidence. How did this occur? The Pentagon Papers, the late 1970s US Department of Defense investigation into the Vietnam War, posit that strategic calculation preferred to support French colonialists than allowing communism, incarnated in Vietminh, to advance in Southeast Asia and conquer Indochina. The Pentagon Papers suggest that the global and strikingly binary strategic thinking that characterized the early Cold War and the recently proclaimed Truman Doctrine relentlessly pushed for communism to be stopped in its tracks before another domino fell.[2] It is therefore not surprising that young Congressman Kennedy was uncomfortable with American involvement in the French effort to prolong colonialism in Indochina. By the time of his visit in 1951, the US found itself supporting a radical French imperial military administration in Indochina bent on retaining the colony at all cost in the face of Vietnamese nationalism. Tragically, this was an anticolonial nationalist cause that, in principle, many Americans sympathized with.

This contradiction was, however, a new and potentially unnecessary one. During the Second World War Vietminh and OSS, America's pre-CIA military intelligence agency, collaborated in the struggle against the Japanese occupation of Indochina. The Việt Nam Độc Lập Đồng Minh Hội, (League for the Independence of Vietnam, abbreviated Vietminh), was formed in 1941 as an alliance of Vietnamese nationalist, socialist, communist, religious and even monarchist parties to fight French colonialism. In March 1945, after years of wartime Axis cooperation, the Japanese suddenly dismantled the Vichy French administration of Indochina under Admiral Ducoux and assumed direct rule. The momentary respite in the fierce French repression of Vietnamese nationalists that had driven the rebel alliance to the mountains allowed Vietminh to expand and consolidate.[3] Vietminh chose to fight Japan as a prelude to preventing the re-establishment of French administration and, crucially, its leaders immediately sought contact with the Allies.

In 1945 Vietminh did not bear the signs of a communist bogeyman. US intelligence and military personnel that came into contact with them during joint anti-Japanese operations sympathized with their goals of decolonization and independence. In late August 1945 a rare constellation of factors came together to favour Vietminh: the French were no longer in power in Indochina, the Sûreté générale (the dreaded colonial political police) and French military were under Japanese internment and on 15 August the Japanese Empire surrendered to the Allies. On 2 September 1945, Vietminh leader Ho Chi Minh declared the independence of Vietnam in Hanoi and announced the foundation of the Democratic Republic of Vietnam (DRV). His speech, witnessed by American OSS officers, opened with a verbatim quotation from the preamble to the US constitution: 'All men are created equal. They are endowed by their Creator with certain inalienable rights, among them are Life, Liberty, and the pursuit of Happiness.'[4]

Vietminh actively sought American and UN assistance between 1945 and late 1948 to prevent the French from re-establishing colonial rule. This little-known diplomatic communication, dug out of French, Vietnamese, British and

American archives and analysed in detail in this book, reveals another possible future, one desperately sought by Ho Chi Minh for over four years and reiterated over every diplomatic communication channel Vietminh could open. Had this correspondence flourished into a relationship, US foreign policy might have enjoined the postwar role imagined for American power by Vietminh rather than that sought by French and British diplomacy.[5] The US might have declined to acquiesce to the French return to Indochina in 1945, perhaps even assisted in preventing the war, declined support for the French reconquest of the colony in 1948, and never launched its own military intervention from the late 1950s. In this might-have-been imaginary, Ho Chi Minh would not have sought Soviet and Chinese assistance in 1949, becoming instead an 'Asian Tito' as some US policymakers had thought possible.[6]

In the late 1940s this question was not foreclosed. Indeed, in December 1946 Abbott Low Moffat, head of the State Department's Southeast Asian Division met with Ho Chi Minh in Hanoi and broached the question of whether Vietminh's goal was communism. Ho replied that 'he knew that the United States did not like communism, but that that was not his aim. If he could secure their independence that was enough for his lifetime.'[7] But between late 1945 and 1946 the US remained silently neutral on French plans for reconquest. France dispatched an expeditionary force led by Second World War hero General Leclerc to recover the territory while French diplomat and spy Jean Sainteny negotiated a temporary settlement with Vietminh on 6 March 1946. That agreement, and a subsequent Franco-Vietnamese Modus Vivendi signed on 14 September 1946, was violated in November 1946 by what historian Stein Tønnesson called a 'colonial triumvirate' of French colonial and military officials hell-bent on reopening hostilities and re-establishing colonial sovereignty by force.[8] During this crisis the US administration remained keen to stay out of a conflict it considered an unpleasant bout of European imperialism.

The misgivings of lawmakers like Kennedy observing the effects of US support for France in 1951 belie and indeed hide the origin of the move from a policy of vague acquiescent neutrality to active support of France. The shift in policy between 1947 and 1948 was predicated on two key developments: recognition that Vietminh was part of a global Communist threat and a liberal French plan to guide Vietnam towards independence under a non-communist regime. Though between 1945 and 1947 US diplomacy had encouraged a negotiated settlement between France and the Vietnamese rebel alliance, by March 1948 American diplomats were considering alternatives to negotiation with Vietminh. In a July 1948 memorandum, the US State Department broke cover and declared support for French proposals for 'a non communist solution to the Indochina problem relying on the cooperation of real nationalists in the country.'[9]

'Real' nationalists were anybody but Vietminh. By mid-1948 US State Department officials were briefing that, despite the lack of concrete evidence, Vietminh was a dangerous scion of international communism. In November 1948 diplomatic and material support for France against Vietminh formally became US policy. In the context of the 1948 Malaya Emergency, the approaching 1949 "Loss of China" to Mao, and the beginning of Senator McCarthy's anticommunist witch-hunts, Vietminh came to be considered by the State Department and the White House as a greater danger than French colonialism. This was a marked departure from previous hesitation and even outright dismissals to accommodate French requests. US–French diplomacy between late 1944 and 1949 is replete with French diplomatic initiatives to obtain US material, financial and diplomatic support for the reconquest of Indochina. These French diplomatic moves were unsuccessful until 1948.

Between 1946 and 1947, French colonial administrators at the Ministère des Colonies worked hard to improve the image of French colonialism. In 1946 the Ministry itself was renamed Ministère de la France d'Outre-Mer (Ministry of Overseas France) and since 1947 had sought to utilize deposed Vietnamese Emperor Bao Dai, then in exile in Hong Kong, to front a puppet non-Vietminh Vietnamese administration within a "progressively reformed" French Empire (also renamed as Union Française, French Union). Crucially, this pliant French-installed government would forgo demands for Độc Lập, independence.[10] At the same time, French diplomats launched yet another campaign to convince their American counterparts that Vietminh was a dangerous Moscow-directed communist bid for power in Southeast Asia. The Bao Dai solution was unspecific and ungenerous since its inception, and the drive to tar Vietminh with the communist brush decidedly unsubstantiated, even for the newly created CIA. Furthermore, both approaches were similar to diplomatic attempts to gain US support dating back to 1945. However, starting in 1948, the 1947 French diplomatic campaigns bore fruit. In sum: somehow the 1947 diplomatic presentation of French colonialism and Vietminh communism were clearly far more persuasive than their 1945 to mid-1947 incarnations.

How was French diplomacy able to persuade anticolonial US diplomats that Vietminh was more communist than nationalist – and France less colonialist than anticommunist? Why had these late 1947 efforts at representing Vietminh and French colonialism succeeded where previous ones had failed?

The rest of this chapter considers how scholars have hitherto sought to answer this question. In the first instance it reviews American, French, Vietnamese and then transnational developments in historical approaches to understanding how and why the US, which had at most acquiesced to the French return to Indochina in 1945–46, made such a shift. It concludes that scholarly understanding of the move to support France in 1948 points to an understanding of Vietminh and France that placed Indochina as the next domino. Secondly, it reviews and discusses two key recent efforts to account for the role of diplomacy in constituting understanding of the political identity of France, America and Vietnam by historians Mark Philip Bradley and Mark Atwood Lawrence. These are the developments in researching First Vietnam War diplomacy that suggest the need for and lay the groundwork for the analysis offered in this book. Building on Bradley and Lawrence's efforts, the last section of this chapter sets out a research-driven theoretical and methodological shopping list necessary to finally answer how representations of identity greatly responsible for US involvement in Vietnam were constituted.

Early American Vietnam scholarship focused on identifying the last 'missed opportunity' to avoid disaster. That is, the instances at which the Roosevelt and Truman administrations might have avoided early involvement in Indochina.[11] The first of these missed opportunities was Roosevelt's cancelled International Trusteeship plan for Indochina. Driven by an extremely negative view of French colonialism, between 1943 and 1944 Roosevelt planned to hand the colony to UN Trusteeship rather than return it to France. Roosevelt's interest in the colony not only represented the very first time the US became concerned with the fate of French Indochina, but also reflected a powerful anticolonial current within American liberalism. Debate on this missed opportunity focuses on the extent to which FDR was willing to enforce his postcolonial vision and, particularly, when exactly it was reversed. The relevance to American involvement, it is argued, is that reversal of Trusteeship was key to obtaining American acquiescence of French plans to reconquer the colony in 1945, which led to a gradual sliding of policy towards supporting France.[12] This debate therefore focuses less on US policy attitudes to French colonialism in Indochina or Vietnamese nationalism than the significance of the 1945 policy shift to the 1948 escalation to support of French anti-Vietnamese military efforts, somewhat conflating the two policymaking instances and their diplomatic circumstances.[13] The missed opportunity approach, however, misses key diplomatic factors due to its US-centrism. American freedom to impose policy on this scale upon France, a key American ally, is assumed, which is debatable. However, of greater relevance to our present study, it is taken as given that the Truman administration understood the situation on the ground in Vietnam – which they clearly did not, as demonstrated by their febrile 1945–48 reporting studied in this book.[14] Another effect, probably worsened by lack of access to archival sources in early studies, is that the crucial diplomatic dynamic occurring 1946–47 is assumed to be part of a continuum spanning 1945–50.[15] This obviates and flattens the crucial diplomacy-led policy shift of 1947–48.

Revisionist scholarship added considerable and nuanced understanding of mid-1940s diplomacy. This included the effects upon Vietnam of the Yalta Conference, the beginning of Soviet–American friction, the gradual disintegration of the KMT in China, and the increased urgency of building an anticommunist alliance in Europe.[16] The late revisionist consensus that emerged in the late 1980s was that Trusteeship was not abandoned. Rather it was watered down at Yalta and only overturned after Roosevelt's death in May 1945.[17] The 'lost opportunity' and revisionist accounts are problematic in two significant ways. Firstly, they lay the onus of later policy shifts on the death of Roosevelt's Trusteeship, resulting in the insight that between 1945 and 1948 US policy regarding Indochina was gradually and continually moving in the same direction: from Trusteeship to 1945 acquiescence of the French reconquest, and onto full support of France in the late 1940s. This seriously undersells the flexibility and dynamism of US policy at the time and its significant internal debates and shifts. Secondly, this approach assumes total American diplomatic agency and catastrophically ignores the role of French, British and Vietnamese actions and diplomacy while overestimating the extent to which US policymaking was independent of outside influence.

My first encounter with French scholarship on the First Vietnam War was spectacularly colonial. Admiral d'Argenlieu's own account of the conflict, written from his perspective as Haut Commissaire of Indochina 1945–47 but also as a historical chronicle, posits the diplomacy of the time, the war, and his own actions as an effort to save Indochina from Vietminh's fascist racism and Stalinism.[18] Notably, it is representative of early French scholarship on this war: torn between colonial apology, critique of French anti-war liberals, strongly flavoured with Gaullist nationalist imperialism and despair to restore France's proper place among nations – *la grandeur*. It is important, however, to note that this scholarship is useful to apprehend the role of two discourses that to this day mark French colonial history.[19] Firstly, normative radicalism in the defence of the *œuvre coloniale*, (the French equivalent of the 'white man's burden') and the extent to which belief in bettering the lives of racially, politically and socially backward peoples sustained the political role of colonial violence in metropolitan France. Secondly, the extent to which the *colons*, the French established in the colonies, were willing to take racially codified violence to protect their way of life. In this book we shall encounter this radical dual colonial logic expressed in French diplomacy when dealing with d'Argenlieu's fanaticism about native need for French rule, the *œuvre*, and even the use of thousands of former Wehrmacht soldiers recruited into the Légion Étrangère to defeat Vietminh.

Later encounters with French scholarship were far more fruitful, particularly the Paris–Saigon–Hanoi approach.[20] This meta-diplomatic and multi-archival account of the diplomacy of the conflict pioneered by Philippe Devillers revolutionized study of the First Vietnam War. It demonstrated that understanding this conflict necessitates transnational study spanning at least diplomatic and colonial institutions in France and Vietnam.[21] The Paris–Saigon–Hanoi approach added consideration of a multiplicity of international actors, including the emergent Vietnamese state and various colonial and anticolonial factions in Saigon and Paris that were key not only to colonial policy, but also – and of greater interest to this book – to French diplomacy towards Britain and United States. The results were spectacular. It was demonstrated that underestimated Vietnamese factors were as important to Vietminh's success in the 1945 revolution as the Japanese takeover, temporary French impotence and the Japanese surrender. Furthermore, it became clear that Vietminh success lay in the coalescing of disparate factions from Confucian monarchists to bourgeois intellectuals around the banner of national liberation focused by Vietminh against grievances including the 1945 famine, a long-seated, culturally coded loathing of exploitative French colonialism, repression and humiliation, a sophisticated understanding of Vietnamese history and identity, and even poetry.[22]

At the international level, the Paris–Saigon–Hanoi approach resulted in sophisticated and transnational accounts of diplomacy and decision-making in 1944–46. It challenged American revisionist consensus, demonstrating that Trusteeship lasted until Truman revoked it – almost accidentally– in June 1945.[23] Returning to our own question of how America went to Vietnam, this approach redirected research attention towards the concern of 1940s policymakers to determine whether Vietminh and Ho Chi Minh were nationalists or communists.[24] This was exquisitely refined by cross-institutional analysis of parallel decision-making hierarchies, particularly the Saigon colonial establishment by d'Argenlieu and the colonial and foreign affairs ministries in Paris coordinated by the Comité Interministériel pour les affaires d'Indochine (the COMINDO, Interministerial

Committee for Indochinese Affairs). This research showed that the outbreak of war in November 1946 was the result of deliberate plotting by a colonialist 'Saigon Triumvirate' including Haut Commissaire d'Argenlieu, political advisor Léon Pignon and General Valluy who defied directives from Paris in seeking a purely military solution.[25] This colonial establishment had major effects on French diplomacy: they conducted their own diplomacy with China, Vietminh and US diplomats in Indochina and, crucially, managed and censored reporting to Paris so as to control French policy and diplomacy, particularly with the US.[26] The implication for study of US involvement in Vietnam is that the diplomatic work of the Saigon colonial establishment is crucial and must be investigated.

Early Vietnamese scholarship on the conflict was official history. Led by former Vietminh figures like Truong Chinh and Tran Van Giau, it focused on the evolution of communism in Indochina and its conceptualization of mass class revolution out of Vietnam's existing cultural and intellectual traditions. Their value, however, is that they provide fascinating background to the evolution of ideology in Indochina before the 1940s, precious detail about the mobilization of Vietminh support and finer constitutional understanding of the early DRV, including the abdication of Bao Dai and the organization of its army under Vo Nguyen Giap and diplomatic corps under Pham Van Dong.[27]

Later Vietnamese research has added significant qualification and understanding that challenge earlier scholarship. Key among these is a nuanced – and perhaps unexpected – account of the economy of ideological currents prevalent in 1940s Indochina. Vietminh had an arduous task in raising support for an uprising against the French, especially considering the savage French repression of the 1941 rebellion.[28] Vietminh built a new and far more organized idea of Vietnamese nationhood and statehood. A key contribution drawing on recently available Vietnamese archives determined a key ideational factor for the present book: Vietminh did not pursue any communist agrarian, foreign, social and economic policies until 1949, when a policy of 'communistification' began, possibly in a bid to attract Chinese Communist and Soviet support. This late-blooming communism might well be the result of internal struggles within Vietminh, or the result of a pragmatic approach to uniting the disparate nationalist parties of Vietnam. What was certifiably communist about Vietminh 1945–48 was the previous affiliation of leading figures like Ho Chi Minh and Vo Nguyen Giap, who had merged their Communist Party of Indochina with nationalist parties of the Sun Yat-sen mould and even with monarchists, to form Vietminh.[29]

The transnational and later Vietnamese research avenues are crucial for our enquiry. They substantiate diplomatic difficulties in determining who Vietminh were and suggest that attempts to understand could and did lead to a spectrum of ideological possibilities that reflected Vietminh's constitution as a rebel alliance and an ideological mix that reflected the spectrum of support it sought to recruit. In other words, all were true. Vietminh was anticolonial, revolutionary, republican, nationalist as well as communist. Transnational approaches determined that US–French–Vietminh diplomatic communication 1945–48 is the key site for research on this US shift. It is now more commonplace to understand American involvement in Vietnam as originating in misunderstanding as to who Vietminh were because all subsequent events were predicated on an understanding of Vietminh as a Soviet stooge.

The debate as to who they were exactly in 1945 is ongoing, primarily opposing those that feel that Ho had a more pragmatic approach to communism, preferring to achieve independence first,[30] and the view supported by Vietnam's government today, which argues that Vietminh had always been an all-communist party with communist and Soviet-aligned goals all along.[31] This book adheres to the position that, while containing some diehard communists truly committed to immediate Soviet-style communism, particularly former ICP hands like its early 1940s former Secretary General Truong Chinh, Vietminh was a far more pragmatic alliance committed to independence first. Crucially, it remains vital to emphasize that Vietminh was truly a rebel alliance in the sense that it contained Communists as well as KMT-type right-wing nationalists, French-style republicans and even monarchists. This book's research contributes to this position with a broader international and diplomatic perspective, for instance showing in some detail how high-ranking Ho lieutenants like Pham Ngoc Thach and Pham Van Dong made vast efforts to communicate with non-communist states and obtain US assistance against France long before formal links were established with the USSR and Mao's CCP. Further, this book contributes to a nuanced understanding of Vietminh, where different factions agree and disagree on different levels. For example, monarchists and communists agreed on demanding immediate independence, but disagreed on what to do with the deposed emperor – fascinatingly Ho was in the middle of these, forcing Vietminh into long negotiations with the French at Fontainebleau against the wishes of the old communist ICP guard led by Chinh.

Misunderstanding Vietminh was (and is) therefore very possible. Vietminh was an alliance of otherwise very disparate parties led by some old Communist hands in a context of a war with near-total French control of information that led to many conflicting claims as to who they were, with one US diplomat at one point even calling them the 'Vietnamese KMT'. This book finds that all the details and subtleties of Vietminh's "real" political identity were completely lost to many foreign diplomats, making any description of Vietminh. This misunderstanding is frequently attributed to instrumentally manipulative French diplomacy that sought to tar the Vietnamese rebels with communism. However, the question as to *how* this was possible and occurred remains difficult to answer.

Colonial and postcolonial Vietnam was an imagined reality. The map in Fig. 1 shows the extent to which colonial power and identity-shaping administrative practices constructed understanding of the country.

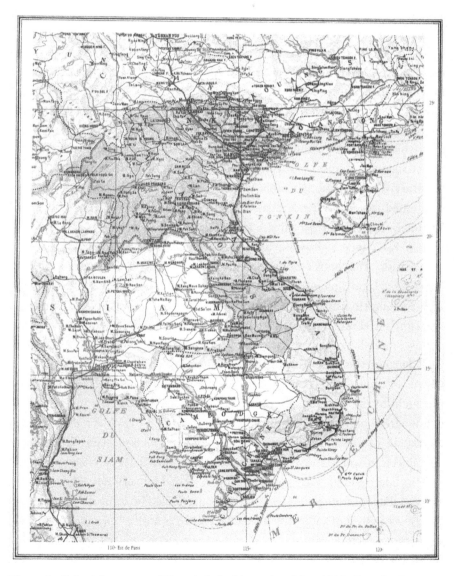

Figure 1 Colonial-era map of French Indochina printed in a 1930s French atlas.

It is a map from a 1933 French atlas. It does not show Vietnam; the ancient empire no longer exists. It has been erased from the map by French colonialism which has divided it into the three Kys (provinces) of Tonkin, Annam and Cochinchina. The French Empire treated the Kys as countries as distinct from one another as Cambodia and Laos. This would bring major problems when Vietminh sought to reunify the country 1945–75. The very name of Vietnam has disappeared, replaced by the orientalist term Annam, a name given to the country by the Han when it was a Chinese colony until 938 CE, when after nearly a millennium of struggle and war, the Viet achieved their independence. These terms, the words of French imperialism, were so pervasive and decisive in constructing the identity of Vietnam that until 1949 even the name of the country remained decisively colonialized. Western foreigners including journalists, the diplomats studied in this book, anthropologists, political scientists and even Graham Greene knew only of Annam, a country populated by Annamese.

Constructing diplomatic understanding of France and Vietminh

We now enter the terrain of representations. That is, the understanding of the conflict and its actors that determined policy at that time. If understanding of Vietminh as communist, nationalist and revolutionary republican were all factually possible even if to varying extents, our quest requires not determining which they were, which idea of Vietminh was lie or truth. Rather, it is necessary to understand which ideas of the conflict and its actors flourished around policymakers, the ideas upon which policy choices were determined. The point is not to determine how communist or nationalist Vietminh was and how rapaciously colonial or enlightened anticommunist France was. Rather we seek to determine how diplomacy and its construction of policy-worthy knowledge constituted understanding of these actors and the conflict itself.

Despite perception of 'the character and power of the Vietminh' having been identified in the *Pentagon Papers* as key to America's early involvement in the conflict, the question remained almost entirely unexplored until recently.[32] The problem for the Department of Defense analysts studying this question in the late 1960s and 1970s was the same as for us scholars. Several visions of Vietminh, France and the conflict were to some extent factually possible or at least somewhat believable and, furthermore, dynamically functioned with or against one another in different ways: French actions as those of rapacious colonials or enlightened developers, Vietminh as a group of Moscow-controlled commies or lefty nationalists bent on achieving self-determination. Some of these, however, clearly emerged more convincingly than others and came to determine policy choices. It is therefore an ideational problem that we are facing, a deeply conceptual rather than factual problematique.

We now delve further into *how* this understanding of the actors involved in the conflict came about. Two very serious attempts to resolve this question deserve some detailed attention at this stage. They are the direct historical – though not conceptual – predecessors of this book and set the stage and need for the analysis offered in this research.

Mark Philip Bradley's *Imagining Vietnam and America* accomplishes a veritable tour de force. Convincingly linking culturally inscribed understanding of the two countries to the historical diplomatic record, it demonstrates that accounting for US–Vietnamese relations must retrieve the cultural constructions of one another in the background of diplomacy. Conceived as an intellectual history, it offers an analytical history of cultural imaginaries and myth-making 1919–50. Drawing on sources from Ho Chi Minh's early writings on American history to 1930s American journalism on Indochina, substantial depth is added through analysis of academic, religious, colonial, propaganda accounts of Vietnam and America. Tracing the background of 1940s Vietminh ideas, the experience of Marxism among early twentieth-century Indochinese intellectuals attracted Ho Chi Minh's generation as a liberation strategy – then disappointed when Stalinism receded on ideas of liberation from colonialism.[33] The book retrieves even more influential if little appreciated influences on Vietnamese revolutionaries, including the early twentieth-century Chinese Restoration movement yearning to save the Empire and particularly Sun Yat-sen's revolutionary republicanism.[34] Another crucial strand of Indochinese thinking is the idea of America that Ho and Vietnamese intellectuals held as a model for national liberation, postcolonial prosperity and modernity. This conceptualization of America born out of violent revolution against colonialism, Bradley argues, was formative of 1940s Vietnamese hopes for American sympathy and assistance.[35]

Despite Ho's hopes, American exceptionalism could not contemplate any anticolonial cause as comparable to its own.[36] This is because of discourses of orientalist development, race and backwardness. Initially racial in a Darwinian sense (climate made tropical peoples indolent and unengaged beyond the next meal), over the early twentieth century they shifted to inability for self-government ascribed to immutable cultural unpreparedness and incapacity for creative politics.[37] This frame of Vietnamese race, society, culture and political agency contributed to the notion that Vietminh organization, ideology and goals were necessarily exogenous – from China or the USSR.[38] Despite America's own colonialism, exceptionalism drove aggressive critique of French colonialism based on the normative comparison between French exploitative imperialism and American paternalistic development of its colonies. American colonialism in the Philippines, for instance, "prepared" backward races through education, governance and ethical development. Belying this exceptionalist differentiation, Bradley's intellectual history retrieves that most American understanding of Indochina – diplomatic, cultural, historical, even intelligence – in fact drew primarily on French sources.[39]

Bradley argues that these culturally constructed images made a US–DRV rapprochement unlikely. This was ultimately because of the suspicion that unlike American postcolonial subjects, the Vietnamese were unable to govern themselves. Ho Chi Minh's strategy to divide US policymaking from French plans and obtain American assistance failed because Jefferson Caffery, the staunchly pro-French US ambassador in Paris who believed in colonial incapacity for self-rule, superseded sympathetic American diplomats in contact with Vietminh.[40] This slightly underwhelming conclusion on the diplomatic record, however, points for the desperate need to take Bradley's far more powerful lessons on the pervasiveness of cultural and racial perspectives into a comprehensive and systematic analysis of the diplomacy of the conflict. It remains to explore how these discourses of Vietnam and America affected diplomacy, how they intervened and persuaded at the key policymaking instances that drew America into Vietnam's war of independence.

In *Assuming the Burden,* Mark Atwood Lawrence seeks to understand firstly the diplomatic moves that brought the US to Vietnam and, secondly, the role of constructions of Vietnam's identity in this policy decision. For the first task he builds on the trans-archival cross-institutional diplomatic analysis of the transnational historians discussed in the previous section. The transnational perspective is expanded to include Britain, a crucial move not attempted on this scale before which greatly expands understanding of the diplomacy that involved the US. We could call this a Hanoi–Saigon–Paris–London–Washington approach, and it is exceptionally successful. It wades into debates seeking to identify moments of policymaking import, determining that 1948 was the key chronological moment of policy shift. Lawrence's most important finding, however, concerns the hitherto little considered role of British diplomacy in assisting France to draw the US into Indochina in 1948.[41]

As part of the British-led Allied Southeast Asia Command (SEAC), in September 1945 British forces were tasked with the surrender and disarmament of Japanese forces in Indochina. When US acquiescence to the return of the colony to France did not bring material assistance, British forces led by General Douglas Gracey freed and rearmed the French interned by the Japanese and, with only partial SEAC approval, assisted in anti-Vietminh operations around Saigon.[42] Lawrence finds that this intervention, coupled with 'medieval' French methods of repression and retaliation against the Vietnamese attracted considerable criticism from the then-new Labour government. SEAC commander Admiral Louis Mountbatten quickly ordered forces to be withdrawn as soon as the Japanese surrender and disarmament was completed.[43] In 1947, still reeling from the 1945 debacle and keen to be dissociated from French colonial ruthlessness due to Britain's new policy on Indian self-determination, British diplomats were extremely reticent to accommodate renewed French requests for assistance. However, by late 1947 they were persuaded of Vietminh's similarity and links to Chinese and Malay communist threats and to persuasively communicate these concerns to their US counterparts.[44] When the Malaya Emergency exploded in 1948, Britain energetically supported French requests for US assistance in Vietnam.

French diplomatic framing of Vietminh was crucial in persuading US policymakers of their part in an international communist offensive. Furthermore, Lawrence suggests that reframing France as modernizing its colonial practices played a role, but this is not precisely retrieved. Lawrence had set out to chart the diplomatic construction of identity from a Constructivist perspective. But this aspect of the research does not work because it is not executed. Lawrence initially mentions Alexander Wendt's Constructivist theory to posit the project as an exploration of 'how a particular set of ideas about a particular country took shape'. However, he never analyses how diplomatic texts and relations among them represented Vietnam, ultimately identifying the presence of various constructions of identity but, disappointingly, without dismantling their construction or charting the emergence of this construction through diplomatic interaction.[45] As a review of Lawrence's book concluded, '[i]t would have been interesting to see how Lawrence would have seen the utterances of British, French and American officials in the light of constructivist thought'.[46]

Though Lawrence does not examine *how* the text of these communications achieved this feat, his contribution is crucial for the present book. It determines the chronological timeframe for research as the run-up to the policy turn of mid-1948, and demonstrates that the way France and Britain painted Vietminh in diplomacy was crucial in securing US support for France in 1948, setting our research agenda. However, this book departs from Lawrence's research in two aspects. First, to the perceptions Lawrence identifies as key to the diplomatic communication I add the racist and colonial representations of Vietnamese unpreparedness found by Bradley. Furthermore, I add those conveyed by Vietminh that I found in the diplomatic record: the physical, social, cultural, economic and gender violence of French colonialism; the will and readiness of the Vietnamese to rule their country, and Vietminh's claim to a universal right to self-determination. The second departure is more conceptually and analytically substantial. France and Britain clearly exercised powerful agency on US foreign policy through diplomacy and Lawrence partially supports Bradley's case that understanding Vietminh's political identity was key to French diplomatic persuasion of Britain and the US to assist in Vietnam.

Addressing how this occurred requires firstly retrieving the dynamics of representation in the diplomacy of the conflict and, secondly, understanding how these representations developed over time. Most importantly for our understanding of this diplomatic history, the second aspect of this task entails determining which representations were successful in convincing foreign diplomats and which were not, thus revealing the instances, context and exact textual as well as ideational means of diplomatic persuasion.

Understanding representation in diplomacy: historical and conceptual requirements

The unanswered questions that emerge from scholarship on the diplomacy of the First Vietnam War can now be clearly conjugated: how did diplomatic communication constitute representations of the actors in the conflict? And, building on answers to the first, how did they develop and come to persuade foreign diplomatic and policymaking establishments?

This book addresses this gap in understanding the diplomacy that led to US involvement in Vietnam. It substantiates Lawrence's identification of the main representations that the diplomacy of the conflict traded in by analysing how they were constituted in and through diplomatic text. This analysis takes in its stride the need highlighted by Bradley to retrieve the colonial, revolutionary and racial dimensions of representations of Vietnam and America – ultimately to understand how they were politicized in diplomacy. This contributes significantly to understanding the diplomacy of the conflict by expanding a crucial detail first raised in Lawrence's research into a key problematique: how did French representations of Vietminh communism come to be absorbed into US diplomatic text in 1948? In other words, what made them convincing in 1948?

Context endowed this representation of Vietminh with meaning. The emergence of several communist threats in Malaya, India, Burma, Berlin and China in mid-1948, interpreted as a Moscow-concerted offensive to conquer Southeast Asia, meant that any group understood as communist would be considered part of that Stalinist conspiracy. The Truman Doctrine meant US policymakers might consider containing it. This only increases our urgency to understand how Vietminh came to be seen as such when there was no evidence of Vietnamese–Soviet relations and Vietnamese leaders kept begging for an agreement with the US.[47] Lawrence argues that the turning point was the beginning of the Malaya insurgency in June 1948. But this alone did not overcome contradictions and reservations about French representations of Vietminh, the groundwork had already been laid in the preceding years and in this book we go on the trail of the representations that were so convincing in 1948.

This book therefore investigates the background and constitution of the representations that were so important to momentous decisions of 1948. This imposes a number of precise historical requirements that take us to the very heart of the diplomatic practices. The first requirement is to determine how an individual diplomatic text constitutes subjective representations of political actors, their motivations, their relations and circumstances. The second is to understand how these representations develop over time within a diplomatic institution – for instance, which representations are prioritized and which are dropped as irrelevant. The third entails identifying representations that crossed from one international actor's diplomatic establishment to another's. These crossovers denote instances of vast diplomatic power, when a foreign policymaker is persuaded of a representation via diplomacy. Their circumstances additionally reveal the conditions that made some representations persuasive. This is how in the understanding of policymakers and probably most you readers, the idea of a "First Vietnam War" defeated that of a "Vietnamese War of Independence".

These purely historical requirements, however, perpetuate a problem. Bradley showed that narratives and images that framed and contributed to understanding Vietnam and America were present in diplomacy. Lawrence individuated the key moves in the diplomacy of American involvement and determined identity was key to them, but failed to apprehend how representations were constructed or developed. The difficulty they faced was accurately conceptualizing representations in diplomacy and, as a consequence, employ the appropriate methodological toolkit.

The first aspect of this conceptual problem, perception, can be quickly ejected. There are empirical limitations to ascertaining which perceptions inform individual policymakers. However, since political scientists and historians make poor brain surgeons or psychiatrists and cannot empirically access perception, determining the individual mind of a policymaker beyond their own declarations is frequently futile. We must return to the historical documentary record of diplomacy and policymaking to look for how it *represented* the conflict and its actors to policymakers. This is an important distinction: researching perception assumes it is possible and fruitful to investigate what you are thinking and why, whereas researching representation involves understanding what informs you, what you read, the information you seek. In our case, this quest involves investigating the documents that bear and develop representations: from the reports originating on the ground to the analysis presented to policymakers.

The second and principal challenge is conceptualizing representation so as to devise accurate analytical methods. This involves thinking conceptually, doing theory not for its own sake but with the above historical requirements in mind. These conceptual requirements, our philosophical shopping list, is therefore focused on the historical methodological requirements of this project: 1) Conceptualization of the diplomatic text firmly binding the practice of delivering representations on behalf of the state leading to a methodological data selection rationale; 2) Conceptualization of the internal machinery of a diplomatic text's constitution of representation. This involves drawing on Poststructuralist identity concepts and particularly methods to rigorously dissect representations. This is to understand firstly how they work and secondly identify textual markers that betray the presence of specific representations; and 3) Conceptualization of diplomacy's machinery of knowledge production. Combined with the above textual markers that act as signposts, this allows analysis to transpose and follow the development representations across thousands of texts within a diplomatic establishment and to compare developments between the diplomatic establishments of Vietminh, France, Britain and the US.

With this clear understanding of the specific requirements of this research, the next chapter can address these conceptual challenges. It delineates a theory-powered historical methodology to explore how US, British, French and Vietminh diplomacy dealt with representations and so ultimately address the puzzle of America's diplomatic road to Vietnam.

2

Reading diplomatic knowledge: analytics and sources

This book's approach to understanding diplomacy's constitution of representations is unique. Drawing on theories of identity, it conceptualizes how diplomatic communication constituted representations of the actors in the conflict and their contexts. The method consists of an integrated set of analytical techniques, an analytical engine made of several parts rather than a single analytical move.

This is how we respond to the methodological requirements laid out in the previous chapter. The method involves three analytical steps and is designed in the light of Poststructuralist conceptualizations of identity, text and language. It first explores how individual texts constitute key representations: how the words on a page, how their articulations, references and linguistic devices tell you that Vietminh was dangerously Communist. Secondly, the analytical engine follows the development of these descriptions through a country's diplomatic establishment, seeking to understand which description became dominant within it and how. Thirdly, analysis compares the evolution of representations across the diplomacies of different actors. This determines how and in what discursive and historical circumstances communication persuaded one of the representations carried by another.

Together, these methods enable analysis of how diplomacy constitutes representations of identity and to gauge their development and effectiveness. To expound this method and its analytical capacity the first section of this chapter briefly introduces the reader to the philosophical developments on which this book relies for its analytics. The second section links these theoretical insights to the methods developed by the author method to analyse how diplomacy deals with and constitutes identity, additionally detailing how the method is applied in the rest of the book. Finally, the third section details the selection of archival sources analysed.

Conceptual developments: Poststructuralism, identity, and text

Poststructuralist philosophy focuses on understanding the constitution of subjectivity. It addresses questions such as how we know that something is evil or dangerous, the ideas that govern much of human existence. Through the constitution of categories like good and evil, mad or sane, even terrorist or freedom fighter appear structural, they are constituted in and through the means by which we know them: language and the practices that taught and delivered them to us such as learning, science or religion. Language and the practices that convey its articulations do not unproblematically convey meaning, but indeed create and qualify it. Nietzsche, who once warned that language did not simply designate, is back with a vengeance.[1]

Subjective ideas rule the world. Michel Foucault would point out that you can only read this because you have not been condemned to a madhouse, an act of normative categorization based on dividing sane from insane. Normative categories like sanity/insanity coalesce into discourses that also include subjects (sane and insane people), which structure assumptions (the insane are dangerous) that result in seemingly logical consequences (lock up the insane). Power therefore lies in the agency to enunciate categorization ("you are mad, she is not") and discipline (go to the madhouse). Categorization, logic, discipline and the agents that execute them depend on discourses, the articulations of ideas that lead to the creation, justification, prioritization and execution of these practices. These knowledge transactions – categories, subjects, the hierarchies and discourses that order and make sense of them – are constituted in language. It is thus in language that we can research how this power is wielded to put you in a madhouse or declare somebody a global threat.[2]

This is not to say that material factors or indeed identity do not exist. Rather, this philosophy argues that the material world is governed by the ideas that make sense of it. There is no divide between material reality and the discourses that account for how we read its significance, nature and causality. In our case, this means no understanding of political identity can be completely and unproblematically grounded. An anthropologist might suggest that my love of spaghetti originated in regular pasta feeding during my childhood in Italy – and she would be correct. However, grounding my identity in this way cannot address the political identity or foreign policy of the Italian state. If one seeks to link spaghetti to politics, for instance, culture too is revealed to be a trope.[3] This is how Poststructuralist thought revolutionized the study of politics and international relations, by addressing the problem of how one subject or group of subjects became categorized as the good to protect or enemy and threat. The constitution of these categories, most often simply called identity, is thus firmly linked to the language that enunciates it, that speaks its name, inscribing and classifying it within existing categories.[4]

The practical consequence of these theoretical insights is to research identity-formation through analysis of the discourses that categorize them. Discourses constitute what we know of any identity and by their internal logic can also propose policy solutions.[5] In this conceptualization diplomacy emerges as a powerful practice in international relations. Diplomats report on international actors; in these reports we find representations, the fruits of practices based on language and text that describe and categorize. Representations articulated in language are the basis for inscription into categories that inform policies, which can in turn enable violence and conflict.[6] This is how we come to know that the Other can be killed for the greater good. This is how, once Vietminh was inscribed as part of a global communist offensive, anticommunism posited its logical solution of strategic containment.

Discourse analysis involves the conceptual move of treating text as literary production.[7] It does not seek to ascertain a text's objective truth, but rather admits that regardless of its lies and truths the political effect of its words justify analysis. This position leads to analysis of the means by which a text constitutes subjectivity, the means by which it represents subjects and their contexts and makes sense of them. In analytical practice, the approach seeks to retrieve the inscriptions of subjects in a variety of contexts and depending on the object of analysis along other axes of differentiation and alterity.[8] In our case we are looking to understand how words and textual devices in diplomatic practice constituted the visions of reality that informed policy in Vietnam.

Accounting for diplomacy's constitution of representations whilst adequately considering its processes and practices poses challenges. Diplomacy is so involved in constituting how international relations are understood that international relations are often called 'diplomacy', which confusingly obfuscates diplomacy as an actual practice. Poststructuralism conceptualizes diplomacy as a practice at the very core of international relations, constituting but also mediating estrangement among actors. Diplomacy achieves this by perpetuating the fiction of representing states as single-will sovereigns, for diplomatic practice itself depends upon saying 'I represent Britain' and therefore making a claim as to what 'Britain wants'.[9] Diplomacy additionally contributes to informing leaders in the capital as to whom the Other is – the part we investigate in this book. In this conceptualization of both functions, language emerges as the all-powerful site where the constitution of Self and Other occurs.[10] Language is the site where discursive practices order material and ideational reality and where we must analyse how its power operates.

There is unfinished business in Poststructuralist thinking about diplomacy. Accounting for language's discursive power in the context of diplomatic knowledge production practices is challenging because it involves hundreds of agents and millions of individual texts.[11] Poststructuralist discourse analysis is effective in retrieving how a single text politicizes, but is challenged by systematic examination of and across thousands of texts. This means we need to systematize discourse analysis across multiple texts as well as conceptually and methodologically resolve source selection.[12] Keeping these conceptual issues in mind, we can now return to our list of methodological and historical requirements.

Analysing representation of identity in diplomacy: from concepts to methods

The first requirement laid out in the previous chapter was conceptualization of the diplomatic text to inform data selection. It is a preliminary step, the filter that chooses data to feed into our analytical machine. It is important because from a theoretical perspective diplomacy does not include many activities usually associated with diplomatic institutions – and we must care for the conceptual if we are to account for representations of identity. The embassy's laundry and Ferrero Rocher bills have nothing to say about representations of the international actors that diplomacy reports on, while the opposite is true of Admiral d'Argenlieu's contacts with Vietminh and foreign powers despite the admiral not being a diplomat.

The answer to conciliating diplomatic practice and representation lies in conceptualizing diplomacy as both concept and profession, theory and praxis. Poststructuralist approaches to diplomacy conceptualize 'the diplomatic' as a delegation of sovereignty. Representing the sovereign (historically an individual, later the state) and diplomatic praxis exist in a mutually constitutive loop. By representing it abroad diplomacy reifies the theory of the sovereign state while the latter enables the practice of representation by practising its need to be represented.[13] This theoretical solution does not consider practices such as visas or consular assistance as 'diplomatic' since they do not involve the theory–praxis nexus of representing the sovereign. By the same token, individuals that occasionally perform the representation of the state like politicians and leaders are in those instances considered diplomatic – and crucially for this book, so is their textual production.

To be conceptually 'diplomatic' communication with foreign diplomats has to be reported into diplomatic structures. It is only at this point that diplomatic institutions can process the demarche and lead to policy or action. In 1945 for instance, American consul Harry Reid might have visited a Hanoi opium den to find information, while French representative Jean Sainteny relentlessly wined and bribed Chinese officials to help reach agreements.[14] However, before Reid's information or Sainteny's deals could pay off they would have to be reported up the diplomatic structure so other diplomats and their governments can benefit or take action. Had they been too intoxicated or hungover to recall the information or deals and not reported them, their demarches would have been in vain, never to affect international relations.[15] I conceptually define this event as the 'diplomatic moment': when an individual diplomat's demarche is linked to the sovereign she represents by submitting information to its diplomatic establishment.[16] These events occur in text, leaving a paper trail of these ephemeral instances of practice that helps historians document and take these diplomatic practices into account.[17] The diplomatic moment conceptually drives the selection of data, separating the diplomatic from the non-diplomatic not on the basis of institutional affiliation but on the basis of practice.

The diplomatic moment marks the entry of a text into a process. It is copied, resent, disseminated, edited, quoted, marked as important or dismissed as irrelevant. This process is conceptualized as a cascade of diplomatic knowledge production where information goes up while feedback, requests and instructions go back down with compliments for the author, requests for further information, or polite notice that no further reporting is necessary. From the report scribbled as Hanoi was bombarded, to the analysis handed to the Prime Minister, conceptualizing this process as a cascade of texts helps consider documents as evolutions of one another and identify when extraneous ones enter carrying new representations. As a metaphor, "cascade" highlights that this is an ever-moving flow of information. The cascade is a practical concept when analysing a series of documents, ordering discourse analysis, compelling it to account for how texts and their representations evolve within diplomatic knowledge production. It additionally orders how analysis is written in this book: for each time period in Part III the cascade of each actor is explored in turn, allowing for quick and methodologically transparent comparison.

The second requirement is analysis of the constitution of articulations of representation. The form of discourse analysis used is Foucauldian archaeology. Exploring articulations and inscriptions, it examines how their use in a text politicizes, classifies and inscribes.[18] This type of semiotic analysis is extremely detailed and effective in demonstrating and deconstructing a text's subjectivity.[19] However, to systematize analysis so that it can be repeated and deliver comparable results I draw on literary commentary analysis. The bane of undergraduate literature students, commentaries contextualize what a short piece of literature says and identify the literary techniques that achieve feeling, expression and aesthetic effect. I deploy the version developed by Roland Barthes geared towards retrieving the constitution of subjectivity from the apparently objective normal.[20]

This form of commentary requires determining how structure (thematic order for example), language (register, tone, vocabulary), articulations ('a rebel alliance') and references ('rebels like the Indonesians') in texts produce representation of subjects and their contexts. Commentaries are also ideally suited to individuating textual markers related to each representation so that the next stage of this book's analysis can follow them across other texts. Commentaries identify topoi, short rhetorical textual markers used in literary analysis to recognize common specific normative positions.[21] One or more standard labels that always refer to the same normative construct indicate the presence of a topos. For instance the labels 'from Moscow and Stalinist' betray the topos of a Soviet-directed Communist expansionist conspiracy. In a text a topos is more than any single word: it is a short reference rather that links to a specific normative discourse. For instance, not unlike the 1940s references to 'Moscow' encountered in this book, Berlusconi's references to 'Reds' sixty years later were direct links to his oft-used argument that there was a Communist plot to take over Italy and destroy his prime ministership. A topos thus clearly signposts a specific normative position.

Commentaries in this book deconstruct and retrieve the mechanics of representation. To achieve precision representation is broken down into representation of subjects and the referent contextual dimensions that make sense of their politicization: temporal (the Vietnamese as backward), spatial (the Vietnamese as tropical), normative (the Vietnamese as corrupt), and sometimes gender (the Vietnamese as effeminate). For ease of reference, I occasionally refer to these same categories as representations of subjects in time, territory and conflict.[22] These inscriptions are mutually constitutive and supportive since they draw on, refer to, and are supportive of one another. Take this sad example written during the First Vietnam War:

To take an Annamite to bed with you is like taking a bird: they twitter and sing on your pillow. There had been a time when I thought none of their voices sang like Phuong's. I put out my hand and touched her arm – their bones too were as fragile as a bird's.

"Is he [still in love with you], Phuong?"

She laughed and I heard her strike a match. "In love?" – perhaps it was one of the phrases she didn't understand.[23]

In this passage Graham Greene inscribes Phuong into a collective Annamese (Vietnamese) gendered subject. The language constitutes a referential space of sex, intimacy and love that is inscribed as both individual and collective by the back-and-forth between Phuong's name and the pronoun 'they'. A direct quotation splits the description, handing to Phuong an instant of agency where she is tragically made to reaffirm the unsentimental normativity into which the author inscribes her.

From here we link language to politics. Phuong is situated a spatial context where Vietnam (thus the Orient) defines her culture and her racially inscribed 'fragile' body. The (British) narrator inscribes her within two temporal frames of his own: when he thought she was unique, and the present when he knows she is no different from other Annamites. This is sequentially linked back to a racial and gendered inscription of their bodies ('their bones') as easily available sexual objects ('an Annamite'). These temporal, gender and racial inscriptions work towards a brutal normative inscription: Vietnamese women do not truly love; they behave the same with any man. The representation thus constitutes a normatively perverse Vietnamese gendered subject. The topoi or textual markers that signpost this representation are cheerful sexual availability ('to take' 'tweet and sing') and particularly race ('fragile'). This is how archaeological discourse analysis ordered as commentaries uncovers how subjects are constituted.

Part II of this book is devoted to this analysis. It firstly determines how individual diplomatic texts constitute representations and, secondly, identifies the topoi signposts that allow Part III to follow the development of these representations across thousands of Vietminh, French, British and American documents 1948–45. Part II features eight commentaries, two Vietminh, French, British and American texts. The selection of documents, in some instances pairs of similar documents, is informed by the need to analyse the minute textual detail that constituted the key representations this research has individuated as formative of the relationships that emerged. For the convenience of the reader, each analysis begins with a large extract from the text studied. As far as possible, these extracts are here printed in font and formatting as close to the original as possible and several are translated by the author. The analyses focus on the key representations encountered in this research: Vietminh communism, Vietminh as Soviet Stooges, French anticommunism, French colonial progressivism, racist and colonial representations of Vietnamese inadequacy and unpreparedness, exploitative and inhumane French colonialism, Vietnamese readiness to govern, and Vietnamese right to self-determination.

The third methodological requirement was to follow representations across the historical series of diplomatic texts to chart their evolution. This final part of the analytical engine draws heavily on the previous two to map the evolution of representations across the cascade of diplomatic knowledge production of an actor. Firstly, it benefits from the "the diplomatic moment" to inform the selection of texts for analysis. Secondly, it takes the understanding of representations and topoi signposts individuated in the commentaries to follow the appearance, presence, disappearance and evolution of specific representations across thousands of diplomatic texts. Mapping the evolution of representations is resolved as a Foucauldian genealogy. Inspired by Nietzsche's approach to understanding the evolution of ethical concepts, it explores the history of the present: how ideas evolved and came to occupy their current place.[24]

In this book genealogy finds, maps and accounts for the shifts, interventions and discursive relationships that enable and constitute representations of subjects and their contexts. It draws on two philosophical insights. Firstly, rejecting 'power's internal point of view', it does not seek to understand what diplomats or leaders thought but rather, how their reports, analysis and writing contributed to the knowledge informing policy.[25] There is rarely a silver bullet in the diplomacy of the First Vietnam War, a groundbreaking choice by a grand strategist that explains all policy decisions. Because policy was based on understanding as to who was fighting and why, the history of this understanding is found in countless cables, policy recommendations, analysis, requests for more information; the work of myriad diplomats filing reports. Secondly, the concept of intertextuality warns us that no text is entirely new; it draws on, exists in discussion with and references other texts.[26] Its analytical consequence is that discourses are to be investigated across the many textual sites that reproduce, modify, develop, challenge or promote them.[27] The Other emerges from the juxtaposition of different genres, forms of knowledge making and articulations.[28] Intertextuality allows us to appreciate in fine detail how some texts become more important than others, are recopied and subsequently cited.[29] Thanks to topoi that signpost their presence, this book can hunt representations across diplomatic intertextual space.

In this book the genealogical history of representations is researched and written backwards. It begins with the US decision to support French military and diplomatic efforts in 1948, and then backtracks to 1945 in its exploration of how representations of the actors in the conflict contributed to informing this decision. Even Foucault never executed genealogy in this way, but this Nietzschean radicalism allows analysis to be driven by the very means that allow ideas to triumph, the means and instances of their entry into common knowledge rather than their narrative.[30] In practice, this means tracing the history of a representation by letting texts tell us when it first emerged rather than imposing a timeframe. To reinforce this, my reader will notice that I rarely refer to the diplomats by name – because of the commitment that regardless of the person or their motives, the policy-affecting act here studied is the report submitted, not the individual. Rather than rejecting or ignoring it, this method embraces the chaos of studying the very text of thousands of diplomatic documents because this intertextual plurality is a core part of diplomacy's constitution of knowledge. What is offered here is a journey back up the trail of the representations that were so powerful and convincing in 1948.

Genealogical analysis of representations in diplomatic text offers key advantages to historical understanding of the diplomacy of the First Vietnam War. The backtracking genealogy makes it transparent to the reader how the history of a representation itself determines the path and extent of analysis. We trace the history of powerful representations backward in time until we find its first instance in diplomatic texts. Chasing topoi individuated in commentary to follow representations across intertextual space permits analysis to follow the journeys of representations across diplomatic processes, allowing us to map their presence and evolution. In Part III a large diagram of these evolutions charts the journey of the most important representations. This approach accounts for the introduction of texts into the cascade from the 'diplomatic moments' of the organization's own diplomats. Because it can look across various cascades as parallel processes, it can also individuate representations that cross over from foreign diplomats. When analysis finds that a representation common in one cascade crosses over to another and is positively reviewed we know it was believed.

This book is powered by an analytical engine composed of various conceptual devices and methods. This chapter has expounded the conceptual developments that resulted in its three methodological steps: data selection filtered according to the 'diplomatic moment'; commentaries that reveal how diplomatic text constitutes representations of subjects and their contexts; and genealogy that explores how representations evolved in the diplomacy of the actors involved in

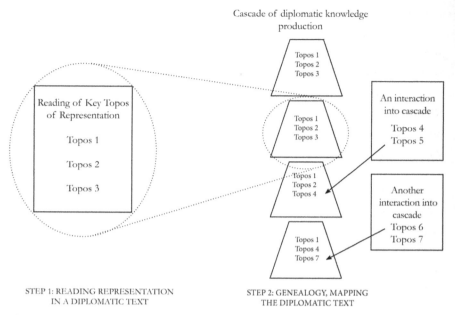

Figure 2 Diagram summarizing the methodology of the analytics of this book. Arrows denote the crossover of representations – signposted by their topoi – from one text to another.

the First Vietnam War to inform the policy results we are familiar with. The following diagram (Fig. 2) summarizes the two-step method executed in Parts II and III of this book.

The first step, on the left, analyses the constitution of representation in single texts and individuates the topoi that denote their presence. On the right is the second step, the genealogy of these representations across time and texts and identification of crossovers. As illustrated in the diagram, the method identified which representations cross over (signposted by Topoi 4 and 7) and those that do not (Topoi 5 and 6). This diagram features only one cascade for simplicity, but Part III features the textual cascades of Vietnamese, French, British and American diplomacies so that the crossovers of representations from one to another – the instances of persuasion– can be identified.

On the archival trail of the First Vietnam War: sources

This last section offers a brief exposition of the archival sources this book draws on. As a consequence of the data selection informed by the 'diplomatic moment' concept, many of the sources are not institutionally diplomatic. Documents consulted also include military documents and sources from colonial and central government archives as well as the personal papers of some key personalities.

As an archivist in Paris once commented to me, French Archives are 'balkanized'. The most important for this research was the Diplomatic Archives at the Ministère des Affaires Étrangères. The key series of documents were the Communication avec les États Unis (communication with the US) and the Fonds États Associés ('Associated States' was the colonial euphemism for the 'French Federation of Indochina' and its component entities of Cambodia, Laos, Cochinchina, Annam and Tonkin). Their files comprise mostly colonial administration, but among them lie precious documents covering communication between the colonial administration and Vietminh as well as Chinese, Thai, American and British diplomats.[31] It is worth highlighting that many of these files were restricted or not released until the late 2000s, making this one of the first studies to include them.

This research analysed the personal papers of Georges Bidault, who served as foreign minister during the wartime Free French Provisional Government and as prime minister in its aftermath; those of Admiral Thierry d'Argenlieu who was governor of Indochina 1945–47; some documents from the Présidence du Conseil des Ministres (the Prime Minister's Office) including part of the COMINDO files, all of which reside at the French Archives Nationales. The Archive Historique at Sciences-Po Paris keeps the documents of Jean Sainteny, the head of the first Free French intelligence and diplomatic mission to land in Indochina in the aftermath of the war. This exceptional series of documents is very enlightening from the perspective of France's early acquaintance with Vietminh 1945–46. Completing the cycle of French archives, this research includes documents from the Archives d'Outre-Mer (the colonial archives), particularly the documents of the colony's political and diplomatic staff (Fonds Conseiller Politique and Conseiller Diplomatique), which maintained communication with local foreign diplomats and reported back to France, as well as the larger part of the COMINDO files (designated Indochine Fond Nouveau).

To understand Vietnamese diplomacy, this research has had to piece together and triangulate multiple sources. In the first instance, it draws on a large cache of DRV documents kept at the Archives d'Outre-Mer and labelled Fond Gouvernement de Fait ("de facto government"). They were collected by the French military over a number of occasions, most importantly when a huge trove of Vietnamese government files were sacked when the French took Hanoi in late 1946. More comprehensive and representative for the purposes of this project are the large numbers of Vietnamese diplomatic communications found in French, British and American diplomatic archives. It is not only suggestive to find them there, but it is also proof that they were received, for though receipt was rarely acknowledged, they were mentioned and analysed internally.

All British sources used in this book were found at the National Archives. The key groups were the Allied SEAC diplomatic and communication records; Foreign Office (FO) diplomatic files that included all levels of diplomatic communication from reports from the ground to analysis handed to the Foreign Secretary and the Prime Minister's office. For the top echelon of policymaking this book draws on the Cabinet Office (CAB) papers, which include details as to how the Cabinet was informed as well as requests and instructions sent back down the cascade of diplomatic reporting.

At the US National Archives, the State Department Fund (RG59) is vast but very conveniently includes the totality of American diplomatic knowledge production, from mission reports to the analysis and policy papers handed to presidents. Furthermore, they also kept copies of presidential papers that would otherwise have had to be found at the Roosevelt and Truman Presidential Libraries. Like their British counterpart, the US National Archives were a researcher's dream: all the files pertaining to the First Vietnam War had long been declassified (French classification rules were the most extreme I encountered) and were to be found at a central location.

This brief description of archival sources is the consequence of the methodology of the diplomatic moment. It is to be considered in conjunction with the short study of each of the actor's diplomatic establishments and their reporting structures in the next chapter.

3

Diplomatic pathways

'Genealogy is gray, meticulous, and patiently documentary. It operates on a field of entangled and confused parchments, on documents that have been scratched over and recopied many times.'[1] That is the field that our method operates on: thousands of documents written by hundreds of diplomats and agents: texts that reflect, contradict, follow, complement and draw on one another. Genealogy is a potent tool that powers exploration of how representations of the Vietnam conflict and its participants were constituted across the thousands of 'confused parchments' of diplomacy's efforts to inform. Before exploring how diplomatic texts constituted representations and studying their genealogical history, one last preliminary demarche remains. Genealogy was indeed grey and meticulous, but for the historian of this diplomacy the earliest and most striking revelation of the archives concerned the adventures of the diplomatic documents themselves.

This chapter maps and outlines the journeys made by the diplomatic documents of the First Vietnam War. This is not a small aside to our study. The pathways taken by diplomatic information are crucial to understanding the history of the representations that in 1948 brought the US to this conflict. Tønnesson for instance found that the capacity of the Saigon establishment to slow down and divert communication headed for Paris was a crucial element of the descent into war in 1946. Another important example is the conflict between the Far East and Western Europe offices at the State Department: the former favoured self-determination, the latter advised the restoration of French *grandeur*. They clearly dealt with reports about Vietminh differently, which means that who processed a report about Vietminh had a bearing on its ultimate significance. These examples serve as warning that the continuities and discontinuities of diplomatic information pathways and diversions such as military or intelligence interventions were integral parts of diplomatic knowledge production.

The exposition in this chapter addresses diplomatic reporting pathways. The most procedurally common that is, and which are therefore not comprehensive of every instance of reporting. It is important to take into account that reporting occurred along simultaneous pathways, with copies sent to various offices. In more commonplace reporting pathways we find telegrams from missions in capitals and key cities such as Saigon and Hanoi. Telegrams were encrypted and, though formally addressed to the chief of diplomacy ('to the Secretary of State'), they arrived at central sorting offices (Division of Central Services in the 1940s State Department) from where they were distributed, sometimes in several copies. They were then received and assessed by various offices depending on their relevance to regional, security and other categories. These offices decided whether to include their contents in wider analytical and policy reports. If the contents were considered of maximum importance, they were copied and distributed, usually further up the cascade towards policy executives such as the Secretary of State and the White House. At the archives, historians can follow the paths taken by the documents by the numerous stamps adorning the documents.

There were, however, many surprising and informal diplomatic pathways. Vietminh ran a series of 'cultural associations' that discreetly maintained communication with foreign diplomats while Ho Chi Minh wrote numerous letters directly to Roosevelt, de Gaulle, Truman and Attlee. Contrary to expectations, Vietminh was not alone in improvising. For most of 1945 a small detachment of US OSS agents were the only American source of direct information on Indochina and link to local actors including Vietminh. In the same period Free France relied on a ragtag set of missions led by Jean Sainteny for contact with Vietminh and Chinese military leaders. Sainteny's reports illustrate the occasionally threadbare quality of information pathways, sometimes reading like fretful imitations of Joseph Conrad's *Heart of Darkness* in their depiction of missions and contact with the Vietnamese.[2] His communication with Chinese Allied leaders in Indochina was even less conventional, requiring ample wining, dining and bribing – and at one point buying a "cowboy" revolver to bribe a recalcitrant Chinese general.[3] Some diplomats were more phlegmatic in the face of circumstances. The British consul, for instance, remained in Hanoi throughout the French siege of the city, which saw heavy shelling and machine gunfire in the streets, but sent his secretary to Hong Kong for her safety.[4]

The unexpected pathways of diplomatic knowledge production vividly demonstrate the limits of diplomatic practice. The archives preserve the tale: Sainteny wrote several of his reports on the back of military report forms and often ran out of coding sheets, resorting to fascinating puzzle-like sheets handwritten in pencil on requisitioned school stationery with the coding on the side.[5] In 1945 the French stationery crisis was so dire that I found a report, typed on a single sheet of airgram paper, which was typed over twice on both sides and in which even the margins were covered in text.[6] This vividly demonstrates the material circumstances in which information was sent back to France and, thinking conceptually, the importance of the diplomatic moment, of reporting back to the diplomatic institution. Diplomatic pathways also suffered from rather sillier problems. The American consul in Hanoi, Reid, telegraphed such frequent and extensive reports back to his superiors that he would often run out of coding stationery and money for telegraph fees, for which he was constantly requesting resupply. In a parallel strain of unconventionality, Vietminh strained to add diplomatic dignity and gravitas to their memoranda and communications with foreign diplomats. In 1945 they produced a polished English-language booklet outlining DRV foreign policy. It had red card covers, a yellow star on the front, was stitched in silk thread, perfectly printed and was distributed to British and American diplomats.[7] On other occasions printing was entirely unavailable and thousands of Vietminh documents have handwritten headers, slogans and even logos.[8] In 1946 Vietminh lost thousands of mid- and low-level administrative files when the French sacked the DRV ministries in Hanoi when the city fell. This research benefits from that incident since those papers ended up at the French colonial archives in Aix-en-Provence.[9]

An understanding of diplomatic communication pathways is vital to understanding how diplomacy constituted representations of the First Vietnam War and its participants. It not only helps map which texts bearing representations influenced which other texts, but also, by revealing unconventional practices and pathways, tells us of the circumstances and conditions of their creation and delivery. This chapter describes the institutional and sometimes less structured paths taken by diplomatic texts to communicate with foreign diplomats or inform policymakers.

The remainder of this chapter maps the pathways taken by French, Vietminh, British and American diplomatic communication (Figs 3, 5, 7 and 8). The concept of the cascade of diplomatic knowledge production described in the previous chapter is helpful to visualize the processes of each diplomatic institution and reminds us that at every stage there is a text. For each actor, the pathways are firstly shown in diagram form. Each diagram is divided by a dotted line that separates diplomatic pathways at the capital, above, and abroad below. Boxes indicate major institutions such a Foreign Ministry; lines indicate reporting, feedback and instruction pathways. The diagrams are not exhaustive, but rather show the conventional institutional paths taken by diplomatic knowledge production and serve as reference for the analyses in Parts II and III. They are not representative of the *entire* diplomatic apparatus of each actor, but rather of the parts most involved in the diplomatic communication studied. After the diagram for each actor, the multi-institutional pathways taken by its diplomatic texts are expounded.

French diplomatic pathways are the most complex in this study due to colonial arrangements that involved two vast institutional bureaucracies. The first was the Colonial establishment, which included the Ministry of Colonies (later of Overseas France) in Paris, led by a Minster, as well as the colonial government of Indochina, the Haut Commissariat of France for Indochina in Saigon, led by the Haut Commissaire (HAUSSAIRE). Secondly we find the more familiar arrangement of the French Ministry of Foreign Affairs, which

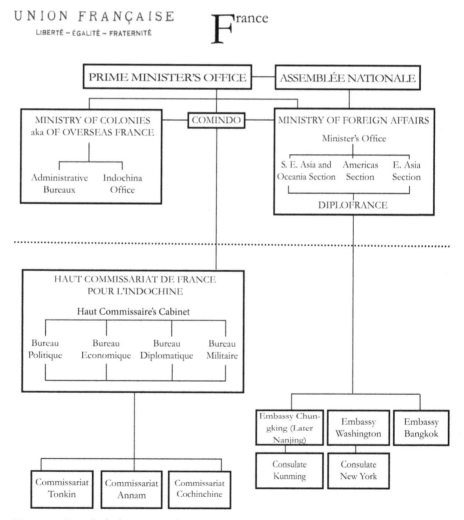

Figure 3 French diplomatic pathways 1945–48.

operated through embassies and consulates. The Ministry of Foreign Affairs was the chief conduit of relations with the UK and the US through its embassies and consulates. As discussed below, however, the colonial establishment occasionally bypassed the Foreign Ministry.

When it came to Indochinese affairs both the Foreign and Colonial establishments had the prerogative to maintain diplomatic communication with foreign powers. The nightmare of running parallel diplomatic and policymaking bureaucratic establishments at a time when Free France was desperate to recover Indochina was evident and in February 1945 de Gaulle established the Comité Interministériel pour les affaires d'Indochine, (COMINDO) to coordinate Indochina policy. Technically under the leadership of the Minister of Colonies, between 1945 and 1947, its authority was in reality frequently and successfully challenged, 'short circuited', and entirely bypassed by d'Argenlieu's establishment in Saigon.[10]

In 1945 de Gaulle's Free French government, recently re-established in Paris after its Second World War exile, had no contact with the colony. Until March 1945 Indochina had been under Vichy control and under direct Japanese control thereafter. To resolve this, on 22 August 1945 Captain Jean Sainteny established the Mission Militaire Française in Hanoi. He made first contact with Vietminh when on 27 August he met DRV Interior Minister Vo Nguyen Giap and until mid-1946 remained the main communication channel to Vietminh.[11] Initially confined by the Japanese to the top floor of the French Commissariat in Hanoi, in August 1945 he witnessed the successful Vietnamese Revolution and Ho Chi Minh's 2 September declaration of independence. While nominally de Gaulle's personal envoy with 'power to engage in talks',[12] he was restricted by d'Argenlieu to securing intelligence and contacts.[13] Sainteny reported to d'Argenlieu in Calcutta until the Haut Commissariat was re-established in Saigon in October 1945. When d'Argenlieu re-established the Commissariats (governorships) of Tonkin, Annam and Cochinchine (the 'Kys' into which Imperial Vietnam had been divided in the 1880s French conquest) on 4 October 1945 Sainteny was appointed Commissaire for Tonkin and North Annam. He met Ho and Giap frequently and in early 1946 was authorized to discuss terms with the 'Gouvernement Révolutionnaire Annamite', resulting in the 6 March accord. Sainteny remained a key French–Vietminh channel of communication until he was wounded in May 1947.

Admiral d'Argenlieu's Haut Commissariat in Saigon operated as a parallel government and had unprecedented diplomatic powers. D'Argenlieu directed diplomatic representation of France in the Far East for all Indochinese affairs.

This included representation of France to foreign diplomats in and around Indochina and, crucially, made him sole French representative to all 'domestic' Indochinese organizations and 'parties' including Vietminh (Fig. 4).[14] This exclusive channelling of communication, fiercely defended by the Haut Commissaire,[15] is reaffirmed when Vietminh representatives in Paris are informed of this ultimately colonial diplomatic arrangement in November 1946.[16] D'Argenlieu's independent diplomatic powers demonstrated their consequence when in August 1946 he convened the Dalat II conference with Laos, Cambodia, Annam and Cochinchina. This coincided with the Fontainebleau conference, which hosted Vietminh–French talks to discuss limited independence and the reunification of the three Kys. At Dalat, d'Argenlieu established the Indochinese Federation as formed of five states – ignoring claims for Vietnamese reunification – and proclaimed the puppet 'République de Cochinchine', irremediably scuppering the Fontainebleau talks.

Correspondence was processed by one of the Commissariat's five principal offices: the Haut Commissaire's Cabinet and the Political Affairs, Military, Economic or Diplomatic Bureaus. The latter forwarded documentation to Paris, always through the COMINDO from where it was distributed to the Quai

Figure 4 D'Argenlieu at his desk in Saigon, undated. Archive Sainteny.

d'Orsay's communications office ('DIPLOFRANCE') and the Ministry of Colonies. Updates and instruction from Paris to the Haut Commissariat were routed through the COMINDO as well as more direct channels. In communication with local British, American and Chinese envoys the Diplomatic Bureau acted as a mini-Ministry of Foreign Affairs, issuing communiqués, memoranda and convening the Consular Corps in Saigon for policy announcements and clarifications of their respective governments' policies on Indochina. The Political Affairs Bureau, led by Léon Pignon until 1948, had a very wide remit including espionage, the dreaded Sûreté political police and political reporting. It provided analysis, reports and recommendations on Indochinese political individuals and movements. As the Political and Diplomatic Affairs Offices fulfilled most reporting requests from the COMINDO and the Quai d'Orsay, a great deal of French information on Vietminh and its leaders is to some extent derivative of Pignon's work. The military Bureau communicated with Vietminh between late 1946 and early 1947 via General Jean-Étienne Valluy. This communication consisted almost entirely of Valluy's ultimatums to Giap, one of which caused the outbreak of war in December 1946.[17]

Vietminh was established as a political and military alliance in 1941 and quickly started to seek foreign backing. The backers it sought reflected the rebel alliance's nationalist and liberal components, rather than its socialist ones, and its vision for postwar independence. KMT China was the first target, though it initially proved entirely unreceptive and occasionally arrested Vietminh representatives including Ho Chi Minh. From 1943 Vietminh actively sought contact with British and American diplomats, probably on the basis of their war against Japan (Indochina aligned with Vichy and had welcomed Japanese forces), and the Atlantic Charter's vague reiteration of Wilsonian principles of self-determination.

Vietnamese diplomacy was by far the smallest and least bureaucratic of the diplomatic operations studied in this research. Vietminh's necessarily spartan diplomatic efforts are especially striking compared to the far wealthier, experienced and long-established French, British and American operations. Another feature of these efforts to obtain foreign backing was that it depended upon a network of individuals rather than an institutional structure. An early and touching effort was the distribution of a beautifully printed 'Letter to the San Francisco Conference' pleading for UN assistance to achieve self-determination. To the great chagrin and surprise of French Foreign Minister Bidault, the successful distribution of this pamphlet to many diplomats at San Francisco was achieved entirely through volunteer Vietnamese expatriates in the US.

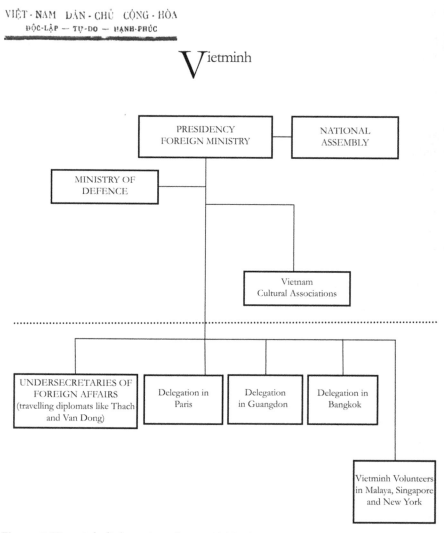

Figure 5 Vietminh diplomatic pathways 1945–48.

Vietminh made every effort to proclaim these individuals as DRV diplomats. However, lack of recognition made their efforts individual and, by necessity, their contact with foreign diplomats uneven in reporting, writing, style and form. Communication with foreign diplomats depended on the efforts of individuals like the medic Dr Pham Ngoc Thach and Ho Chi Minh confidant Pham Van Dong (who later became foreign minister and subsequently prime minister after the Second Vietnam War). Between 1945 and 1948 they were sent to US missions in Kunming, Shanghai and Bangkok and also travelled to meet with French representatives. Most notably, Pham Van Dong led the Vietnamese delegation at Fontainebleau in 1946 and later at Geneva in 1954.

Vietminh's improvised diplomats reported to the DRV Foreign Ministry, which was integrated with the Presidency since Ho held both posts. Ho wrote many of the letters these diplomats carried, including missives to de Gaulle, Roosevelt, Attlee, Nehru and their foreign ministers. Another key Vietminh official was Vo Nguyen Giap, who was in this period Interior and then Defence minister – the roles were more compatible than might be expected considering that in 1945 the first entailed anticolonial revolution and the second anticolonial military insurgency. Ho, Giap and Dong had leading roles in meetings with foreign officials like the OSS officers, the US consul in Kunming, State Department Southeast Asian Division Chief Abbot Low Moffat, as well as Sainteny, Valluy, Pignon and d'Argenlieu (Fig. 6).

Lack of means was not the only reason for Vietminh's diplomatic paucity. A key factor was a French diplomatic, military and intelligence campaign to prevent Vietminh diplomatic efforts from succeeding. This included surveillance, interception of documentation and telegrams (even US diplomatic cables from

Figure 6 (Left to right) Ho, Sainteny, Leclerc and d'Argenlieu meet in 1946. Archive Sainteny, Paris.

the Saigon consulate bearing Vietminh messages), assassination, incarceration, destruction of documents as well as an initiative designed to prevent Vietminh sympathizers and agents from obtaining visas to any Western country, particularly the US where Vietminh intended to present its case at the UN.[18] From 1941 Vietminh used a group of 'Vietnam Cultural Associations', nationalist front organizations extant from the 1930s and 1941 anticolonial uprisings that printed propaganda and raised funds. In 1945–48 they produced documents and official DRV foreign policy documents distributed to foreign diplomats in Southeast Asia.

In 1945 communication with France was initially impossible. Until the 2 September Vietnamese declaration of independence the Free French Far East mission in Kunming did not believe that Vietminh was a significant group and de Gaulle claimed it did not exist and that the Indochinese ardently desired to return to France's bosom. Upon arriving in Hanoi Sainteny became Vietminh's main channel to France. Sainteny, Ho and Giap negotiated the 6 March accord, which established a ceasefire and provided for the return of French forces to north Vietnam and a Peace Conference at Fontainebleau in July 1946. After Fontainebleau, Vietminh left Duong Bach Mai in Paris to act as chief of the 'Vietnamese delegation in Paris'. He was emphatically ignored due to French insistence that all exchanges should proceed via d'Argenlieu in Saigon.

British diplomacy was the most impressive, accurate and reliable in its reporting on Indochina, especially compared to US efforts. This was due to extensive diplomatic and imperial experience of the wider Southeast Asia region, the assistance of numerous long-established British expatriates in Indochina as well as a slightly more extensive presence on the ground. I would argue, however, that the most important factor was espionage-worthy attention to detail and willingness to research in depth rather than take previous reports for granted. As Graham Greene might have said, less York Harding and more observation. This is borne out in British diplomatic dispatches from Indochina, which often contradict or correct previous ones and are happy to contrast received French or American reports. British diplomatic pathways were complex and did not always consistently follow procedural lines of communication. This is because they included a multitude of cooperating departments and missions and reporting was often copied across departments horizontally to then re-emerge unexpectedly.

Britain's two key diplomatic offices in Vietnam were the Consulate-General in Saigon and the consulate in Hanoi. Hanoi reported to Saigon, which prepared large sets of documents, reports, analysis and numerous copies of French colonial administrative documents (willingly lent, leaked or corruptly purchased on a

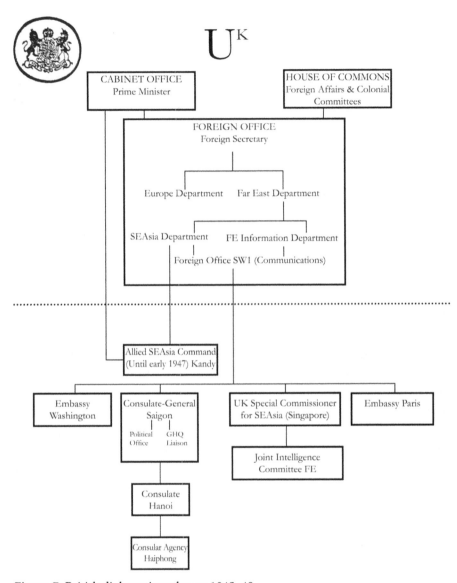

Figure 7 British diplomatic pathways 1945–48.

regular basis). These large packages were sent by safe diplomatic pouch back to the Foreign Office in London. Urgent and time-sensitive reports were laboriously coded and telegraphed, most often by way of British India or Singapore. The Saigon consulate included a political office that not only gathered information but also provided first-hand analysis and advice. The consulate's operations included a General Headquarters (GHQ) Liaison that dealt with information of military and intelligence relevance. British diplomacy in Indochina ran a small Consular Agency in Haiphong consisting of two enthusiastic volunteer diplomats, employees of a British bank and BOAC. They had first-row seats to the beginning of the war in late 1946 and reported in minute detail. Before their re-establishment in Indochina in 1945–46 and in parallel until 1947, information about Indochina came via SEAC, the Allied Theatre command centre led by Admiral Louis Mountbatten based in Kandy, Ceylon.

The operation in Indochina benefitted from a large British diplomatic and colonial presence in Southeast Asia. From 1946 UK appointed a Special Commissioner for Southeast Asia based in Singapore with a very unconventional colonial and diplomatic remit. As Governor-general, the Commissioner was to coordinate the development of the British colonies of Malaya, Sarawak and Singapore towards autonomy while coordinating diplomacy with the surrounding European colonies and independent states.[19] The Special Commissioner's office produced huge volumes of reporting of its own and through its oversight of the Joint Intelligence Committee Far East and its role near diplomatic missions such as the Saigon and Hanoi consulates.

All reporting was sent to the Foreign Office's communications receipt office, referred to in cables simply as 'Foreign Office SW1'. At the Foreign Office also arrived dispatches from the embassies in Washington and Paris, Britain's main postwar conduits of communication to the US and France. The receipts office decoded, copied and distributed correspondence to the various Departments and Desks, chief among them in the case of Indochina the Southeast Asia Department, which was to some extent subordinate to the Far East Department (which had its own extensive Information Office). These high-level Departments reported analysis and information to the Foreign Secretary who subsequently reported both to the Prime Minister, the Cabinet and the Cabinet Office as well as the House of Commons and its various committees.

A key development, globally commonplace in the early twenty-first century but which was unique in the 1940s, was the practice of printing the most relevant and highly regarded reports, regardless or origin or mission, in booklets called Confidential Print. This is because there were serious limitations to making multiple copies in typewriters and the task of printing long runs of Confidential Print was better left to the Foreign Office's Stationery Office. They were widely distributed to all Departments in the Foreign Office and diplomats on mission concerned with any one region (in our case France, French Indochina and Southeast Asia were the key Confidential Print editions) or issue so as to homogenize information and intelligence across reporting and policymaking.

They have the additional advantage of telling us which reports, documents and briefings were widely distributed in British diplomacy and policymaking. The practice ended with the arrival of photocopying, but we still find its contemporary incarnation in State Department, Foreign Office and Quai d'Orsay cables, where we see key documents centrally distributed electronically by issue or region.

US diplomatic knowledge production was sophisticated, clear and extensive but, unlike Britain and France's, its pathways remained relatively simple due to procedural clarity. During the Second World War its only consistently open and staffed missions in the Far East and Southeast Asia were the embassy at Chungking (later moved back to Nanjing) and the Kunming consulate. As the war drew to an end, the critical consulates in Hong Kong and Shanghai were

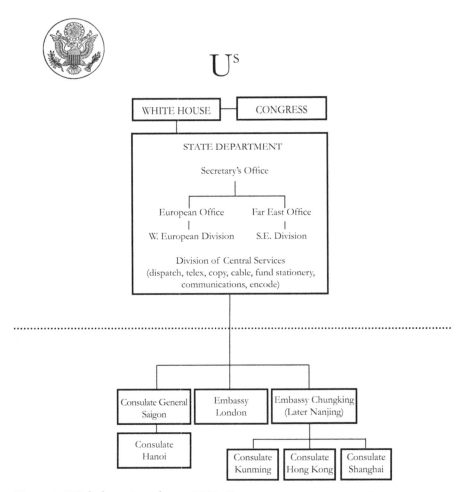

Figure 8 US diplomatic pathways 1945–48.

reopened. These were crucial for it was through these, particularly the mission at Kunming, that Vietminh made its first approaches to the US. All of the Chinese missions reported to the embassy, which in turn reported to the State Department.

OSS officers with Operation Deer were the only contact inside Indochina from mid-1944 until January 1946. Sent to recover downed American pilots, gather intelligence and sabotage Japanese operations, they collaborated with Vietminh and witnessed the August 1945 revolution and 2 September declaration of independence. OSS officers reported back to OSS Chief General Donovan through the military liaison at the US embassy to China until late November 1945. In January 1946 the Consulate-General was opened in Saigon and in February 1946 the consulate in Hanoi was established. The latter was crucial, providing direct contact with Vietminh until the French siege expelled Vietminh in February 1947. Throughout this period the industrious Consul James O'Sullivan cabled near-daily reports and all Vietnamese communications back to the Consulate-General in Saigon, which in turn sent them on to Washington with its own reports and analysis of the Haut Commissaire's activities.

Unlike British reporting from Indochina, which was more or less independent from the UK embassy in France, US reporting from the colony was cross-referenced and checked with the Paris embassy which often took the position of the French Foreign and Colonial ministries and appealed to them for clarifications. When both strains of diplomatic reporting, from Indochina and Paris, arrived at the State Department, it would appear from the archival evidence that reports from Paris were given some preference.[20] Correspondence arrived at the State Department Division of Central Services where it was copied, translated if necessary, and distributed to the relevant Offices and Divisions, in our case the European and Far Eastern Offices and their subsidiary Southeast Asian and Western Europe Divisions.

The Divisions at the State Department processed reporting and documentation into briefs, reports, research, analysis and policy recommendations. They additionally sent requests for further information and feedback back down the cascade. With approval and direction from the Secretary of State, they could also initiate demarches and meet foreign leaders. Thus under a Southeast Asia Division initiative we find its chief Abbot Low Moffat meeting Ho Chi Minh in 1946. The Offices in turn reported to the Secretary of State and his office, who regularly briefed the White House. Unlike Britain and France, in the US the White House rather than the State Department, was in charge of briefing Congress.

The preliminary overtures are now concluded. Having considered historical debates in Chapter 1, developed methods and analytical sequences in Chapter 2 and mapped and diagrammed the diplomatic pathways of the diplomacy under scrutiny, we can now move onto analysis. We are now on the trail of how diplomacy constituted representations of the First Vietnam War and its participants. The next step of this book's enterprise, Part II, analyses how a selection of individual diplomatic texts constitute identity. Part III then follows on the trail of diplomatic communication 1948–45 to understand how, in the understanding constantly constituted and re-constituted in diplomacy, Vietnam moved from being represented as a local colonial war to a global battlefield in which the US had to intervene to contain global communism.

Part II

Diplomatic Text and the Words of Identity

Not so very long ago, the earth numbered two thousand million inhabitants: five hundred million men, and one thousand five hundred million natives. The former had the World; the others had the use of it.

Jean-Paul Sartre, Preface to *The Wretched of the Earth*

4

The Vietminh rebel alliance: universal rights and self-determination

PROVISIONAL GOVERNMENT OF THE DEMOCRATIC
REPUBLIC OF VIET-NAM
HANOI, October 22, 1945

The Minister of Foreign Affairs
to the SECRETARY OF STATE DEPARTMENT,
WASHINGTON, D. C.

EXCELLENCY,

The situation in South Vietnam has reached its critical stage, and calls for immediate interference on the part of the United Nations. I wish by the present letter to bring your Excellency some more light on the case of Vietnam which has come for the last three weeks into the international limelight.

First of all, I beg to forward to your Government a few documentary data, among which our Declaration of Independence, the Imperial Rescript of Ex-Emperor BAO DAI on the occasion of his abdication, the declaration of our Government concerning its general foreign policy and a note defining our position towards the South Vietnam incident.

As those documents will show your Excellency, the Vietnamese people has known during the last few years an evolution which naturally brings the Vietnamese resistance, we at last saw France defeated in Europe, then her betrayal of the Allies successively on behalf of Germany and of Japan. Though the odds were at that time against the Allies, the Vietnamese, leaving aside all differences in political opinion, united against the Japanese. Meanwhile, the Atlantic Charter was concluded, defining the war aims of the Allies and laying the foundation of peace-work. The noble principles of international justice and equality of status laid down in that charter strongly appealed to the Vietnamese and contributed in making of the Vietminh resistance in the war zone a nation-wide anti-Japanese movement which found a powerful echo in the democratic aspirations of the people. The Atlantic Charter was looked upon as the foundation of future Vietnam. A nation-building program was drafted which has been fully carried out these last years: continuous fight against the Japanese bringing about the recovery of national independence on August 19th, voluntary abdication of Ex-Emperor Baodai, establishment of the Democratic Republic of Vietnam, assistance given to the Allies Nations in the disarmament of the Japanese, appointment of a provisional Government whose mission was to carry out the Atlantic Charter and San Francisco Charters and have them carried out by other nations.

As a matter of fact, the carrying out of the Atlantic and San Francisco Charters implies the eradication of imperialism and all forms of colonial oppression. This was unfortunately contrary to the interests of some Frenchmen, and France, to whom the colonists have long concealed the truth on Indochina, instead of entering into peaceable negotiations, resorted to an aggressive invasion, with all the means at the command of a modern nation. Moreover, having persuaded the British that the Vietnamese are wishing for a return of the French rule, they obtained, first from the British command in Southeast Asia, then from London, a tacit recognition of their sovereignty and administrative responsibility as far as South Vietnam is concerned. The British gave to understand that they had agreed to this on the ground that the reestablishment of French administration and, consequently, of Franco-Vietnamese collaboration would help them to speed up the demobilization and the disarmament of the Japanese. But subsequent events will prove the fallacy of the argument. The whole Vietnamese nation rose up as one man against French aggression. The first street-sniping which was launched by the French in the small hours of September 23rd soon developed into real and organized warfare in which losses are heavy on both sides. The bringing in of French important reinforcements on board of the most powerful of their remaining warships will extend the war zone further. As murderous fighting is still going on in Indonesia, and as savage acts on the part of Frenchmen are reported every day, we may expect the flaring up of a general conflagration in the Far-East.

As it is, the situation in South Vietnam calls for immediate interference. The establishment of the Consultative Commission for the Far-East has been enthusiastically welcomed here as the first effective step towards an equitable settlement of the pending problems. The people of Vietnam, which only asks for full independence and for the respect of truth and justice, puts before your Excellency our following desiderata:
1o. - The South Vietnam incident should be discussed at the first meeting of the Consultative Commission for the Far-East;

2o. - Vietnamese delegates should be admitted to state the views
of the Vietnamese Government;
3o. - An Inquiry Commission should be sent to South Vietnam;
4o. - The full independence of Vietnam should be recognized by
the United Nations.

I avail myself of this opportunity to send your Excellency my
best wishes.

Respectfully,
President HO CHI MINH[1]

October 1945. The Second World War has recently ended; on 2 September Ho Chi Minh declared the independence of the Democratic Republic of Vietnam in Hanoi and established an administration throughout the country (see Fig. 14). Following the armistice, in September 1945 Allied troops occupied Indochina to disarm them. The Chinese in the north tolerated the DRV government, while British troops occupying the south rearmed French soldiers and set about dismantling the DRV administration and violently clearing Vietminh forces. French troops and colons (settlers) were keen to re-establish French rights throughout the colony, a sentiment driven by racist frustration with having been ruled for a year, firstly by the Japanese and then Vietminh. The letter, quoted above in full, is signed by Ho Chi Minh, DRV President and Minister of Foreign Affairs, and reached US Secretary of State James Byrnes by way of the US consulate in Kunming. It accompanied and summarized two beautifully produced booklets, one detailing DRV foreign policy and the other, analysed in detail in the next section, denouncing the violent takeover of Saigon by French troops and colons in late September. Stamps on the document reveal that it was read at the State Department's Far East, Southeast Asia and the Secretary's Offices, but no reply was ever sent to DRV. The letter is representative of 1945–48 Vietminh efforts to present the case for independence to major powers and particularly of how it sought international backing – especially American.

The letter summarizes Vietminh's core diplomatic arguments: Vietnamese right to self-determination and French aggression. It appeals to the right to self-determination established under the Atlantic and San Francisco Charters, interpreted as providing for 'the eradication of imperialism and all forms of colonial oppression'. By the same logic, framed in this letter as both political but also legally binding, Vietnam requests UN intervention ('interference') to stave off French aggression and abuses. The letter outlines French collaboration with the Axis during the Second World War and the violent reoccupation of Vietnam after the

Japanese and DRV interregnum. Surprisingly, it is not radically opposed to France. Rather, it blames French 'colonists' (colonialists) for deceiving the French public and the British military so as to carry out an 'aggressive invasion' with 'savage acts', a conflict compared to the troublesome British re-establishment of Dutch sovereignty in Indonesia that very year. Ho's letter concludes with a request for a UN investigation into French abuses during the reconquest of September 1945, a Vietnamese voice in that process, and recognition of Vietnam's independence.

This is a significant set of claims. By appealing to the Atlantic and San Francisco Charters, the foundational basis of the UN and contemporary international law, the text assumes Vietnam's place as a member of the international community and as a holder of universal rights. This is firstly located in the context of the Second World War: France is represented as a traitor to the Allied Cause and Axis collaborator, whilst Vietnam is represented as a small actor that carried out Allied 'resistance in the war zone' and 'continuous fight against the Japanese'. Secondly, Vietnam's assumption of rights is inscribed as legitimate by the identification of 'the Vietnamese nation' in a process of determining its own future, 'nation-building' and establishing of a 'united' government 'in the democratic aspirations of the people'. In addition to its Allied wartime record, by representing Vietnam as democratically exercising self-determination this text locates Vietnam among politically comparable Western democracies and claims their international rights. Against these rights the letter posits France as an aggressor and perpetrator of atrocities. Thus, it is as a consequence of Allied collaboration and the universal rights enshrined by the UN that the letter requests that the UN defend Vietnam from France.

The structure and form of this text are deeply implicated in constituting these representations. Its structure posits two axes of differentiation repeated in the second, third and fourth paragraphs. The first separates French collaboration with the Axis powers against the Vietnamese who 'united against the Japanese', while the second pits Vietnamese self-determined nationhood and its rights against French abuses. French influence is evident in vocabulary such as 'interference' to mean intervention, or the cardinal numbering marked '1o', '2o', French abbreviations for 'primo', 'segundo'. This is to be expected considering that much of Vietminh's elite was educated in French and many had studied in France – where many became socialists and communists. This is also apparent in the header, which reflects de Gaulle's Free French 'Provisional Government of the French Republic'. Structure and form, however, are remarkably un-Gallic: the letter is direct and does not feature the long constructions, florid formalities and intricate argumentation typical of French diplomatic writing.

The structure of this letter temporally inscribes Vietnam's existence. The events leading to the letter are written in the past tense, making Vietnamese independence a fait accompli. The narrative embeds highly relevant, political and legal vocabulary into the narrative representing the steps for a 'nation-building program which has been fully carried out': fighting the Japanese, 'national independence' and the 'abdication of Ex-Emperor Baodai', 'establishment' of the DRV government and assisting the Allies in disarming the Japanese. These events justify (Allied assistance) and legitimate ('recovery of independence', abdication, 'unity') DRV's claim to represent Vietnam and claim statehood. Writing about these events in this way linguistically posits a fait accompli: DRV exists and is there to stay. Vietnam's legal rights as an Allied state and as provided for under the Atlantic and San Francisco Charters are also claimed linguistically: DRV 'calls' for assistance, 'only asks' for its rights, and requests 'interference' (intervention). This is posited against French treachery in the Second World War and abuses in the reoccupation of the colony, which in UN terms are framed as 'aggression' – as tried at Nuremberg the following month. Thus the linguistic differentiation is complete: Vietnamese rights, rightfully deserved by their actions, are pitted against French violation of the international rights of states.

Vietnamese nationhood is relentlessly reiterated in smaller linguistic choices. The letter combines the legal language of the San Francisco and Atlantic Charters with some formality for the benefit of the Secretary of State and to reflect Vietnam's status as a state. 'Vietnam' is the only name used to refer to the country; the colonial terms 'Annam', 'Tonkin', 'Cochinchina' are never mentioned while 'Indochina' is only used once. Except for Vietnamese nationalist circles, this nomenclature was rather unusual at the time and until 1948 all French and foreign diplomats use the colonial names and the demonym 'Annamese' for the Vietnamese. The use of the endonym Vietnam is relevant in terms of Vietnam's national self-identification and deeply political, denoting historical pride and independence. The Tang Dynasty name 'Annam' (安南) means 'Pacified South' in Chinese, a contraction of the administrative name "Protectorate General to Pacify the South" (安南都護府) that reflects the violent measures the Tang took to pacify that colony. Upon independence in 938 CE the Ngo dynasty named the country 'Dai Viet' ('Great Viet' Empire). The word 'Viet' would be retained in all subsequent variations of the empire's name until the French conquest in the 1850s reimposed the name Annam and the demonym Annamese.[2] Using only Vietnam and rejecting all other terms was itself a nationalist political statement, an act of self-declaration borne in language.

Vietminh appears only once in this text. When it does, it is powerfully inscribed into the representation of Vietnamese self-determination. It is linguistically and structurally framed as a natural expression of Vietnamese self-determination, resistance against the Japanese and French invasions, and the new international norms: 'the Vietnamese, leaving aside all differences in political opinion, united against the Japanese' which, combined with 'the noble principles' of the Atlantic Charter, 'contributed in making of the Vietminh resistance'. The text constitutes Vietminh as the expression of Vietnamese Allied resistance who then turned to the equally just cause of Vietnamese independence. Forged in the crucible of anti-Japanese resistance, Vietminh brings together various political groups around the common cause of Độc Lập: independence.

The representation that emerges most powerfully from this text is Vietnamese right to independence and French colonial ruthlessness. Vietminh is only its institutional expression, the expression of national awakening. Vietnamese will and right to self-determination is constituted on the basis of the Charters and, crucially, the will of the Vietnamese made manifest. This was demonstrated by unity against the Japanese and especially the French – a core part of the interwar international conceptualization of self-determination.[3] This representation is marked by textual markers (topoi) reflecting international legal language (references to the Charters like 'aggression', 'self-determination'), popular will ('united', 'as one man', 'democratic aspirations of the people') and the act of statehood ('appointment of a provisional Government'). Vietnam's desire to exercise international rights are signposted by language and references such as Vietnam 'calls for' and 'equitable settlement'.

Vietnamese nationhood and its rights are pitted against the powerfully inscripted representation of French imperialism. The letter assumes colonialism is no longer widely considered legitimate under the Charters and was further delegitimized by Vichy Second World War collaboration. To this it adds deceit in 'having persuaded the British that the Vietnamese are wishing for a return of the French' and even treachery to the French public. These are strong accusations to make against a democracy, and clearly reference Vietnamese accusations about the difference between French republican democratic and rights-based ideals and colonial practices that disenfranchised every Vietnamese. The representation of colonialism as illegal – at least postwar – is reinforced by allusions to military violence and military aggression ('instead of entering into peaceable negotiations'), something that had recently been made illegitimate under the San Francisco charter. This representation is signposted by vocables such as 'betrayal', 'the colonists', 'aggression', 'murderous' in the context of references to brutality, war and violence. In this letter, internationally supported independence emerges as the only solution.

5

The French Empire strikes back: aggression against Độc Lập

PROVISIONAL GOVERNMENT OF THE REPUBLIC OF VIETNAM
DECLARATION OF THE FOREIGN OFFICE

September 1945
Blood is being shed in South Vietnam. The situation is aggravating every hour, threatening the security of the Far-East.
False propaganda and insinuating reports have disfigured the world opinion on the Vietnamese question. We wish to expose in the following note, the development of the Vietnamese situation since the establishment of the French domination up to the present day.
[. . .]
By the end of August 1945, the Japanese surrendered to the Allies unconditionally. China and Britain were to send troops to occupy Indochina temporarily, until the disarmament of the Japanese is achieved. Big spontaneous demonstrations, and enthusiastic expressions of the free press, showed that the Vietnamese, backing up their Government, were ready to welcome the Allies Nations into Indochina. The Chinese forces to the North of 16th and British forces to the South moved in without the slightest incident.
But in the meanwhile, radiobroadcast from French General De Gaulle, M. Bidault, General Leclerc and Amiral d'Argenlieu, to quote only a few, as well as the provocative attitude of French residents in the main Indochinese towns evinced the dark aims of France, whose representatives openly menaced Indochina of a second aggression. On September 23rd, in the morning, the threats became facts and the French, with the complicity or at least with the connivance of the British troops launched a night attack in the streets of Saigon against the Vietnamese civilian population.
[. . .]
CONCLUSION
In the light of the preceding statements, the following facts are established:

1. France was militarily incapable of defending her colonial Empire, contrarily to the treaties signed with the protected countries.
2. From 1940-1945, France, breaking all her promises, yielded to Japanese pressure and cooperated with the axis-powers, while the Vietnamese resisted and stuck to the Allies.
3. France carried out an inhuman and destructive food policy in Vietnam, whereas it had been stated in every quarter that after the war food situation will be very serious in the whole world.
4. Vietnam has wrested her independence out of the Japanese, and from August 19th has been a de facto independent republic with all the organs of a legitimate government supported by the whole nation.
5. French troops, excited by French propaganda and smoke-screened by British occupation forces, violated Vietnamese national rights, territorial integrity, as well as the principles laid down in the Atlantic Charter and in the agreements reached in subsequent peace conferences.
6. The Vietnamese, people is determined to fight to the last man for its independence and for the cause of international Justice and equality of status, against French aggressors.

In conclusion, the Provisional Government of the Democratic Republic of Vietnam, appealing to the United Nations, has decided:
1. To lodge a most emphatic protest against the British Disarmament Mission in South Indochina for having connived at and favoured a French aggression on the Vietnamese people, aggression contrary to the principles laid down in the Atlantic Charter, in the Teheran, San-Francisco and Postdam conferences.
2. To lodge a most emphatic protest against the use of the British, Japanese and Gurkha indian troops to help the French aggressors under pretence of trying to reestablish order, whereas the responsibility for the disturbance of order can only be imputed to French troops under French Colonels Cedille and Riviere.
3. To apply to the United Nations for an urgent settling of the Indochinese situation on the basis of full respect for the independence and freedom of the Vietnamese people.[1]

The above extracts come from a booklet that accompanied Ho Chi Minh's letter to the Secretary of State analysed in the previous section. Titled 'Declaration of the foreign office', it focuses on the initial reimposition of French rule in Saigon on the night of 23 September 1945, when French troops retook control of Saigon from Vietminh and terrorized the population. They had been rearmed by the British occupying force and had reoccupied the city with their blessing. In a racist *libération* of Saigon, the French settler population joined the soldiers in acts of revenge against those that had momentarily overturned the tables of colonialism and their French *collaborateurs*. In an act of brutality analysed later in this book, settlers and soldiers shaved, stripped and publicly paraded a French woman that had written a tract against French colonialism in support of Vietminh. De Gaulle had announced that France would not tolerate terrorism and would re-establish order by force if necessary. An expeditionary force led by Second World War hero General Leclerc was to be sent from France to re-establish order and assist the new Haut Commissaire of the colony, Admiral Thierry d'Argenlieu. This team was de Gaulle's personal choice of loyal nationalist personnel to re-establish and secure French sovereignty over Indochina.[2] The booklet, highly polished and bound in red covers with silk thread, was an explicit effort to give the new Vietnamese state a voice with the great power that had just defeated Japan and established the UN, the only power that could be expected to favour decolonization and counteract France.

This text sets out to denounce colonial aggression. It lays the blame for the violence in southern Vietnam on French troops and settlers let loose and armed by a British force led by General Gracey occupying Southern Indochina to disarm the Japanese. In the first three pages of the booklet (not included in the above extract), the events of 1945 are set in the context of a long history of ruthless conquest and repression of Vietnam beginning with the French conquest in the 1850s. The text is at pains to stress that Vietnam had been a state, a highly organized empire. Against the backdrop of colonial conquest, the booklet's second half and conclusions (in the extract above) achieve far more than lay the blame for recent violence on the French military and racist settlers. They denounce the entire colonial enterprise and, in this narrative, make the present a point of crisis that justifies international censure of French colonialism in Indochina and support for Vietnam's independence. The arguments are effective without rhetorical drama: France has failed to protect its colony (technically a protectorate), collaborated with the Axis, purposefully left millions of Vietnamese to starve in the famine of 1944–45, seeks to re-establish control at the cost of a new war, while an indigenous government has already replaced French rule. Like the letter analysed in the previous section, it concludes with a request for international intervention, but its focus is to convey the Vietnamese side of the story of the French reconquest of Indochina.

The structure of the text is primarily narrative. After summarizing the 'establishment of the French domination', the first part of the extract distinctly separates between Chinese toleration of the DRV government from French demands for the complete and unquestioned re-establishment of sovereignty 'in France's own terms'.[3] The representation of a colonial conspiracy against legitimate Vietnamese actions and claims is completed by the collusion of the British, who 'use British, Japanese and Gurkha indian troops to help the French aggressors'. The second part of the extract summarizes the Vietnamese view of French crimes and, clearly as a consequence of them (whence the analytical focus on narrative), the actions advocated by the DRV for itself, resistance, and international protests, and which it requests from others: international arbitration and recognition of Vietnamese rights. The text's linguistic choices support the narrative leading to these conclusions. The vocabulary inscribes a deep division, opposing French colonial cruelty against Vietnamese legitimate rights, although the focus is almost entirely on the former. While Vietnamese actions are described as 'spontaneous' and 'enthusiastic expressions' of their political will, French acts constitute a 'second aggression' (after the Japanese) by a state 'incapable of defending' those in its charge, 'breaking' international commitments and carrying out 'inhuman' and 'destructive' acts fuelled by 'propaganda'.

The booklet constitutes a more detailed and defined set of inscriptions that work towards constituting representations. The text primarily achieves a temporal location of France as an advanced nation that for a century has been using its power for illegitimate ends in Indochina while neglecting the basic duties of a colonial power such as defence or basic food supply. Specifically, it is the French colonial enterprise, the oeuvre that de Gaulle and d'Argenlieu were so keen to defend, that is thus inscribed as entirely abusive and primarily violent. Likewise, Vietnamese subjects emerge from this temporal inscription as century-long victims of colonialism and racial abuse. The language of this anticolonial narrative is not new. It was typical of an emerging anticolonial position in France itself, one advocated for instance by André Malraux, that focused on administrative abuses, inhumanity and repression very much through the lens of individual rights and sought at least improvements in conditions for the natives and some degree of self-government.[4] Remarkably, in this booklet the violation of rights is combined with French fiduciary ineptitude to result in a call that is partially codified as divestment of responsibility for Vietnam.

Drawing on this temporal frame, the normative inscription of French colonialism and Vietnamese nationalism is further differentiated. References to the Allied Cause, the foundational United Nations Charters and the right to self-determination and decolonization work towards locating French colonialism in the wrong side of the Second World War and postwar normative divide. This is corroborated in the conclusion, which lays out in plain terms French collaboration with Japan, the breach of the Charters and self-determination principles, the wartime food policy that caused famine in 1944–45, as well as aggression against Vietnam.[5] The DRV, by the same token, emerges on the Allied side, having fought with the Allies against the Japanese, being democratically proclaimed and having established a 'legitimate government supported by the whole nation'. Vietminh does not appear at all as it is subsumed within the DRV Government. The actions of this government are legitimate and the will of the Vietnamese, and this extends to foreign affairs, where 'the Vietnamese backing up their government' welcomed the Allies.

Độc Lập, independence, is the conclusion of the narrative, language and representation of French colonialism, Vietnamese subjects and DRV in this text. It is firstly inscribed as a normative necessity by the extent of French violence against Vietnamese subjects over a century. Secondly, it is posited as a normative and narratively constituted conclusion of colonial repression and incompetence during the Second World War. Thirdly, it is constituted as the practical desert of DRV which 'has been a de facto independent republic'. Finally, it is normatively inscribed as the democratic will of the Vietnamese, who 'wrested her independence out of the Japanese'. It is worth highlighting that this text, linking Vietnamese identity to the will to independence, is not simple rhetorical drama, it is a deeply inscribed historical facet of Vietnamese national identity that is 1,500 years old and which celebrated the millennium of struggle against Chinese rule, with heroes such as the Trang sisters. This is evident in this booklet and in most Vietnamese texts on Độc Lập (Độc Lập was even part of the DRV motto) where the drive for independence is assumed and linguistically referenced in heroic terms. This narrative is a historical given in Vietnamese identity-formation and is part of its normative inscription. Like the title character's passionate filial love in the Vietnamese epic poem *The Tale of Kieu*, the very existence of anticolonial sentiment is inscribed as immanent, natural and righteous.[6]

Representation of Độc Lập as Vietminh's and DRV's sole goal reappears consistently both in articulation and language until 1948. As Vietminh came under pressure for the Communist background of key leaders like Ho and Giap, and its 1941 amalgamation of the Communist Party of Indochina (CPI) with several nationalist parties to form Vietminh, its national liberation objective remained consistently represented. For comparison, in 1947 American Ambassador in Bangkok E. F. Stanton submitted written questions to DRV Undersecretary for Foreign Affairs Dr Pham Ngoc Thach. Here is the embassy's paraphrase of Thach's answer to 'Can a definition be given to Communism as it exists in Vietnam?'

> In reply to the third question for a definition of Communism as it exists in Vietnam, Dr. Thach stated that since 1932 it has embodied the spirit of national resistance against French

colonialism and that it has changed little since the government
of Vietnam assumed power in August 1945. Dr. Thach refers to the
dissolution in November 1945 of the Communist Party of Indochina
with a view to stopping internal and external bickering in order
that the national cause might triumph. Dr. Thach asserted that
Communism for the majority of its adherents is no more than a
means of achieving independence. He referred to the serious damage
inflicted upon the doctrinaire position of Communism in Vietnam
by the unexpected support given by the French Communist Party to
the expeditionary force of Gen. Leclerc. Dr. Thach summed up
Communism in Vietnam by stating that basically it ''advocated
production of sufficient to feed and cloth the population, to give
instruction to all, to respect personal liberties and to respect
property rights. He also emphasized that the economic program of
the government advocates neither nationalism nor division of
private property but on the contrary favors utilization of foreign
capitalism in the reconstruction of the country.[7]

This extract from 1947 offers the same normative inscription of Vietminh as a league of many parties with independence as its unchanged goal since 1945, and features the same articulation (anticolonialism, rights) and language ('national cause', 'achieve independence'). It is updated with the anti-independence position of the French Communist Party, which places it at odds with Vietminh, the latter's lack of socialist economic programmes and the sententia (unsubstantiated rhetorical argument, like a maxim) that communism was to Vietnam the provision of basic rights and independence.

The booklet containing the 1945 extracts has a red cover with a yellow star in the middle, the flag of the DRV. Though this clearly has a communist origin and is commonly interpreted as such, it also bears an interesting link to Vietnam's Imperial past. The flag of the Nguyen Imperial Dynasty (of which Bao Dai was the last) sported a red circle in the middle of a red field. The Nguyen, however, not unlike the Qing in early twentieth-century China, were widely derided as inept traitors for failing to resist European conquest. The previous dynasty, the Later Lê, had a standard remarkably similar to the Vietminh flag: a yellow circle in the middle of a red field. The Later Lê, 1428–1788, unified most of contemporary Vietnam and was the longest-lived dynasty in Vietnamese history. This is not to suggest a direct link between Vietminh and the Later Lê. Rather, to educated children of Imperial Mandarins such as Ho and much of the Vietminh elite, the Vietminh flag had crucial nationalist associations beyond communism, as it did for the founders of the Đại Việt Quốc Dân Dảng (the KMT-like Nationalist Party of Greater Vietnam), founded two years before Vietminh, whose flag had a white star on a blue circle on a red field.

The representations of French, the colonial crimes of the French Empire, and Vietminh's struggle for Độc Lập are signposted by the most stable and consistent textual markers encountered in this entire project. French colonialism is to be consistently found within articulations marked by the 'inhuman', 'destructive', and treacherous attitude of empire that 'violated' rights. Conversely, the cause of Độc Lập is represented as an individual and national right, and its articulation is found signposted by the language of 'international justice', 'right' and 'freedom', which is furthermore often historically contextualized. After all, Việt Nam Độc Lập Đồng Minh Hội means 'League for the Independence of Vietnam'.

6

Vietminh as Fascists: Vietnam does not exist

Dalat, the 26th April 1946   HAUT COMISSAIRE DE FRANCE
                                pour l'INDOCHINE

/ <u>VERY SECRET</u> /   Le Haut Commissaire
                    <u>MEMORANDUM</u>

SUBJECT: Political turning point in Indochina

I. As the work of the conference at Dalat begins, it is important to locate the question of the future of Cochinchina in the context of the Indochinese problem.

The goal of our policy, first and well-defined object of my mission, was to re-establish French sovereignty.

This sovereignty -let us call it authority- already exists.
- in Laos: we are at the gates of Vientiane and Luang-Prabang.
- in Cambodia: the situation develops favourably, under our control
- in South Annam: up to the Ban-Me-Thuot - Van-Gia parallel
- in Cochinchina: the regional and federal governments are there. Our authority was established in the liberal spirit of the 24th March 1945 declaration, well received by all.
- in Tonkin and North Annam: our forces are now implanted and our political authority shines weakly to the extent permitted by the Hanoi Government's strict interpretation of the 6 March Convention. The presence of Chinese forces is still significant and they are distinctly hostile, forcing us to act with extreme reserve for some time.
[. . .]

[reuniting the three Kys] is not without risk. The most normal course of action would be to continue as we had done before the signing of the convention. A [Cochinchinese] government is ready to be declared. It would be up to them to guide Cochinchina towards its destiny through the preparation of the referendum. The work of establishing the electoral system has already been underway for a good few weeks and will be completed by the end of June.

Without directly intervening in the electoral campaign,
France, seeing the nature of its interests at stake, must have
a political position. She can favour the autonomy of Cochinchina,
to the keen displeasure of the Hanoi government. Conversely,
she can, favour the reunification of the three Ky to the
detriment of French authority.

She can therefore act in Annam one way or another. She can
abstain.
III. Only an ideological and doctrinal position favours the
reunification of the three Ky and our stepping behind the
initiative of the Hanoi government.
Not geographically, historically, or economically is the
concept of the reunification of the three Ky the necessary one.
Rather it's the contrary.
Not geographically, for the Mekong basin solidly welds
together Laos, Cambodia and Cochinchina. The Annamite mountain
chain completes their isolation in relation to Annam.
Not historically, for the plantation of Annamites from the
North replaced the centuries of occupation of these lands by the
ancient Khmer people. This plantation was accidental and brief.
That of France succeeded it for nearly a century.
Not economically, for the Mekong with its delta ties together
Laos, Cambodia and Cochinchina. It is France, France alone,
that has made Cochinchina the masterpiece of the Indochinese
economy (rice, rubber, etc. . .).
As to the argument derived from linguistic unity, it is
either a puerile or embibed by a racist slant.
Was the argument of linguistic unity not the one used by the
Führer to force the Germanic minorities to meld into the great
Reich?[1]

April 1946, the first Dalat conference begins. This memorandum is the precursor to the second Dalat conference in August, which coincided with Franco-Vietnamese negotiations at Fontainebleau, Paris. The memorandum, sent to Minister of Colonies Moutet, lays the groundwork for how Haut Commissaire d'Argenlieu's diplomatic actions scuppered Fontainebleau and helped bring war about in 1946. The July–September 1946 Fontainebleau conference brought together a DRV delegation including Ho Chi Minh and Pham Van Dong and a French legation including Moutet and Foreign Minister (and then Prime Minister) Bidault, to discuss and reach agreement on the future basis of Franco-Vietnamese relations. On the agenda were the reunification of the three Kys (see map, Fig. 1), the powers of the Vietnam Government, and the extent of its diplomatic, political and military competences within the framework of the French Union – the renamed French Empire. These talks had been arranged in the 6 March 1946

(Ho–Sainteny) accords that allowed the return of French troops to north Indochina. It was the only time until 1954 that France would officially engage with the DRV and consider its delegation as representatives of a country.[2]

Concurrently, d'Argenlieu's second conference at Dalat brought together representatives from the five parts of French Indochina. In a perpetuation of the 1887 colonial break-up of the Empire of Vietnam, he insisted in treating Indochina as five equal parts. This conference accepted his creation in June of the Republic of Cochinchina – which may have been informally approved by Moutet. This memorandum outlines his arguments against the reunification of Vietnam and for the permanent separation of Cochinchina from Annam and Tonkin. It was the only official warning he issued to the French government of his inclination to permanently separate Cochinchina, which he effectively executed at the second Dalat conference. By thus prejudicing negotiations on reunification, d'Argenlieu irremediably scuppered the talks at Fontainebleau.

Despite having overstepped his authority in inventing the puppet Republic of Cochinchina, the arguments in d'Argenlieu's memorandum remained a key part of the Vietnam reunification debate long after him. The French would not again contemplate reunification until the late 1948 Baie d'Along version of the Bao Dai solution, when the new non-Vietminh French-supported Central Government of Vietnam was established.

Reunification was never effected, and Vietnam was separated again in the Geneva negotiations of 1954, pending a referendum that never took place, when North and South Vietnam were created upon the defeat of the French at Điện Biên Phủ. Some of these arguments would be found again in US 1950–70s discourse against reunification, with the difference that French progressive influence was replaced with Catholicism, one of Ngo Dinh Diem's main claims to South Vietnamese nationhood.

This Memorandum argues that Vietnam does not exist. It is furthermore a perfect definition of how a text can inscribe and constitute understanding (policy-relevant in this case) of subjects, territory, history, and even the material economy. The nationality of subjects is simply circumscribed within the extent of the colonial Kys of Annam, leaving aside the extent of the Vietnamese language, culture, history, institutions or political history.[3] Annamese subjects are, furthermore, subtly inscribed as imperialist and violent, pitted against helpless Cochinchinese that need France to help them retain their freedom. Spatially, Indochina is codified and internally differentiated in geospatial and geopolitical terms, subjugating other human factors that play into the establishment of areas of shared political, linguistic, agricultural and other social identity. For instance, Cochinchina's geographical location at the mouth of the Mekong 'solidly welds' it to Laos and Cambodia while mountains separate it from Annam. The seventeenth-century Vietnamese conquest and settlement of the Mekong delta is historically inscribed as a single act of aggression, which in a fascinating colonial contradiction, appears revoked by the French conquest. In relation to the same temporal frame, Cochinchina is presented as wealthier thanks to longer French rule and the establishment of more French businesses – which makes it distinct from the north's smaller economy.[4]

Furthermore, Vietnam should not exist. The memorandum argues that seeking reunification of the three Kys is an unreasonable demonstration of doctrinaire and ideological extremism. In the second part of the extract Vietminh's aim and negotiating position is equated to Nazi ideological ethno-nationalism, a deeply normative Second World War contextual inscription that draws on fascist German and Japanese expansion to represent Vietnamese reunification as normatively perverse, violent and repressive. Vietnam's Führer-like expansionist extremism constitutes a set of identities at risk (Laos, Cambodia, Cochinchina and minorities within Vietnam such as the Muong) that are at risk from Vietnamese aggression. Vietnamese unification is a risk for all in Indochina – and thus France is needed to arbiter and protect. Despite appearances, this representation was not contradictory with d'Argenlieu's other common representation of Vietminh as communist. French colonial discourse at the time linked extremists such as fascists and communists not as mutually opposing as my reader and myself might, but in terms of their 'anti-white' extremism, where fascist Japanese anti-Europeanism was perfectly compatible with communist anti-Westernism.

The language is geared towards reinforcing the colonial five-way division of Indochina. In its syntax, long sentences with several sub-clauses refer to Cochinchina and France, which contrast sharply with the truncated brief constructions discussing Vietminh, which rhetorically suggests that only simple and succinct argument rebuttals are necessary for poor arguments. In a formatting and alliteration feat at the end of the extract, 'not' is repeated four times to begin short paragraphs – in the original French all seven paragraphs begin with a negative particle. Grammatical gender and number are implicated in this differentiation too. France and Cochinchina are personified (addressed as 'she') as per the French convention for countries ("La France"), while 'the government of Hanoi' is referred to as 'them', withdrawing from Vietnam the grammatical treatment reserved for countries, inscribing it within the linguistic convention used for political parties and other groups.

Inscription of the 'Annamese' as violent imperialists is reinforced in vocabulary. For instance, by the use of terms like 'plantation', 'imperial' (not in the extract), 'expansion' in reference to Vietnamese conquest of the south in the seventeenth century. Furthermore, the memorandum makes heroic linguistic efforts to avoid the word 'Vietnam', even when mentioning the language or DRV, which is referred to solely as 'Hanoi' or 'Hanoi Government'. To use the name Annam is a colonial linguistic choice. Meaning 'Pacified South', it comes from the Han term for Vietnam when it was a Chinese colony. Vietnam has explicitly not used it since independence from China in 938 CE and it was imposed by the French administration of Indochina in the 1880s. A year later, d'Argenlieu called 'brilliant' the 'idea of reviving the ancient name of Vietnam' and demanded that the Foreign Ministry 'bans usage of the term Viet Nam for all official documents'.[5] It should not be surprising that d'Argenlieu was deeply invested in Empire, its very words and history. He began his navy career during the 1911–13 colonization of Morocco, when he had the opportunity to appreciate the order established by Hubert Lyautey, the 'French Empire Builder' whom he admired.[6]

Three important representations emerge from this memorandum.

First, Vietminh's extremism and fascist 'doctrinal ideological position', the most important representation in this text. This is because Vietminh ideology and goals, whether fascist, communist or anticolonial, would be represented by French and US diplomacy on the basis of exactly the same dynamic and articulation for thirty years and through various reincarnations. Vietminh's anticolonialism – rather than anticolonialism more broadly – is inscribed as illegitimate, an effect of underdeveloped native immaturity that results in ideological extremism. The vital core articulation links Vietminh goals and means to oriental political inadequacy, backwardness and lack of development. In 1946 French diplomacy of the period described anticolonial struggle as 'terrorism' or 'anti-white' racism, linking Vietminh not only to other anticolonial movements and extremism, but also to Japanese Second World War ideology and anti-Western militancy. This representation is signposted by topoi textual markers such as 'doctrinal', 'ideological', 'extremist', 'racist', references to 'them' (as opposed to 'it' or DRV, denying identity beyond a political party) and by references to Second World War fascism. This would be crucial in 1947–48, when, ironically, Vietminh political and battlefield successes led French diplomats to suggest to British and American counterparts that Vietminh ideology, organization and success must be the product of foreign agents. Representation of extremist and backward Vietminh linked to the broader orientalist discourse to posit that 'indolent' Vietnamese could not possibly challenge France with such political determination without a

Western guide, Soviet in this case. This representation of 'ideological' extremism is politically powerful, for it normatively destabilizes the violence, efforts, organization and ultimately the very cause of anticolonialism.

Related but distinct and far older, the second is Annamese imperialist expansionism. Much as British colonialism did with some Indian ethnic groups, the 'Annamese' were qualified as violent, expansionist and themselves colonial.[7] This imperial ethnographic idea is signposted by markers such as 'plantation' when referring to Annamese populations where they should not be, and 'Annamese' imperialism over less developed races and peoples. This representation is directly related to and mutually constitutive of early twentieth-century French colonial discourse that proposed France as a mature more developed neutral arbiter of native violence. Representation of the French *œuvre coloniale* and pride in its achievements and *mission civilisatrice* is usually marked by 'œuvre' or references to progressive achievements and tutelage of less developed peoples. They are very present in this Memorandum's discussion of Cochinchina, the 'masterpiece' of Indochina thanks to the benevolence and progress of 'France, France alone'. In other words, Indochina is at risk from Vietnamese expansionism – only the French Empire, civilizing mission and protection can save and develop Laos, Cambodia and the minorities.

The third and most scandalous representation, that Vietnam does not exist, draws on the above two. It is based on an articulation that leaves the cause of Vietnam as a racist and expansionist dream of oriental Imperial glory promoted by Nazi-like fascist extremists. It is marked by the relentless avoidance of the vocables 'Viet' and 'Vietnam' and use of the colonial 'Annam' or 'Hanoi Government' ('the communists' in later texts) and insistence on the existence and distinctiveness of 'Cochinchina' and 'its destiny' that France must protect – while 'seeing the nature of her interests at stake'.

7

Vietminh as Communists: 'Moscow's interest in Indo-China'

This telegram must be   Paris
closely paraphrased be-
fore being communicated
to anyone. (SECRET)

Secretary of State,
Washington.

September 22, 4 p.m.

According to Baudet the French feel greatly reassured about the intentions of the Chinese Government regarding Indo-China. He referred to certain apprehensions France had some days ago that the Chinese Government might possibly be giving Lou Han a free rein and said that they are now convinced that this is not the case and that they are doing what they can to keep him from acting independently. He added that when Soong was in Paris he received a telegram from Ching-Kai-Chek stating that the French should be informed that China had no territorial ambitions in Indo-China and would do nothing to prevent the French from reestablishing their former position there.

He then discussed the so-called "Viet Minh Movement" and said that it was organized somewhat along Communist lines with secret cells, etc.. He also said that the French have evidence that it is in touch with the Soviet Mission at Chungking. Despite this he expressed the opinion that the "Viet Minh is not a Communist organization although the Communist Party in northern Indo-China (which he said had been quite active at one time) "has now more or less disappeared as such and appears to have been absorbed in the Viet Minh."

Speaking of the statement of the French Communist Political Bureau (my 5639, September 22) Baudet said that while the statement was couched in "rather moderate terms" it nonetheless indicated Moscow's interest in Indo-China.

In speaking of the reestablishment of French authority in Indo-China he said that the French intend to modify the statute for Indo-China but that the Foreign Minister believes it would

be an error to modify the statute until French authority has
been restored and the situation studied on the spot. He added
that the evolution of events there made it obvious that the
former French conception of the status of Indo-China must be
revised "taking into consideration the desires of the nationalist
groups in Indo-China."
He concluded by expressing deep appreciation for shipping the US
has offered to make available in the Pacific and emphasized the
importance of obtaining ships from the British to send to Indo-
China the French military forces necessary to restore order.

CAFFERY

Sent Department 5645, repeated Moscow 336 Chungking 16[1]

September 1945. The Second World War has just ended and Allied Chinese
troops occupy north Indochina to disarm the Japanese. Vietminh declared the
independence of the DRV twenty days before. In this cable US ambassador to
Paris Jefferson Caffery reports a conversation with Philippe Baudet, Director of
the Asia-Oceania Division at the French Ministry of Foreign Affairs. This cable
represents a key type of diplomatic correspondence: an account of a conversation
among diplomats, textualized by one of them for reporting. We are analysing this
American document as an instance of French diplomatic communication
because, lacking a recording of the conversation, this is the exact version,
language and ultimately representations that US diplomats and policymakers
garnered from Baudet. Stamps on the original document denote that it was read
at the Southeast Asia, European and Secretary's Offices at the State Department,
and was resent to the US embassies in Moscow and Chungking. That same week
French intelligence agent and later colonial diplomat Jean Sainteny met with Ho
Chi Minh for the first time. He had been parachuted into Indochina at the head
of a small corps to gather intelligence on the situation on the ground, about
which de Gaulle's government knew remarkably little.

Since de Gaulle's declaration on Indochina of 24 March, French policy for
Indochina was to 'liberate' the colony and restore order from the effects of the
Japanese occupation, including Japanese-inspired terrorists. While early French
reports on Vietminh treated them as Japanese stooges and their eradication as
part of the *liberation* of France, this conversation is one of the first instances they
are linked to communism and particularly to international communism directed
from Moscow. Significantly for this book, it constitutes a representation of
Vietminh ideology that draws on similar orientalist discourses as the text in
the previous analysis, but this time locating Vietminh within international
communism.

The main concern expressed by Baudet is the 'reestablishment of French authority in Indo-China'. That is, the recovery of northern Indochina from Chinese occupation, followed by the necessity to either placate or repress Vietminh once Chinese troops left. The Chinese occupation under General Lou Han was particularly concerning as this force, larger than a division, were reportedly sacking northern Indochina, living off local resources and failing to protect French interests and population – not least from the Vietnamese. Despite Chiang Kai-shek's statement that 'China had no territorial ambitions in Indo-China', this Chinese force would prevent the return of French forces to north Indochina for another six months. In what might partly have been a show of Republican Nationalist solidarity (for Vietminh included within itself and in its government coalition two nationalist KMT-inspired parties), they tolerated Ho's DRV government, though not without attempting to manipulate it. Furthermore, through the threat of delaying withdrawal, the Chinese forced the French, in the person of their representative Sainteny, into talks with DRV, leading to the 6 March 1946 agreement.

The manner in which Baudet discusses the communism of 'the so-called Viet Minh Movement' appears highly ambiguous at first. Vietminh is partly communist and has 'absorbed' a communist party, Baudet explains, and yet 'is not a communist organisation'. He then asserts that it definitely has links to Moscow, proven by declarations of the French Communist Party and 'evidence' of contact with Soviet diplomats in China. Baudet is keen to show that French policy towards Indochina is progressive, though reform remains conditional on French restoration in Indochina. This progressivism is not surprising considering that the US had only recently withdrawn its plans for International Trusteeship over Indochina and France was requesting American shipping for the expeditionary force being dispatched to Indochina. This conversation sets the stage for dismissing Indochinese anticolonial resistance as the ploy of foreign-led communists, arguing that repossession is necessary before even declaring changes to French colonialism to accommodate 'nationalist groups'.

Analysing the language of the conversation through the report of the US ambassador is fascinating, for this is a text bearing complex and multi-layered ideational structure and linguistic choices. Structurally the conversation moves from the (apparently) resolved question of Chinese occupation to the unresolved issues of Vietminh and the shipping needed to take a French army to 'restore order' in Indochina. Despite Baudet's tone appearing generally sympathetic to 'nationalist groups in Indo-China', analysis of the language shows the extent to which he was constructing the basis for a hard dismissal of Vietminh and particularly of any anticolonial grievances.

Vocabulary choices suggest a certain level of uncertainty as to Vietminh itself: 'so-called', 'somewhat', 'more or less'; words that denote and indeed promote vagueness as to what Vietminh or its goals are. Remarkably, in the very same sentences, certainty is invested by vocabulary choices onto references to Vietminh's foreign communist credentials. We find, in contrast, strong definitive statements and words like 'communist lines', 'secret cells', 'absorbed', and particularly 'Moscow'. Uncertainty as to Vietminh's goals with the certainty of its foreign-directed communism powerfully combine to constitute a representation of Vietnamese subjects relegated to puppets in a Moscow-directed conspiracy. This is a subjugation of the agency of Vietnamese anticolonialism to Western ideology, evidently also discursively subjecting Vietnamese subjects and agency to Western ones. This articulation draws the same discourse of colonial political inadequacy as the previously analysed d'Argenlieu memorandum, representing the ideology of backward colonial subjects as necessarily foreign and Western. In this text, however, it is more subtly written, appearing far more normalized.

Language is heavily invested in the French repossession of Indochina. Potential Chinese 'territorial ambitions' are negatively posited against France's 'former position'. And the fact that this is a return is the most heavily emphasized linguistic feature: 'reestablishing', 'restore'. Such words posit the legitimacy of French sovereignty over Indochina and its re-establishment as a legitimate return, de Gaulle's *libération*, not a reconquest despite the need for military forces to 'restore order'. The conversation suggests French willingness to 'modify the statute' of Indochina to accommodate the 'desires of the nationalist groups' as the US had pressured France to do (not least through Trusteeship) and Baudet's language might have mirrored American discourse on the subject – though this is uncertain, as this aspect of the conversation's language is particularly vulnerable to having been reported this way, accommodated in translation as it were, by US diplomats taking notes. In this way, Baudet's language constructs a temporal frame that posits France as progressive and legitimate in the future, accommodating past colonialism and legitimizing the present need to re-establish French rule.

Two representations of vital importance emerge. First, the presence of Soviet international communism in Indochina, which depends on a twofold articulation. On the one hand 'Moscow' communism is a monolithic global conspiracy infiltrating organizations and countries. It is ultimately illegitimate and, at least in terms of anticolonialism, false because it is a Soviet power play. The presence of this representation is signposted by exceedingly familiar topoi markers such as 'a communist organisation' (replying on the assumption that they are all the same or centralized) featuring typically conspiratorial 'secret cells' working on 'Moscow's interest'. On the other hand, representation of Vietminh is entirely subsumed into international communism, effectively obscuring the individuality of the cause of anticolonialism and particularly its agency to take such an initiative. This is clearly signposted by markers such as the communists being 'absorbed' into Vietminh (more commonly found as 'infiltration') and organization 'along communist lines'. The second representation is France's new drive for liberal colonial reform. It is signposted by markers such as the 'obvious' need for 'consideration of the desires' of colonial subjects and future 'modification' of colonial governance. Its commencement is, however, marked by conditioning depending on 'the reestablishment of French authority'.

A brief comparison with the representation of Vietminh communism prevalent in the later 1940s is worthwhile. Representing Vietminh as part of an international communist conspiracy was discontinuous, incoherent and at some points unusual in 1945 and would only reappear consistently in late 1946. Rather, French diplomatic writing about Vietminh between 1945 and mid-1946 was characterized by the representations in d'Argenlieu's memo and "Vietminh fascism".[2] Fascist-communist inconsistency in representation is most probably due to the composition of French government coalitions in 1946. They included the French Communist Party, making it difficult for civil servants to write about communism as an anti-French conspiracy. Communism took a significant place in French–US diplomacy in late 1946 and would gain serious consistency, including links to the USSR, in late 1947. The change in emphasis is reflected in a 1948 report tasked with suggesting improvements for French diplomacy, information and propaganda in the US. It concludes that Franco–American relations would 'thrive' on common enmity with the USSR, which is described in the precise terms common during the Red Scare. In the extract below, the report's author, Claudel, suggests how French diplomacy should represent the 'reciprocal position of our two countries':

> It is dominated by one fact. Both are on the same boat, both are in mortal danger. For the first time perhaps since the creation of the world, the equilibrium of the planet is under threat. In the Old World, circumstances have given a crushing dynamic superiority to a State that does not share any of its ancient Christian principles, that no longer speaks the same language and that is increasingly, as was the case with Hitler's Germany, animated by an undeniable will to aggression. What remains of Europe has insufficient means of defence against this terrible danger. Europe has need of two things: the first is an understanding between its component parts; the second is the persistent and solid support of America.[3]

8

A 'united front' and 'the left-wing trend of the Viet-Minh'

FO memo (M. Anderson),

FRENCH INDO-CHINA

[. . .]

Amongst the Annamites there had always been underground movements for severing the French connection. These included a strong Communist element, but included many other schools of political thought including purely "nationalist" movements, on a racial basis. On the outbreak of war severe steps were taken against the Communists on the same lines as in France, and many of the Annamites leaders were arrested, some of them prominent persons in public life. The anti-French movement, with the tacit approval of the Japanese, was prevented from giving trouble throughout the period of French administration under Japanese direction. When de Japanese suppressed that administration in March 1945 they did so in the name of Annamite independence, but gave the Annamites little actual authority. On the collapse of Japan the principal Annamite nationalist party (Viet-Minh) seized actual power and secured Japanese arms. The true extent of their present following amongst their countrymen is very difficult to judge. The leader of the Viet-Minh party is Ho Chi Min, a man of considerable force of character, who studied in Moscow for a period of time after 1918 and who has a very considerable prestige and a large personal following. It is understood that the French authorities are at present negotiating an agreement with Ho Chi Min whereby they hope to regain a measure of control in Northern Indo-China in exchange for concessions to Annamite nationalism.

The Viet-Minh is the most important party but other parties exist. Of these, the next in importance is the Viet-Nam Quoc Dang Dang (VNQDDO, a traditionalist party, as opposed to the left-wing trend of the Viet-Minh. It is this party which is said to count the former Emperor Dao-Dai (see 3 above) among its supporters. There is also an extremist terrorist organisation which recruits its members mostly among youth trained on Hitler

```
jugend lines and which raises party funds etc. by intimidation.
These three main political parties, including the Viet-Minh,
concluded a political truce recently in order to present a
united front. In the elections which followed shortly after
this truce was concluded Ho Chi Min was confirmed as leader of
the whole nationalist movement.¹
[. . .]
```

September 1946; India is on the road to independence from British rule. In Indochina war has recently been averted by the Ho–Sainteny negotiations that culminated in the 6 March agreement. The previous year French forces, with assistance from the British, took over Saigon in a quick and bloody coup de main. In south Vietnam, General Leclerc is restoring order and French rule, whereas in the north Chinese Allied occupation prevents the return of France. These conditions have allowed the DRV led by Ho Chi Minh to establish a government and hold elections for a national assembly where multiple parties are represented. Eleven days before this memorandum was drafted, the 6 March agreement had established a temporary arrangement that allowed French forces to return to Hanoi while Franco–Vietnamese negotiations were held at Fontainebleau in the summer.

This Foreign Office Memorandum was produced to update and inform diplomats concerned with French Indochina, France and Southeast Asia. Remarkably, it draws very little on contemporary French claims and reports about the political and military situation in the colony. It contains details of the five territories of the colony, their status, population, religion, a summary of recent events and nationalist groups. The above extract is the latter section. It was widely distributed among UK diplomats through Confidential Print. It is brief but comprehensive, seeking to give a factual historical perspective and details to help policymaking. In this regard it is a standard example of Foreign Office documentary research production. It is, however, of great relevance to British understanding of Vietminh and Indochina, for we would see its analysis, linguistic choices and ultimately representations were repeated in various iterations through 1946 and 1947.

British diplomats were in sudden need of detailed and reliable information on French Indochina and especially the Vietnamese question. On the one hand French claims about Vietminh and Ho Chi Minh dominated the broader understanding of the situation, for instance in the press. In March 1946, for example, *The Times* emulated d'Argenlieu's contradictory communist and fascist assertion that Vietminh, 'under Communist control, had established itself with the connivance of the Japanese'.² On the other hand, a mid-March Foreign

Office file 'of particular secrecy' reveals an internal debate as to how to respond to a 18 March telegram from Ho Chi Minh to Prime Minister Clement Attlee with a request for 'the Government of Great Britain to recognize the Democratic Republic of Vietnam as a free state'.[3] The Foreign Office had no intention of replying until the diplomatic status of Vietnam was settled between France and Vietnam in negotiations. They did, however, feel the need to be informed as to that process, whether peace would last, and about the actors involved, spurring the Foreign Office's vast information-gathering and analysis machinery into action. For the majority of the period studied in this book it would manage to gather, collect and analyse much information about French Indochina, most often independently of French sources and far more accurately and comprehensively than their American counterparts. In the context of UK diplomacy, this memorandum marks the beginning of a constant and consistent stream of knowledge gathering and analysis concerning Vietminh and Vietnam.

The extract deals primarily with Vietminh, situating it in the colonial political context. Vietminh is located as one of various 'Annamite' 'movements for severing the French connection' that ranged from communist to the extreme right. The Memorandum is very factual and information is expounded as narrative. In the extract it moves from the French oppression of communist anti-French groups, through the wartime creation of Japanese-controlled nationalist puppets, to the Vietminh takeover at the end of the Second World War. The extract focuses on Vietnam's 'most important party', which has reached an accord with the Viet Nam Quoc Dang Dang, the Sun Yat-sen-inspired Vietnamese nationalist party, and an extremist group, to form a united 'nationalist movement' against French rule. This was remarkably accurate, and this nuance would soon be lost for six decades.[4]

To articulate representation of the nationalist Vietnamese political scene, this text relies on narrative, categorization and references. Narrative is a powerful discursive tool. It constitutes representations and the context they inhabit by inclusion, exclusion, depth and prioritization. It can even suggest causality by the very order of historical events in text and of links between them, even when such links are not explicitly written. Along this chronological organizational axis we find the permanence of Vietnamese resistance against French rule. Over time it has included communists and 'other schools of political thought' such as traditional 'purely "nationalist" movements'. During the Vichy France regime the repression of communists recrudesced and, after the complete Japanese takeover in March 1945, the Japanese installed a puppet Vietnamese government. At the end of the war Vietminh seized real power, a situation that France has been unable to reverse, forcing it to negotiate their return to north Indochina. The temporal frame of representation has the effect of contextualizing nationalism as a natural form of politics and, furthermore, constituting it as a permanent feature of Indochinese political life. Unlike their representation in the previous two French texts, this anticolonial nationalism is not the exception, but rather the rule. In this context, Vietminh emerges as the most successful of the nationalist parties.

Categorization in this text locates and groups Vietnamese political groups by ideology, comparing them to one another and linking them to global frames of reference. Articulation and language are considered together since such contextual references depend on use of syntax, language and vocabulary, articulating similes, comparisons or contrast. Vietminh is located within the 'left wing' of the political spectrum, a reference and choice of words that makes their political norms familiar to any Westerner by comparison with their own political parties. In this case, however, it is possibly driven by the communist background of Ho, about whom they have limited information considering the consistent misspelling of his name as Ho Chi Min. Interestingly, Ho's communist background is not overstated nor stretched to all of Vietminh. This is partly because of the awareness of the early 1940s French purges of Vietnamese communists described in the first paragraph. Most importantly, however, it is because of Vietminh's overwhelmingly nationalist focus evidenced by their willingness to form 'a united front' with other nationalists. This is a choice of vocabulary that is reminiscent of the Indian Congress party's then-recent alliances against British rule as well as Sukarno's even more recent nationalist coalition against Dutch rule in Indonesia. This is crucial, for in this text Vietminh is categorized only as a nationalist group and its goal solely as independence from France, a simple categorization linking it to other such nationalist groups in the colonial world. Conversely, the use of the demonym 'Annamite' indicates the power of the European colonial mapping and naming of the world.

In comparison, the Viet-Nam Quoc Dang Dang party is categorized as 'traditionalist', one of the above 'purely "nationalist" movements', its traditionalism reinforced by association with 'former Emperor Bao-Dai'. This party was known to other diplomats as the 'Vietnamese Kuomintang' (the name they used in Chinese in fact) and was supported by China. It was through this party that DRV secured Chinese tolerance of their government during the Allied Chinese occupation of north Indochina. The text also mentions an unidentified 'extremist terrorist organisation' of Nazi-like indoctrination 'on Hitler jugend lines' and fundraising practices based on 'intimidation'. This last description is interesting, because although unrecognizable and unspecific, it still gains political location by the references to German right-wing extremism and terrorism – which at the time would have been reminiscent of anarchist groups. The conclusion, describing elections following the alliance of the three parties, locates nationalism as consensual and popular. Additionally, it emerges as representative of the ambitions of Vietminh, particularly as Ho emerged as joint leader.

Two main representations emerge: Vietnamese nationalist will and the relative legitimacy of Vietnamese nationalist parties. The extent and depth of Vietnamese nationalist sentiment is articulated within the exposition of the various parties through the choice not to categorize them as 'rebels' (despite having fought the French in southern Vietnam in late 1945) and, crucially, the depth of the historical existence of the anti-French that extends as far back as French rule. In this way they appear normal rather than exceptional – which was the case in the previous text, where nationalism was represented as acceptable but Vietminh was represented as a perverse foreign-created exception. This representation of Vietnamese nationalism is signposted by simple topoi markers such as 'nationalist', 'independence' and 'nationalist movement', which we rarely find in French diplomacy.

The representation of the legitimacy of Vietnamese nationalist organizations is related but crucially important. It is articulated by drawing on the nature of Vietnamese nationalist sentiment and linking it to the categorization of its exponents as 'parties' that, furthermore, participate in elections – thus somewhat addressing popular will. This is also true of Vietminh who, despite having a former communist as leader, appears legitimated by the extent of popular support for the party. The exception, however, remains the mysterious 'terrorist' and blackmailing mafia-like party, which I have been unable to identify through other references in Foreign Office documentation. This party, by association to ideological extremism and the indoctrinating of youths, remains very much outside the realm of acceptability in this Memorandum, though not its cause. This representation of Vietnamese nationalist parties is also very simply signposted with markers such as 'parties' and 'movement' that locate them as rather standard political organizations. In this representation of the legitimacy of Vietnamese nationalist parties, their dedication to nationalism appears to be further corroborated by their willingness to ally to present a 'united front' despite vast political differences. If recent British colonial experience was anything to go by, this alliance spelled the end of Empire.

9

D'Argenlieu's 'sudden raising of the Communist bogey'

Saigon, 17 January, 1947

SITUATION IN FRENCH INDO-CHINA

In my despatch No. 156 of 10th December last I referred to the apparent indications that French policy in Indo-China might undergo a radical change on the return of Admiral d'Argenlieu from France. I shall endeavour in this despatch to estimate how the recent events in the Tonkin have affected, or are likely to affect this policy.

2 In my talk with Admiral d'Argenlieu on his return (reported in my telegram No. 405 of 27th December) I obtained the impression that the High Commissioner considered that Ho Chi Minh had played into his hands, and that with the assured backing of the Blum Government in France he would now have a free hand. A lot would, however, depend on M. Moutet's visit and n what his reactions would be to the unexpected turn of events.

3 As a local paper has expressed it, the Minister for the Colonies "veni, vidi . . ..!" and I would like to fill the gap with "d'Argenlieu vicit." It was obvious that by the time the Minister arrived there was little prospect of negotiation and though at all times during his visit he expressed himself as prepared to meet representatives of the Viet Nam Government that his visit would be mainly exploratory. In his first public speech at the official dinner given by de High Commissioner in his honour, M. Montet stressed that France was fully decided to ensure the re-establishment of order and peace in the territory before resuming negotiations;
[. . .]
I still consider that be will aim at consolidating the French position in the south with the support of the new Government in Cochin-China, while assuring a static military control in the main centres in the north until such time as a new Annamite Government has been established, either by the return of the ex-Emperor Bao Dai or by the formation of a puppet-Government in Hanoi on similar lines to the original Government in Cochin-

China, hoping that the dissatisfaction among the native population in the north at the conditions existing there will give the Government sufficient backing to hold its own against the extremists. Whether either of these alternatives will achieve the desired results is another matter. One thing is quite clear, however: the High Commissioner will do everything in his power to avoid outside intervention in Indo-China. Both the Chinese and the Americans are considered by the French as having no small share in the responsibility for the present situation in the Tonkin, the former for the way in which they dealt with the disarmament and repatriation of the Japanese as well as in delaying the French reoccupation of the territory, and the latter for the encouragement and support given to the Viet Nam by their agents in the Tonkin. In addition, both countries are accused of having supplied arms to the Viet Nam.
6. Though in view of the situation in the north the danger of Communist infiltration undoubtedly exists and will require careful watching. I feel that the sudden raising of the Communist bogey by the High Commissioner, both to me in November (see my despatch No. 149 of 22nd November) and a few days later to His Majesty's Ambassador in Paris, was part f the plan to discredit the Viet Nam Government and to obtain support, or at least non interference, from the United States, China and ourselves in their dealings with the Annamites. In this connexion I am enclosing herewith a summary of a French official report on the Indo-China Communist Party and its ramifications in the Ho Chi Minh Government, but neither in this document nor in my recent talks with the head of the French Surete have I been able to obtain any clear evidence of outside control of the Communist movement; what evidence exists would point to Siam as the most likely channel of communication. Be that as it may, I still maintain that the Annamite population as a whole, other than the extremists, is not a particularly favourable breeding ground for communism and if law and order can be restored the large majority of the population will be only too glad to revert to their normal agricultural pursuits rather than to involve themselves in political issues.
[. . .]
I have &c.
E. W. MEIKLEREID[1]

January 1947, the war has been escalating for two months since the Haiphong Incident in November 1946. A negotiated peace seemed less likely with every passing day – and not due to Vietminh reticence. French Minister of Colonies Marius Moutet has just visited Indochina but has not met with any Vietminh representatives. French policy, announced during his trip, seeks 'the re-establishment of order and peace in the territory before resuming negotiations':

defeating Vietminh is to precede any negotiation over Vietnam's status. The despatch above, by British Consul-General William Meiklereid, was an important contribution to British understanding of Indochina in 1947. The most read analysis from diplomats on the ground since the outbreak of hostilities two months before, it explores the situation from the perspective of changing French policy and its potential for success.

A response to a Foreign Office request for analysis, this despatch was widely circulated through Confidential Print. The many 'I consider' remind us that Consul Meiklereid is submitting his opinion and analysis. While opinion is usually of limited significance in the broader process of diplomatic knowledge production, this text's wide circulation warrants focus on the opinion and analysis it carried. Its perspective was vital in the context of how the Vietnam Wars developed in later years. For from January 1947 French policy came to include three goals that would endure until 1954: rejection of any negotiation with Vietminh; establishment of a puppet national government in north Indochina; and the garnering of material assistance or at least non-interference from the US and UK. In the context of these policy objectives, this despatch marks when d'Argenlieu and French diplomacy more broadly began raising 'the Communist bogey'.

The despatch seeks to untangle and analyse French policy and claims about Vietminh's communism. There was much to untangle: French policy was quickly shifting after the collapse of negotiations began with the Ho–Sainteny 6 March agreement and which, after the collapse of Fontainebleau, had produced only a troublesome Modus Vivendi. It would be sixty years until scholars would discern the 'French trap' that began the war in November 1946 set up by d'Argenlieu and the colonial generals.[2] Indeed, the extract begins with speculation that d'Argenlieu might have returned from France with new orders, likely considering that his creation of the puppet Republic of Cochinchina the previous summer had directly sabotaged Fontainebleau. There were no such new orders for the Haut Commissaire, though the despatch makes it clear that he is now firmly in charge of the colony and more in control of Indochinese policy than Moutet.

Our laborious diplomat rather accurately discerns that under d'Argenlieu French policy shifted to include diplomatic disengagement, military control, and the establishment of puppet governments to manage nationalism. He does not, however, conclude whether the new approach will succeed. Turning to the threat of communism, the despatch makes it clear that the documentary evidence provided by the French is unreliable and does not prove Vietminh is under 'outside control'. This is not because the Communist threat in Indochina is not taken seriously in the UK, indeed it 'requires careful watching'. Rather, the consul suggests that in the case of this conflict it is a French ploy delivered via diplomats in Saigon and Paris to 'discredit the Viet Nam Government' and 'obtain support or at least non-interference' from Britain and America. This despatch suggests that the raising of the 'Communist bogey', linking the uprising in Indochina to the global Communist threat, is a French move to obtain British and American assistance or at least acquiescence. D'Argenlieu's and Moutet's ploy was not effective, at least not immediately. Indeed, this despatch is representative of the scepticism that met it. Despite the many French claims about Vietminh links to international communism, throughout 1947 they were not taken seriously by British and American policymakers. Rather, they pointed to French colonial intransigence as the prime driver of events and conflict in Vietnam.

This despatch articulates two representations: French colonial duplicitousness and Vietnamese political and ideological agency. The first is crucial to the diplomatic history of the Vietnam Wars, but the second is a faint reference that exists mostly in contrast to the first. These articulations are inscribed in the international context through structure, narrative, analytical order and vocabulary. The text begins with a summary of Moutet's recent visit, which is thinly criticized for being ineffective, brief, and lacking real willingness to engage with Vietminh. Significantly, the narrative continues with analysis of d'Argenlieu's position – now French policy – with a focus on the ground strategy against Vietminh and diplomatic strategy vis-à-vis the UK and US. D'Argenlieu's claims about Vietminh communism are addressed only at the end, where they are condemned as unreliable and not believable on account of the 'Annamite' temperament.

The structure of the text subordinates claims about Vietminh communism to French diplomatic strategy. This has the effect of inscribing them as a French ploy for the benefit of 'the United States, China and ourselves'. This is an important inscription: it differentiates Vietminh from international communism. It rejects the normative link to the international context attributed to it by French diplomacy and, by opposition to French colonialism, inscribes it as nationalism. Vietnamese lack of political agency is also raised to counter d'Argenlieu's claims. For it is dismissed with the then-common ethnographic assumption positing the political fecklessness and immaturity of oriental peoples who would rather 'revert to their normal agricultural pursuits rather than to involve themselves in political issues'. In other words, in Meiklereid's argument the Vietnamese cannot be natural communists; as orientals they are naturally preoccupied with farming rather than politics. There is a remarkable nuance within this articulation of Vietminh's relationship with communism: it 'undoubtedly' exists but it does not amount to a part in Moscow's international plans as claimed by French diplomats. Had more agency been assigned to this otherwise accurate representation of Vietnamese political drive, a very different understanding of the 1945–46 revolution and war in 1947 would have been possible.[3] As a consequence of this structure presenting a narrative followed by devastatingly contrarian analysis, the only significant representation that emerges is French colonialism. Vietminh communism emerges faintly and only by opposition to French claims, as does representation of Vietnamese political immaturity, which also serves to prove d'Argenlieu's ploy.

The language of the despatch supports subordination of the representation of Vietnamese political ideology to that of French colonialism. As textual presence, the 'Viet Nam Government' is only referred to in relation to French policy regarding negotiations, whereas communism emerges only as 'infiltration' – again from outside sources, assumedly the USSR. Closer to the text, at the level of vocabulary, representations are strongly contrasted by the choice of words and idioms. French colonial determination and d'Argenlieu's ruthlessness emerge through terms like 'puppet government', 'everything in his power' and the ironic 'd'Argenlieu vicit'. This representation of the demon of French colonialism has the rhetorical effect of subtly but effectively removing any reasonable suppositions as to motives and means. In other words, this linguistic frame normatively places d'Argenlieu as an extremist. I would venture that the unwritten comparison (found in many contemporary British documents) pits this attitude against British concessions to Indian nationalists in the 1930s and conceding Indian independence in 1947. Any further claim to the diplomatic legitimacy of the French cause and its means is obliterated by vocabulary like 'the sudden raising of the Communist bogey', 'plan to discredit', 'what evidence exists'. This language and its situation in the construction of this text contribute to the representation of a French colonial establishment hell-bent on keeping Vietnam French on its own terms and willing to manipulate its allies' concerns about communism.

Representation of French colonial duplicitousness dominates this text. Its articulation, as explored, is well defined and contrasted in structure, language and references to the global context. In British – and sometimes American – diplomatic text its presence is signposted by reference to instrumentality such as 'bogey' or 'clear evidence'. This representation is so powerful in this text that Vietnamese ideology is entirely subsumed as a side question. Vietnamese communism, while 'undoubtedly' present, is only part of a global threat in d'Argenlieu's colonial machinations. This subtle differentiation, which inscribes Vietminh within anticolonial nationalism rather than in international communism, is indicated by plain markers such as 'extremist'. The other side of Vietnamese political agency, Vietnamese political immaturity and 'agricultural' backwardness, also functions to disprove that communism was widespread in Vietnam. It is part of the widespread orientalist discourse whose presence is clearly signposted by references to agency-less backward Vietnamese that would rather 'revert' to their 'normal' 'agricultural' condition.

The key representation of this text cannot be underestimated: in diplomacy Vietnamese communism exists in relation to French colonialism. Inasmuch as 'outside control' of Vietminh is concerned – and thus its global role as Muscovite agent – Meiklereid makes the case that it is only a figment of colonial strategy. British diplomacy would continue to believe this for over a year after this despatch. When it ceased to do so, representation of Vietnamese communism did not change on its own, it continued to change in tandem with that of French colonialism. Even the reliability of French intelligence sources, so derided in 1947, was reconsidered when both representations changed together in mid- to late 1948. For a brief comparison, it is worth reading the following note from August 1949.

British Consulate-General

Saigon
27th August, 1949

Dear Department,

We enclose a copy of the French translation of a Viet Minh document which the French have handed to us.
It brings out very clearly the extent to which the Viet Minh movement has been penetrated by the allegedly dormant Communist party. The "UBKC/HC" is the "Administrative Committee of the resistance", i.e., the Viet Minh administrative organisation.
It is interesting to see the communist party actually appearing in black and white once more. It is quite widely held here that the party will in fact shortly announce its official renaissance. We are copying this letter to Paris and Singapore, and to the latter are sending a photostat copy of the original document.

Yours ever,
CONSULATE-GENERAL[4]

When this brief cover note was written Britain was assisting France in drawing the US into Southeast Asia, specifically Malaya. The UK made common cause with France for two years, assisting French diplomacy in selling the 'Communist bogey' in order to obtain American material assistance in their conflicts in

Indochina and Malaya.[5] In 1949 the 'bogey' and French evidence for it are not treated with the searing scepticism we have analysed in 1947. This remarkable and history-changing policy and representational shift, how it was reached in diplomacy, is explored in Part III of this book. For the moment, we move onto study of two US diplomatic texts.

10

Meeting 'radical Annamese opponents of both France and Japan'

November 6, 1945

Voluntary Report
by
Charles S. Millet, F. S. O.

Subject: Political and Economic Report on Northern
             French Indo-China, Based on Observance
             during October, 1945.

[. . .]

Previous to March 9, 1945, the date when the Japanese authorities in Indo-China abandoned their policy of "amicable cooperation" with the French Colonial Government of that area, there had been several factions active in Indo-China, most notably in the northern part where the government has long been centered and where greater friction appears to have existed between the French, the Japanese, the Annamite people and the Chinese influence from across the Yunnan-Kwangsi borders. These factions included the powerful and athoritative French Colonial Government, markedly pro-Vichy; a submerged and little-known body of deGaullist French persons (whose most effective activities were those of espionage and the rescue of grounded American military aircraft crews); a vigorous and large body of anti-Japanese and anti-French Annamites very active in guerrilla warfare and sabotage; and a smaller Japanese-sponsored, group of Annamese collaborateurs who worked with the Colonial Government and with the Japanese. The overseas Chinese in northern Indo-China kept in the background in so far as was possible, it appears.

[. . .]

The collapse of French rule was a signal for greater activity on the part of the radical Annamese opponents of both France and Japan; guerrilla work and sabotage efforts were redoubled, with assistance from American Army personnel operating out of Kunming.

[. . .]

Ho, an old revolutionary of much experience and the record of repeated incarcerations by the French in Indo-China, the anti-Communist Chinese and the British at Hongkong, both Ho and his family members had allegedly suffered gravely at the hands of his French political opponents. His quite closely knit and well organized party took the name of the "Viet Minh", an abbreviation of a long and imposing title. As might be expected, this party is definitely left-wing and is believed to include many Communist members. Ho himself disclaims the title of Communist, and emphasises that he and his group are all simply and definitely revolutionaries, and that party denomination and differences must await the success of the revolution.

Friction between the conservatives of Bao-Dai and the radicals of Ho Chi Minh was apparently subdued during the months that followed the eclipse of French authority, the Ho Chi Minh group being sufficiently sophisticated to realize that their time was not yet ripe and that it would be with the collapse of Bao Dai's Japanese support. This they were apparently willing to await.

On August 19, Japanese power having dissolved in northern Indo-China, the Viet Minh group accomplished a swift palace revolution and took over the reins of power from Bao Dai. The Emperor delayed a week and then announced his complete abdication, in the interest of unity and independence. He soon thereafter accepted the post of adviser to Ho Chi Minh.[1]

This text is the first American diplomatic report on Vietminh. It is based on observations made during a short trip into north Indochina the month following Ho Chi Minh's declaration of the independence of Vietnam. It marks the first time since 1939 that a US diplomat ventured into French Indochina. Foreign Services Officer Charles S. Millet was the second secretary of the US embassy at Kunming.[2] Millet was sent 'to make a short visit to Hanoi for the purpose of observing the situation'.

There was good reason to seek the opinion of a diplomat on events in Indochina following the end of the Second World War. Earlier American intelligence on north Indochina and Vietminh came from OSS Deer Team officers that towards the end of the Second World War assisted Vietminh in anti-Japanese activities and who witnessed the birth of independent Vietnam. Their reports from the field, however, were primarily tactical and military. For a political understanding of north Indochina, particularly its many political factions and the orientation of each, such reports were of somewhat limited value, and they would only be extensively debriefed by State Department officials as late as January 1946. They are better known (and studied) than the above report since chronologically they are the very first American–Vietnamese encounter.[3] But they were not the work of diplomats or diplomatic analysis.

The Millet report might have chronologically preceded the trickle of OSS reports at the State Department, and in any case represents the first encounter of American diplomacy with the Vietnamese rebels. More importantly, since the US Consul-General in Shanghai recommended it as 'of interest and value', we know it was quickly passed on to the Secretariat and the Economic, Development, SEA, FE and European Offices at the State Department. Crucially, as this section explores, this was also the first diplomatic analysis of Vietnamese political determination to reject French rule. The report's stated purpose is to report on the political situation in north French Indochina followed by an account of economic conditions – the latter not included in the extract above.

The report's analysis of the politics and political groups of French Indochina is organized around the temporal and normative frame of the Second World War. The temporal frame is constructed around a narrative account in the first section that summarizes events in the last year of the Second World War in Indochina. It focuses on the period between 9 March, when the Japanese took over administration of Indochina from the Vichy French, and the end of the Second World War, when Vietminh declared the independence of the DRV. Within this frame Millet introduces the 'several factions active in Indo-China'. The various actors are quickly divided as pro-Allied, including the Gaullist French and Vietminh, and pro-Axis, the Vichy French and Vietnamese collaborators. Significantly, the report also betrays some sympathy to the anticolonial cause. This is, however, discreetly integrated into the Second World War ideological divide as well as a decidedly understated but present understanding of Chinese and Southeast Asian politics. This is conceptually and discursively similar to Roosevelt's own integration of international liberalism and anticolonial principles into American and eventually Allied political thinking and postwar planning.

The report articulates four representations divided into radically opposed pairs separated by the Second World War ideological chasm. On one side we find the representation of the Free French who are qualified as 'submerged', 'little known' and who were of very little practical help during the war. Though inscribed in the Allied side of the normative binary that dominates this report, the syntactically contradictory use of the superlative 'most effective' for the rather underwhelming activities of occasional espionage and pilot rescue (indicated in that devastating comparative bracket) qualifies their contribution to the Allied effort as very minor. Conversely, far more attention is paid to the 'vigorous and large body of anti-Japanese and anti-French Annamites'. They are on the right side of the Second

World War, of course, and unlike the Free French they are 'very active in guerrilla warfare and sabotage'. They are in fact so active and 'well organised' that after the collapse of the Japanese they took over government of northern Indochina in a 'swift palace revolution'. As examined in more detail below, their communism is also framed within the terms of the Second World War Allies.

On the other side of the Second World War divide we find pro-Vichy French and Vietnamese puppets of the Japanese. This text summarily consigns them to the dustbin of Axis normative evil. The Vichy French are described by typical Second World War vocabulary. Besides the 'pro-Vichy' French, we also find the Vietnamese puppet government described as 'collaborateurs' and 'Japanese-sponsored'. In a hint of the slightly anticolonial position of this report, the 'French Colonial Government' is not only 'markedly pro-Vichy' but also 'authoritative' and, through references to their treatment of anticolonial rebels such as Ho who 'suffered gravely', portrayed as cruel and repressive.

The report focuses primarily on Vietminh. Besides being located in the late Second World War chronology, it is the subject of the remainder of the political analysis in the report. This is justified by their being the unknown factor in the Indochinese equation, unlike French policy which had already declared its intent to recover the colony. Two vocabulary choices stand out in this section's description of Vietminh: 'radical' and 'revolutionary', that need to be understood in the contexts of the Second World War and East Asian emancipatory ideologies. To call anti-Japanese groups 'radical' was not a dramatic vocabulary choice during the Second World War, especially since, unlike Sukarno's Indonesian followers or Laurel's Philippines, Vietminh did not collaborate with the Japanese occupation and sought complete independence. The Second World War context is also why 'guerrilla warfare and sabotage' are not yet associated to international communist rebels but rather to anti-Axis resistance.

Millet clarifies that Vietminh 'is definitely left-wing and is believed to include many Communist members', but then makes it clear that their relationship with ex-Emperor Bao Dai and other allied conservative groups leaves little doubt as to their nationalist aims. Millet's use of terminology like 'overseas Chinese' (海外華人, the Chinese equivalent of "expats") demonstrates knowledge of China and Southeast Asia not apparent in the reports of the OSS officers who had been in north Indochina. Though the overseas Chinese in this text play no role and 'kept in the background in so far as was possible', Millet's China expertise explains the use of the term 'revolutionary', where it would have been associated to KMT's following of Sun Yat-sen's modernizing revolutionary nationalism ideology. This differentiation between Soviet communism and Vietminh partial communism would be part of the dominant understanding of Vietminh at the State Department for nearly two years.

This non-Soviet qualification, however, depended on a very thin discursive line separating Vietnamese political subjects from foreign influence. This differentiation is entirely defined by and dependent upon discourses of postcolonial political adequacy, which posited that oriental subjects were temporally and racially backward and needed the support and guidance of more advanced nations and races.[4] Millet's report suggests that Vietminh and Ho might not be able to contain and control their followers (not in the extract above). This doubt is raised at the instance in the narrative when Vietminh take over Hanoi – in other words, as soon as they establish a government. The text's great emphasis on Vietminh's troubles containing anti-French violence in Hanoi thus links to assumptions of oriental political inadequacy. In this aspect of Vietminh's textual representation we recognize the primitivism, incontinence and immaturity attributed to Asian peoples in American interwar racial discourses.[5] When effectiveness and organization are recognized, it is with textually reticent expressions such as 'sufficiently sophisticated'. In most instances, recognition of organization or sophistication in Vietminh tended to be seen as the result of foreign intervention, assistance or indoctrination.

For this crucial aspect of the articulation of Vietminh political ideology and agency, it is worth citing a small section of OSS General Gallagher's debrief at the State Department. In the original memorandum of the conversation at the State Department, the same extract is outlined in pencil. As was the case with passages from the Millet report, we find this exact extract quoted partially or in full for around two years, down to the language of 'not full-fledged doctrinaire' and 'their interest in independence'.

> Asked how "communist" the Viet Minh were, General Gallager replied that they were smart and successfully gave the impression of not being communist. Rather, they emphasized their interest in independence and their Annamese patriotism. Their excellent organization and propaganda techniques, General Gallager pointed out, would seem to have the earmarks of some Russian influence. General Gallager stated that the minority Cao Dai group were definitely Communist. In his opinion, however, the Viet Minh should not be labelled full-fledged doctrinaire communist.[6]

The political unpreparedness of colonial subjects is welded to the Vietnamese rebels from America's very first military and diplomatic encounters with

Vietminh. This is clearly represented in the reports of Gallagher and Millet here examined. Why? Simply because racist assumptions made it difficult to believe that 'excellent organization and propaganda techniques' were not the result of more developed Western influence, in this case Russian.

This text bears the very first diplomatic representations of Vietminh and French colonialism, a representation predating the eruption of the conflict between them in late November 1945. The French colonial regime (except for the little-known body of Gaullist French) is clearly inscribed on the wrong side of the Axis/Allied divide by the Second World War classical terminology of 'Vichy', while the pro-Japanese Vietnamese puppets by the term 'collaborateurs'. Vietminh are normatively inscribed on the side of Allies whom they have made efforts to assist against the Japanese. This is signposted by markers like 'guerrilla work and sabotage efforts' 'with assistance from American Army'.

Though somewhat and uncertainly tainted by communism, Vietminh's postwar cause is clearly represented as nationalist and directed at obtaining independence. The text's construction and references to 'authoritative' French colonialism make it clear that this is not unreasonable in terms of the economy of representations dominant at the State Department. This rather Rooseveltian representation of Vietminh nationalism and French colonialism is signposted by markers indicating colonial injustice and repression such as 'authoritative', 'incarcerations' and 'suffered gravely'. Representation of Vietminh ideology, goals and means is completely contingent on race and culture. Vietminh is represented as susceptible to and indeed needful of foreign influence because of oriental political backwardness. The continuous presence of this discourse *within* American representation of Vietminh is signposted not only by references to political immaturity (doubts as to their capacity to govern Hanoi in Millet's report) but also by references that demonstrate the assumption of foreign 'influence' on Vietminh, especially when considering their successes.

The relationship between assumptions of oriental unpreparedness and more developed foreign influence would last until long after the end of both Vietnam Wars. In 1991, former Vietnamese Foreign Minister Nguyen Thach finally had the opportunity to explain to Robert McNamara that 'Mr. McNamara, you must never have read a history book. If you'd had, you'd know we weren't pawns of the Chinese or the Russians. McNamara, didn't you know that? Don't you understand that we have been fighting the Chinese for 1,000 years? We were fighting for our independence.'[7]

11

Creating Pyle's "Third Force": 'a truly nationalist government'

POLICY STATEMENT
INDOCHINA
Department of State
September 27, 1948

A. OBJECTIVES

The immediate objective of US policy in Indochina is to assist in a solution of the present impasse which will be mutually satisfactory to the French and the Vietnamese peoples, which will be within the framework of US security.

Our long-term objectives are: (1) to eliminate so far as possible Communist influence in Indochina and to see installed a self-governing nationalist state which will be friendly to the US and which, commensurate with the capacity of the peoples involved, will be patterned upon our conception of a democratic state as opposed to the totalitarian state which wold evolve inevitably from Communist domination; (2) to foster the association of the peoples of Indochina with the western powers, particularly with France with whose customs, language and laws they are familiar, to the end that those peoples will prefer freely to cooperate with the western powers culturally, economically and politically; (3) to raise the standard of living so that the peoples of Indochina will be less receptive to totalitarian influences and will have an incentive to work productively and thus contribute to a better balanced world economy; and (4) to prevent undue Chinese penetration and subsequent influence in Indochina so that the peoples of Indochina will not be hampered in their natural developments by the pressure of an alien people and alien interests.

B. POLICY ISSUES

To attain our immediate objective, we should continue to press the French to accommodate the basic aspirations of the Vietnamese: (1) unity of Cochinchina, Annam, and Tonkin, (2) complete internal autonomy, and (3) the right to choose freely

regarding participation in the French Union. We have recognized
French sovereignty over Indochina but have maintained that such
recognition does not imply any commitment on our part to assist
France to exert its authority over the Indochinese peoples.
Since V-J day, the majority people of the area, the Vietnamese,
have stubbornly resisted the reestablishment of French authority,
a struggle in which we have tried to maintain insofar as possible
a position of non-support of either party.

While the nationalist movement in Vietnam (Cochinchina,
Annam, and Tonkin) is strong, and though the great majority of
the Vietnamese are not fundamentally Communist, the most active
element in the resistance of the local peoples to the French has
been a Communist group headed by Ho Chi Minh. This group has
successfully extended its influence to include practically all
armed forces now fighting the French, thus in effect capturing
control of the nationalist movement.

The French on two occasions during 1946 attempted to resolve
the problem by negotiation with the government established and
dominated by Ho Chi Minh. The general agreements reached were
not, however, successfully implemented and widescale fighting
subsequently broke out. Since early in 1947, the French have
employed about 115,000 troops in Indochina, with little results,
since the countryside except in Laos and Cambodia remains under
the firm control of the Ho Chi Minh government. A series of
French-established puppet governments have tended to enhance
the prestige of Ho's government and to call into question, on
the part of the Vietnamese, the sincerity of French intentions
to accord an independent status to Vietnam.

1. POLITICAL

We have regarded these hostilities in a colonial area as
detrimental not only to our own longterm interests which require
as a minimum a stable Southeast Asia but also detrimental to the
interests of France, since the hatred engendered by continuing
hostilities may render impossible peaceful collaboration and
cooperation of the French and the Vietnamese peoples. This
hatred of the Vietnamese people toward the French is keeping
alive ante-western feeling among oriental peoples, to the
advantage of the USSR and the detriment of the US.

We have not urged the French to negotiate with Ho Chi Minh,
even though he probably is now supported by a considerable
majority of the Vietnamese people, because of his record as a
Communist and the Communist background of many of the influential
figures in and about his government.

Postwar French governments have never understood, or have
chosen to underestimate, the strength of the nationalist
movement with which they must deal in Indochina. It remains
possible that the nationalist movement can be subverted from

Communist control but this will require granting to a non-
Communist group of nationalists at least the same concessions
demanded by Ho Chi Minh. The failure of French governments to
deal successfully with the Indochinese question has been due,
in large measure, to the overwhelming internal issues facing
France and the French Union, and to foreign policy considerations
in Europe. These factors have combined with the slim parliamentary
majorities of postwar governments in France to militate against
the bold moves necessary to divert allegiance of the Vietnamese
nationalists to non-Communist leadership.

In accord with our policy of regarding with favor the efforts
of dependent peoples to attain their legitimate political
aspirations, we have been anxious to see the French accord to
the Vietnamese the largest possible degree of political and
economic independence consistent with legitimate French
interests. We have therefore declined to permit the export to
the French in Indochina of arms and munitions for the prosecution
of the war against the Vietnamese.
[. . .]

We are prepared, however, to support the French in every way possible in the establishment, of a truly nationalist government in Indochina which, by giving satisfaction to the aspirations of the peoples of Indochina, will serve as a rallying point for the nationalists and will weaken the Communist elements. By such support and by active participation in a peaceful and constructive solution in Indochina we stand to regain influence and prestige.

Some solution must be found which will strike a balance between the aspirations of the peoples of Indochina and the interests of the French. Solution by French military reconquest of Indochina is not desirable. Neither would the complete withdrawal of the French of Indochina effect a solution. The first alternative would delay indefinitely the attainment of our objectives, as we would share inevitably in the hatred engendered by an attempted military reconquest and the denial of aspirations for self-government. The second solution would be equally unfortunate as in all likelihood Indochina would then be taken over by the militant Communist group. At best. There might follow a transition period, marked by chaos and terroristic activities, creating a political vacuum into which the Chinese inevitably would be drawn or would push.
[...]

An increased effort should be made to explain democratic institutions, especially American institutions and American policy to the Indochinese by direct personal contact, by the distribution of information about the Us, and the encouraging of educational exchange.[1]

The promulgation of this document in September 1948 marks a turning point in diplomatic history. The September 1948 US State Department Policy Statement for Indochina formalizes a key shift in US policy: from engagement with nationalist rebels to the need for another, non-communist, solution to the conflict. It posits the need for a non-Vietminh nationalist solution while avoiding another French-installed puppet government, whence my allusion to Graham Greene's fiction of a US-sponsored "Third Force".[2] In honour of Greene's ruthless scepticism I refer to this policy position as the Third Force. This policy statement is part of a series of secret memoranda stating current updating policy objectives and issues. After policy decisions were made at the highest policymaking levels, such memoranda were produced by the regional offices at the State Department, in this case Far East and Southeast Asia. They were then printed as green booklets and widely distributed to relevant missions and individuals to ensure continuity in diplomatic statements of policy and reporting.

The historical and ideational context of this policy statement is vital. American concern with communist advances had been building up for three years. The year between mid-1947 and mid-1948 truly was the year of the Stalinist domino, when conflicts and events worldwide came to appear as a concerted Stalinist bid for global conquest. In early 1947 the UK requested US assistance in supporting anticommunist forces in the Greek Civil War. As a response, in March 1947 the Truman Doctrine was promulgated to 'support free peoples who are resisting attempted subjugation by armed minorities or by outside pressures'.[3] Concurrently the Truman administration issued Executive Order 9835, which established processes to root out communists and fellow travellers from all American Government agencies, including political loyalty reviews. In mid-1947, the military situation in Indochina reached a stalemate, with Vietminh controlling the countryside and the French reduced to static positions around cities. In 1948 more Stalinist drama added to the fire as the Berlin blockade began in April. In June rolling labour strikes by ethnic Chinese labourers in Malaya flared into insurgency. Meanwhile the nationalist KMT seemed ever less likely to triumph in the Chinese Civil War.

In the context of the year of the Stalinist domino, this policy statement marks a significant shift from previous positions. Firstly, it established the Vietminh as irrevocably penetrated and captured by international communism – thus concurring with French policy to not negotiate with Vietminh under any circumstances. Secondly, it criticizes the many wrongs of French colonialism, especially reticence to make any concessions to nationalist aspirations and, for the first time, explicitly marks the French policy of establishing puppet governments in Indochina as particularly aggravating and erosive of trust. The statement expresses concern that French actions might drive anti-Western hatred, which would help the expansion of Soviet influence. Thirdly, on account of Vietminh's untouchability for negotiations towards a settlement, for the first time this statement posits that a Third Force, neither communist nor colonial, must be sought. This Western-friendly Third Force should be assisted in creating 'a truly nationalist government' that can attract non-communist nationalists. Crucially, this Third Force would seek assistance and advice from France and the US. This Third Force is the Bao Dai solution, the French plan to establish a tenuously autonomous Vietnamese government under ex-Emperor Bao Dai. However, the fact that it is not mentioned by name suggests that the Bao Dai solution was at this point not quite acceptable to US policymakers – though it would be within a month.

The significance of this shift cannot be underestimated. It committed US policy to supporting a French-established solution in Indochina 'in every way possible', a shift French diplomats had sought since mid-1947. Unlike previous policy positions (and policy in the case of Indonesia), it completely rejected negotiation with Vietminh, again absorbing one of the three pillars in French policy since January 1947. The position outlined in this memorandum writes into policy the assumption that a Vietminh victory would entail totalitarian communist domination of Indochina. Fascinatingly, this is because the memorandum establishes the relationship between Vietminh and Moscow as given, asserting that there is 'increasing Soviet interest in Indochina'. This is a *sententia* (rhetorical proof): 'there continues to be no known communications between the USSR and Vietnam' and the only evidence is a Soviet 'step up in radio broadcasts' criticizing American Indochina policy.

Thus US policy absorbed the understanding of the conflict and its actors promoted in French diplomacy. As seen in the following paragraphs, French representations of Vietminh and communism in Indochina also crossed over to US diplomatic knowledge production. This memorandum is when US policy decided to save the Vietnamese domino and marks the point of departure of the analysis in Part III of this book, which explores how this American understanding of the conflict, its actors, and context was reached. For this was the representation of the war in Vietnam that led the US to support France and, after French withdrawal in 1954, to assume the burden of saving the Vietnamese domino.

Representations in this text appear contradictory. It would seem perverse that in six pages American anticolonialism would lead to support of French imperialism. Although the Vietnamese are represented as having legitimate aspirations that the US should support, this policy shift comes at their expense. It is not only the case that American norms of emancipatory solidarity were victims of the Cold War binary. The text betrays that racist assumptions meant that Vietnamese emancipation was represented as limited by oriental political immaturity, 'commensurate with the capacity of the peoples involved'.

To entangle this complex web of contradictory normative representations it is helpful to think of them as stacked upon three superposed discursive planes.[4] The topmost discursive plane is the Cold War binary, where our representations pit international communism, expressed through its Vietminh incarnation, against the forces of freedom and democracy represented by France and the US. This takes normative preference over the second discursive plane: the emancipation of 'dependent peoples'. On this plane we find representation of French colonialism, ruthless and reticent to reform, pitted against American sympathy for the anticolonial cause and the principles become part of the Atlantic and UN Charters upon American insistence. This second plane is clearly in contradiction with the first, but it is not only the urgency of anticommunism that leaves anticolonial solidarity behind. On the third discursive plane we find representation of political inadequacy and backwardness of Vietnamese colonial subjects set against the advanced assistance or subversive doctrine of developed Westerners. In this plane the two representations are ordered according to orientalist discourse of racial and culturally driven political inadequacy, which determines that non-Western subjects are unable to govern and are vulnerable to nefarious influences.

Vocabulary is key to this document's textualization of representation. For instance, the word 'communism' does not appear, even though it is the reason for policy in support of France, refusing talks with Vietminh and advocating a Third Force. Instead, words like 'penetration', 'domination', 'aggression', 'capture', 'totalitarian', or 'Moscow' inscribe the subjects and the contexts they qualify, Vietminh and its assumed Muscovite masters, as the normative antithesis. US policy objectives are written with far more reasonable vocabulary that draws further contrast with Soviet objectives: 'self-governing' Vietnam, 'French interests' and 'US security'. Language articulates representations in terms of Cold War binaries, for instance comparing 'a democratic state as opposed to the totalitarian state which would evolve inevitably from Communist domination'. Articulations such as 'capturing control of the nationalist movement' suggest infiltration, a plot exploiting 'ante [sic]-western feeling among oriental peoples'. This language is the same as the more famous late 1940s American communist conspiracy theories of the Red Scare.[5] Language is crucial in textually conjuring the existence and role of monolithic international communism in Southeast Asia, making Vietminh one of its agents and, by *sententia* again, predicting that its objective is to 'inevitably' establish a 'totalitarian state' against US interests. Tragically, just over a year before US–Vietminh contact consisted of 'a plea by the Vietnam Government for the assistance of the United States'.[6]

Understanding of Vietminh is contingent on representation of international communism. The latter is represented as monolithic, a programme directed from a central hub in Moscow that encompasses communists and 'fellow travellers' all over the world – even in the US – and of many nationalities. This representation is articulated as conspiracy to establish a totalitarian regime in every country by 'penetrating', 'capturing' and 'subverting' populations, sometimes through the ploy of capturing control of popular political movements. This monolithic, centralized, ideologically driven conspiracy that can unleash violence is represented as the radical opposite of Western ideals of democracy, progress, prosperity and freedom, and only Western unity can defeat it. It is clearly signposted by allusions to 'totalitarianism', and particularly 'Moscow', which especially recalls the concept of a centralized ideological programme.

Vietminh, as agents of this global conspiracy, are represented as not 'real nationalists'. Consequently, they cannot be negotiated with – a representation we find in d'Argenlieu's 'doctrinal' accusations in the third text (Part II, Chapter 6). The third part of the articulation of Vietminh is also typical of late 1947 French diplomatic discourse; it posits that if Vietminh were allowed to win, Indochina and eventually Southeast Asia would fall to communism. This particular representation of Vietminh is denoted by their subsumption into international communism, which leads them to be textually marked simply as 'communists' and references to the inauthenticity of their nationalism. The articulation of Vietminh as part of a monolithic communist drive in Southeast Asia, denoted by language denoting conspiracy such as 'infiltration', is enabled by the orientalist discourse that posits Vietnamese political unreadiness – whence their vulnerability to foreign 'penetration' and, in an independent future, their need for French and American guidance in their 'natural developments'.

Representation of US anticolonialism is driven by longstanding American opposition to European imperialism. This was particularly strong after 1946, when the US granted independence to the Philippines, an example of progressiveness often cited in American discussions about Vietnam. The US looks 'with favor' upon colonial aspirations to independence. Though tempered by belief in the unreadiness of oriental subjects for self-rule, it is marked by a belief that following the example of American institutions, politics and civil society would lead to better results. The report concludes that an 'effort should be made to explain democratic institutions, especially American institutions', a contrast with concern that French colonialism engenders 'ante [sic]-western feeling', to Soviet advantage. This representation of America's progressiveness is signposted by references to the 'legitimate political aspirations' of colonial peoples. Consequently, American anticolonialism is articulated in relation to peaceful resolution to the war. Due to opposition to communism, this takes the form of supporting a Third Force to establish a 'truly nationalist government', albeit 'consistent with French interests'. The moment French diplomats were able to sell the Bao Dai solution as this settlement – and with the same language – they gained the support pledged in this policy statement.

French colonialism stands in representational opposition to American progressiveness. It is articulated as a failure in several respects. It has lost the respect of the peoples it seeks to rule over through methods such as puppet governments and the complete rejection of the legitimate 'aspirations of dependent peoples'. It has failed to control the country and in any case 'military reconquest' is not desirable. French colonialism is accused of engendering wider anti-Western sentiment to the detriment of American interests. Represented as unreasonably unwilling to concede and develop, French colonialism is marked by references to how France has engendered doubt among the Vietnamese as to 'the sincerity of French intentions', not to mention that 'French governments have never understood, or have chosen to underestimate' Vietnamese nationalism.

Textual analysis of this crucial policy statement found that American Indochina policy was driven by a set of powerful representations. Monolithic communism had infiltrated Vietnamese nationalism in a bid for 'domination' of Southeast Asia. France, though reliably anticommunist, was inconveniently reticent to reform its colonial practices, which compounded the communist problem by fuelling anti-Western sentiment. Politically backward Vietnamese subjects with 'legitimate political aspirations' had been 'captured' by communism. In this equation of representations, the racially informed understanding of Vietnamese political agency as susceptible to advanced ideological power both Soviet and American was key. It drove both the believability of communist control of Vietminh and the need for an American-assisted French initiative in Indochina.

* * *

At the turning point in the history of the Vietnam Wars, we find that reality was at least as puzzling and problematic as a novelist's fiction. Pyle's fictional assumptions about the East and how American values could save it from communism were reductive compared to the complex, overlapping and contradictory representations that informed US Indochina policy. These contradictory representations competed with one another for policy outcomes based on their relative urgency and salience. To support emancipation or not to? To fight communism or assist in European colonialism? Why did some of these triumph over others?

We now know how representations were articulated in the diplomatic communication and reporting of each of the four main actors in the First Vietnam War. These eight short essays have illuminated how each actor's diplomatic practices constituted representation in writing: from the structure of a text to the most minute choice of words that describe and qualify. Words have power, and since communication necessarily relies on expression in language these are the words that represented what was seen, thus constituting how the subjects, space, time and ideas of the First Vietnam War were understood. We have established in-depth understanding of how the chief representations in the diplomacy of the conflict were articulated: Vietnamese readiness to govern, Vietnamese self-determination, Vietminh communism, French anticommunism, French colonial progressivism, French reticence to reform its colonialism, and racial representations of Vietnamese political agency. These eight exercises in detailed textual analysis have additionally identified topoi markers that signpost the key representations encountered. We can now use these markers to follow the presence, absence, concentration, policy salience and development of these representations across thousands of texts.

The next move in this book's analysis, in Part III, follows the development and history of these representations. They are examined through each of the four actors' diplomatic processes over the period 1948–45 to determine how some triumphed and came to inform policy, while others came to be seen as irrelevant. Crucially, Part III works backwards from the September 1948 Policy Statement, to determine how its understanding of the conflict, its actors and their motives originated and developed to bring America to Vietnam.

By September 1948 US policy had resolved to contain communism in Indochina. As set out in the September 1948 State Department Policy Statement analysed at the end of the previous section, US policy had undergone a key shift. This policy decision integrated the Indochinese conflict into the global struggle to contain the advance of communism. The colonial conflict in Indochina became subject to the Truman Doctrine, meaning that the US made it a policy objective to halt the advance of communism in Vietnam by assisting anticommunist actors on the ground. The 1948 US policy decision would grant assistance to France, the only major anti-Vietminh force in Indochina, in order to bring about a non-communist solution to the conflict.

A solution to the conflict compatible with US policy required the emergence of a non-communist entity in Vietnam. It would be Western-aligned so as to remain 'within the framework of US security' and further 'our longterm interests which require as a minimum a stable Southeast Asia'. Because Vietminh had been penetrated by communism, any engagement with it was rejected in favour of the creation of a 'truly nationalist' French-supported alternative. Crucially, American assistance for such a solution was contingent on meeting the conditions of furthering 'the efforts of dependent peoples to attain their legitimate political aspirations' while remaining 'consistent with legitimate French interests'. This was an impossible contradiction, for granting 'at least the same concessions demanded by Ho Chi Minh' to 'a truly nationalist government' ran contrary to French policy of retaining sovereignty over Indochina. American assistance would be forthcoming when these conditions were met. Indochina had just become a theatre in the global struggle against communism.[3]

This policy shift had been based on a specific understanding of the conflict. By late 1948 the conflict was constituted of a set of representations that after years of contradictory instability become dominant and made Vietnam a Cold War battlefield. Understanding of the subjects involved was key: in the previous chapter we found representations of backward but well-intentioned Vietnamese seeking 'legitimate' political rights that had been misled and infiltrated by international communism. This meant that the most popular independence movement, Vietminh, could not be counted upon for reasonable negotiation. The French government was represented as less well intentioned and reticent to grant meaningful self-rule to colonial subjects. However, it could be counted upon to fight communism and could be supported if it were to accept a fair compromise to accommodate nationalist demands. Crucially, by late 1948 US diplomats had come to believe this was likely.

These representations had not previously been prevalent in US diplomatic understanding of the conflict. Until 1948 US diplomacy had been riven by scepticism as to French willingness to make any concessions to nationalist movements. Furthermore, it was believed that the success of radical and even communist forms of nationalism such as Vietminh was the direct result of French intransigence. Vietminh itself had been considered differently, with US diplomats making informal suggestions and offers of mediation between France and Vietminh. Clearly Vietminh had not yet become a simple communist stooge. The French adamantly rejected and came to fear such overtures, making avoidance of any US or UN mediation a major policy objective. This is because from January 1947 French policy rejected *any* negotiation with Vietminh, at least until such time as complete military control had been re-established throughout the territory.

By September 1948 American understanding of the conflict had changed. Vietminh had been subsumed into the monolith of international communism. Though representative of Vietnamese anticolonial sentiment, Vietminh had been infiltrated and seized by communists. Negotiation was therefore no longer possible; any Vietminh victory would lead to the establishment of a Stalinist regime. This position is predicated on the understanding of Vietminh as part of a Soviet drive into Southeast Asia. This representation was so powerful that it required no proof, and indeed none came until 1949. That year saw the beginning of US assistance to France; Vietminh gave up on seeking US assistance or mediation and began its real drive towards communism and alignment with China and the USSR. These representations were reflections of those dominant in French diplomacy. How had they crossed over such that US diplomats made them their own? In other words, how had French diplomats persuaded their American counterparts of this representation of the conflict and those involved?

Support for France was contingent upon the establishment of a non-communist nationalist option. Established and supported by the French, it would supplant Vietminh in Vietnamese hopes for emancipation. This condition was adhered to by US policymakers. Over 1948 France would reframe the policy of establishing a puppet Vietnamese national government under ex-Emperor Bao Dai: the so-called Bao Dai solution. I define it as reframing because co-opting rulers as puppets of French colonialism had been French policy since the conquest of Indochina in the 1860s and had been advocated by French administrators and diplomats from late 1946. However, this time the Bao Dai solution would have to address American conditions, particularly the reunification of Vietnam and concessions little short of independence. The Bao

Dai solution never met expectations, as deplored by visiting Congressman J. F. Kennedy three years later in 1951.[4] However, it is crucial that in late 1948, the representation of the Bao Dai solution was convincing and matched the expectations of US policy.

Vietminh's part in international communism and French willingness to enact meaningful colonial reform informed the late 1948 shift in US policy. These representations were significant developments in understanding of the conflict but were not inevitable – especially as Vietminh was still seeking US and UN assistance and mediation. How did Vietminh become part of the international communist monolith in the eyes of American diplomats? How did the Bao Dai solution become the sought-after Third Force? To ask these questions is to ask one pertaining to specific diplomatic knowledge production processes in the diplomacy of the US, France, Britain and Vietminh: how did these powerful representations come to dominate US understanding of the conflict?

The following three chapters answer this question by examining the trail of diplomatic communication between these key international actors. This genealogical examination determines how, among the different realms of possible representations of the conflict, its actors and context, these representations emerged from thousands of diplomatic documents to eventually inform US involvement in the First Vietnam War. The three chapters trace the history of these representations and the ideas that constituted them in the diplomatic information and communication of France, Britain, Vietminh and the US. Crucially, the analysis individuates instances when representations crossed from one to the other. That is, when they persuaded the diplomats of another actor that made it their own.

The analysis works backwards from the September 1948 Policy Statement. It traces the history of each policy-changing representation, retracing their emergence in diplomatic reporting and communication among and within each of the four actors. This is an extremely detailed analysis through thousands of texts, through hundreds of iterations of each idea of representation. In the trail of diplomatic efforts to inform policy and to inform the policy of other countries, we find that some representations were successful and became dominant, while others were dropped.

The following charts (Figs 9 to 12) summarize the findings of this reverse genealogical history of representations in diplomacy. The diagrams are particularly helpful to locate changes in the presence or absence of representations in their chronological context. The charts map the evolution of dominant representations across time, summarizing part of the findings of this research.

Representations in French diplomacy 1948-45

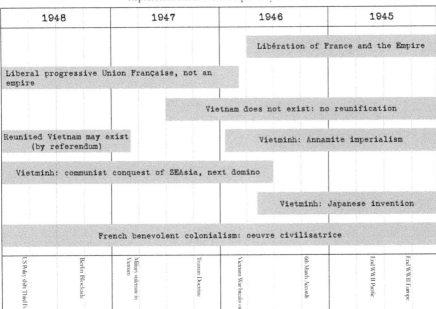

Figure 9 Representations in French diplomacy 1948–45.

Representations in UK diplomacy 1948-45

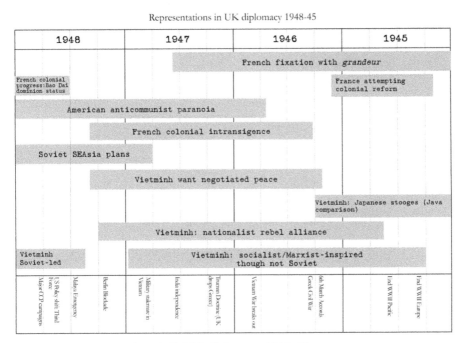

Figure 10 Representations in British diplomacy 1948–45.

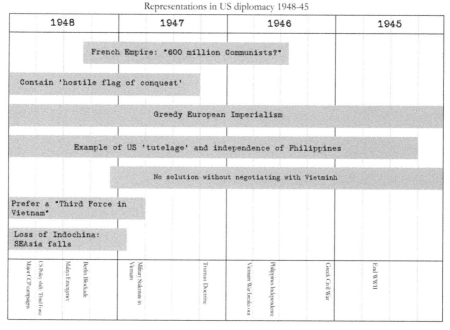

Figure 11 Representations in US diplomacy 1948–45.

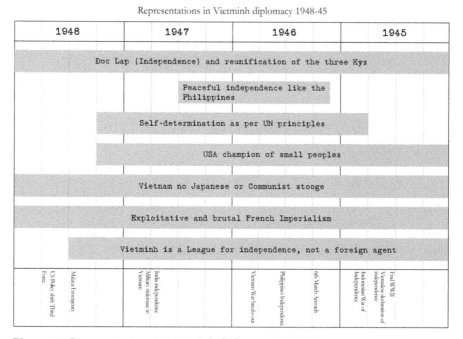

Figure 12 Representations in Vietminh diplomacy 1948–45.

They are not extensive or detailed, but rather seek to give an idea of the dominant ideas present at each time in the diplomatic discourse of each actor. They also serve as a guide for the next three chapters, helping the reader navigate the economy of representations in diplomacy in their chronological context. The end of the bars does not signify that a representation disappeared altogether, but rather that its presence in reporting has become extremely infrequent and is not repeated in the cascade of diplomatic knowledge production. The bar for each representation represents its density and frequency, not policy positions. The vertical order of the bars does not imply hierarchy.

These charts map the chronological evolution of representations, mapping the timing of key changes in representations. Two periods of major change in discursive focus are readily apparent. Firstly, mid- to late 1946 and, secondly, late 1947 to early 1948, when a significant number of representations disappear while others gather momentum. It is appropriate to speak of periods of change because transformations are neither sudden nor radical. As is apparent in the charts, representations, even contradictory ones, often coexist. The historiography reviewed in Chapter 1 established that these were periods of policy change, particularly late 1947 to early 1948,[5] which adds urgency to this book's goal of determining *how* representation of subjects and their contexts changed at these instances.

The following three chapters use the two periods of change as separators, giving us three discursive periods for analysis. They focus firstly on the key representations carried in the diplomacy of each actor to determine how their understanding of the conflict, its subjects and contexts evolved. Each chapter analyses representations carried by all four actors in that period: France, Britain, the US and Vietminh. At the same time, interaction and communication between these diplomatic establishments are analysed to determine which representations crossed over from one to the other – the crucial instances of persuasion – and when they failed to do so.

We now set off on the trail of the diplomacy of the First Vietnam War. We travel in reverse, looking for the instances when the representations that informed such momentous policy decisions in 1948 emerged and the means and pathways by which they developed as they did. This is a genealogy, a history of the ideas that informed policy that will reveal the *how* of the changes observed in the charts. It additionally individuates the rare trophies of diplomatic persuasion: when diplomats persuade their foreign colleagues of their view of events, people, ideas.

Travelling through thousands of archival diplomatic documents, readers will find that most often the original spellings, spelling mistakes, and textual details

12

Late 1948–September 1947: the year of the Stalinist domino

International communism seemed to be on the march on every front around the globe.[1] In Europe, the Berlin blockade had begun in June 1948 and was to last until May of the following year, while in February, the Communist Party staged a successful *coup d'état* in Czechoslovakia. The Iron Curtain divided Europe and close military alliances were quickly forming on both sides. Meanwhile, US public and policy opinion was quickly sliding into the Red Scare. The years 1947 and 1948 saw the beginning of trials of individuals suspected of communist subversion, and measures were put in place to eradicate communists. The Truman Doctrine had been in place since March 1947 to counter the expansion of international communism.

In China the communists were approaching victory. In 1948 they fought on multiple fronts against Chiang Kai-shek's Nationalists, deploying millions of troops in classical rather than asymmetrical offensives. The Liaoshen Campaign, launched in September, captured Manchuria in under two months; the Huaihai offensive launched in November took Shandong and the central Chinese plains, while the Pingjin offensive resulted in the surrender of Beiping (Beijing). All of China north of the Yangtze river was in communist hands and the defeat of the nationalists seemed all but inevitable. Though not well known, the ongoing Huk peasant rebellion in the Philippines was of relevance since American diplomats extolled to French counterparts the US model of colonial 'tutelage' followed by independence and the close Philippine–US relations that followed. By early 1948 President Roxas' 'Mailed Fist' policy, counting on extensive US military and material assistance had failed. In August 1948, negotiations to disarm the rebels collapsed and the insurgency resumed with renewed vigour. The Philippine government had claimed since 1946 that the Huks were supported by the Soviet Union, and in late 1948, the Philippines Communist Party (PKP) decided to support the revolt.[2]

International communism was not only advancing globally. In the late 1940s it appeared monolithic, a single global plan directed from Moscow. In this global context, the war in Vietnam was grinding to a stalemate, with Vietminh dominating the countryside even to the outskirts of Saigon, while the French secured static positions in cities. In mid-1947 there had been a sudden massive unsuccessful rebellion in the French colony of Madagascar that took nearly a year to repress. French resources were overstretched and support was needed to make progress in Vietnam. This chapter locates exactly how, when, and in which circumstances the "new" Bao Dai solution of 1948 became the acceptable Third Force that drew America to assist France in Vietnam. In particular, analysis locates and explores how, and thanks to what ideas, French diplomacy wrote the new incarnation of the solution and the instances when the Bao Dai solution crossed into US diplomatic reporting as the acceptable Third Force.

Among these cables we see the tragedy of the diplomacy of this conflict. In 1948 both France and Vietminh were desperate for American support, but the evidence shows the American choice to support France preceded by around a year the communistification of Vietminh and the subsequent approach to Mao's China. When this happened, British and French intelligence noticed, particularly when in December 1949 they had confirmation that Ho and Mao exchanged telegrams congratulating upon the PRC.[3]

France

Between late 1948 and September 1947 French diplomacy focused on Vietminh's Muscovite association and the benevolent evolution of French colonialism. The representation of Vietminh communism was constituted by association with the representation of monolithic international communism. Carried over from late 1946, it developed to include Vietminh as part of a communist offensive in Southeast Asia but, crucially, one that France was unable to contain alone. Conversely, representation of French colonialism saw major changes in this period. While it retained the discourse of civilizing backward peoples, representation of the new Union Française, which had emerged in late 1946, developed significantly. It was described as an association of willing members which, upon pacification and a referendum, would be amenable to concessions to Vietnamese nationalism, including reunification.

It was extremely difficult to demonstrate French willingness to make concessions to Vietnamese nationalism. Such concessions clearly contradicted

French policy and, worse still, successive governments refused to issue any details. Persuasively representing their Indochina policy as progressive, democratic and emancipatory was therefore a far greater challenge for French diplomats than representing Vietminh communism. It is a tribute to the capacity to represent normative identity and positions in diplomatic communication that they persuaded their American counterparts of a progressive willingness and plan that did not exist. It was crucial since the September 1948 Policy Statement made a progressive French solution a condition for US assistance.

It took until November 1948 to represent the "new" Bao Dai solution as meeting these conditions. While by mid-1948 linking Vietminh to international communism had succeeded in persuading US and British diplomats, it remained extremely difficult to persuade of French willingness to surrender colonial power. That is why the American September 1948 Policy Statement does not explicitly name the Bao Dai solution but rather lays out the conditions it should meet. When France was finally seen as willing to meet them, it was through suggestion that France had finally acceded to longstanding British and American suggestions of greater freedoms for Vietnam. It only came into fruition in November 1948, after Émile Bollaert was dismissed in October as Haut Commissaire and the diplomatically astute and well-informed Léon Pignon was appointed.

Pignon has been credited with 'reinventing' the Bao Dai solution.[4] The diplomatic communication studied here substantiates how this was done. As seen in Part III, Chapter 14, he based his "new" Bao Dai solution – and, crucially, its language – on the 1946 American solution to Philippines independence. Pignon was an experienced colonial hand who had long experience in Indochina's own mini-diplomatic service and was the author of many of its political reports. In November 1948, before departing for Indochina, he announced to US and British diplomats that his administration would effect 'the progressive handing over to the Viet-Nam government of the chief instruments of their sovereignty and independence within the framework of the French Union'.[5] As he arrived in Saigon, this was publicized in a very extensive press conference. Crucially, his version of the solution was written in the exact terms of American expectations of a Third Force.[6]

US assistance was tied to French concessions to a Third Force, the impossibility of negotiating with Vietminh, and the latter's Muscovite links. All three representations had to be persuasive. As Pignon explained to the British Foreign Office in London: 'there were nationalist elements in the Viet Minh ready to break away from the hard Communist core if they were given an opportunity to rally round some alternative government. [. . .] the problem was to find another rallying point for them. M Pignon had impressed upon the French government the necessity of making large concessions if they were to succeed.' The appeal for British help in obtaining US assistance was reinforced by comparison with the Malaya problem: 'Though our particular political problems in our respective territories were different, there were matters of common interest [. . .] in the measures to be taken to prevent the spread of Chinese Communism'.[7] Representation of the conflict in this exact triangular articulation worked to persuade Britain and then America, which is substantiated by finding this exact same articulation in their own diplomatic reporting.

French diplomacy had reason to know what their US counterparts wanted to see. Earlier demarches seeking US support for a solution to the Indochinese conflict had aroused American interest. In March the Ambassador in Washington reports that the State Department is extremely interested in every last detail of the Bao Dai negotiations. He requests that to increase this goodwill they should be 'further enlightened' on the matter.[8] This feedback was crucial. This positive reception in March spurred the development of the "new" Bao Dai solution we encountered in November 1948. This is the beginning of the crossover of French representation of their solution into US diplomacy; the evidence of how the reformulated representation of French willingness to reform was persuasive.

Though French reform was not credible before November 1948, linking Vietminh to the global enemy was well underway. French diplomacy represented the policy of not engaging with Vietminh as predicated on its part in a Soviet Southeast Asian offensive. In May 1948 the head of political affairs at the Ministry of Overseas France explained to the US ambassador in Paris that 'when you strip the situation down to its bare essentials we are faced with the impossibility of dealing with Ho'. Since only Vietminh could 'command any kind of wide support', an Indonesian-style solution including a UN-mediated commitment to independence over time was impossible, for 'the mere Communist character of Viet Minh and of Ho constituted basic difference'.[9] This is how it was absorbed and accepted into US policymaking.

By 1949 French diplomacy framed conflicts in Southeast Asia as part of a communist offensive. The monthly reports submitted by the Haut Commissariat's Diplomatic Counsellor to the Quai d'Orsay between 1948 and 1949 interpret regional events, particularly anticolonial upheaval, as part of an advancing Soviet-planned Communist offensive. In the July 1949 report China establishes 'a state ideologically subject to the Soviets' while 'Communist parties of this region are in turn subordinate to Kong Chang Tang, the only [Asian] belonging to the Far Eastern Bureau of Cominform.' Communism was monolithic, centrally led and on the march. Western powers had to act to halt the offensive, for 'from Korea to the Irrawaddy, the die is cast. From September we can expect to see the extraordinary muddle that we currently see in Southeast Asia become distinctly clearer depending on the position taken by the Western Powers.'[10] This reporting was regularly distributed throughout the French diplomatic establishment.

This representation of a communist Asian offensive is found in communication with America and Britain. Unsurprisingly, diplomatic communication is marked by increasing awareness that communism is the dominant US policy concern and a potential diplomatic commonality. The November 1948 Claudel report (analysed in Part II, Chapter 7) suggests that 'natural' French anticommunism is a cause for rapprochement, a key asset. Diplomats should emphasize that France and the US are partners against 'unchristian' Soviet aggression; 'to sell' (in English in the original) to the American public and government that France is an ally against 'unchristian' barbarism.[11] French difficulties in containing the communist onslaught are widely communicated. In a moment of diplomatic high drama, Defence Minister Ramadier tells the US ambassador France is 'considering a plan to evacuate Tonkin and North Annam [. . .] if Chinese Communists reach the northern frontier.'[12] This was effective. American and British diplomats discussed with alarm the imminent threat of a French strategic collapse caused by a Vietminh–CCP junction in north Indochina.

Representing Vietminh as part of a communist conspiracy needed constant discursive diplomatic reiteration. Soviet links were unclear, not to say untrue, until 1949, and to add contradiction Vietminh persistently sought US assistance. In histrionic displays of collaboration, US and British envoys were supplied with vast quantities of intelligence and analysis concerning Communist 'penetration' of Vietminh, Indochina and Southeast Asia.[13] A June 1949 Haut Commissariat Political Office report passed to the US consulate in Saigon argues that Vietminh's policy to the US can be characterized as 'favourable' 1945–47, 'official prudence' 1947–48, and hostility from August 1948. It explains the last shift on the basis of a meeting of 'Far Eastern communist parties' attended by Soviet envoys.[14]

However, linking Vietminh to international communism had begun much earlier. Throughout this period the key link to international communism was the CCP. An April 1947 French intelligence report on Vietminh–CCP collaboration describes Vietminh organization in terms of 'cells', 'agitators', 'liaisons', and relations between Vietminh and CCP as 'constant'.[15] A report by Pignon, leaked by him to the US consulate in March, expounds Nationalist Chinese–French anti-Communist 'cooperation' against Communist infiltration geared towards establishing communism in Southeast Asia.[16] Even while seeking to secure US material assistance in late 1947, French policymakers resented American encouragement to negotiate with Vietminh. Suspecting ulterior US motives, a comprehensive investigation into American activities in Indochina was ordered. Its findings eerily reflect a scenario in Greene's novel *The Quiet American*, where a US firm (the Indochina Development Corporation in reality) covers for anticommunist intelligence and propaganda activity. Despite deep suspicions, the investigators hoped this meant Americans had 'come round to a more exact conceptualisation' of Vietminh and that communism was a concern for US policy on Indochina.[17]

In 1947 French diplomats worked hard to promote their representation of the conflict, especially Vietminh communism, to US counterparts. The Haut Commissaire was so desperate for anticommunist press coverage of the conflict that an American journalist is afforded every comfort and high-level access because 'he spontaneously told me that if it is the case ['that Viet Minh is essentially Communist'] no effort should be spared to combat them'.[18] Two weeks later the Washington embassy exultantly reports the appearance of an article referring to Vietminh as 'the reds'.[19] In October 1947 Foreign Minister Bidault told US Senator Bridges that 'if we do not succeed in our attempt to pacify these areas in accordance with our present policy, Indochina will definitely be governed by the Communists and perhaps Madagascar as well'.[20]

In late 1947 representation of Vietminh was unstable and contradictory. In response to an earlier Vietminh submission to the UN concerning French atrocities, in December Pignon compiled a counter-report to dissuade third parties from instigating a UN investigation. The report, titled 'Vietminh is a totalitarian regime that reigns by terror and its police organisation', features hundreds of pages of documentation on how Vietminh 'distribute death' to any opposition with a 'truly Gestapo-like police', its ideological extremism since Ho 'is an old Soviet agent' and Vietminh a Japanese 'creature' that can only survive thanks to a 'ceaseless propaganda of extremism'. Amusingly, the paper cannot decide whether the worst of this extremism is fascist or communist, but concludes that both pose risks to France and the world.[21] It is representative of the instability in representation that, due to extreme contradictions (fascist/communist in this case), had the effect of making French allegations less believable and only highlighted French determination to retain the colony by any means.

Earlier in 1947 we see the last cry of representation of Vietminh as Japanese collaborators common in post-Second World War months. An extensive report argues that Vietminh never fought the Japanese. It posits that fascist/communist inconsistency is explained by Vietminh cynicism in seeking military expertise, funding and protection, and clarifies that Vietminh are fascists of 'l'ecole Staline' (the Stalinist school). This is one of the few textual sites where representation overlaps in the then-fading Second World War normative binary and the new Cold War binary. Needless to say, the normative representation of Vietminh that resulted was contradictory, somewhat fantastical and completely unconvincing. American diplomats, for example, had OSS files detailing OSS–Vietminh joint anti-Japanese operations.[22]

All the above representations were sustained by orientalist subjectivity. Throughout the period French diplomacy underscored representation of Vietnamese political subjects with backwardness, incapability and violence. In September 1947, for example, a speech in Saigon by the recently appointed Haut Commissaire Émile Bollaert justifies France granting very little self-governance and no sovereignty on the basis of Vietnamese need for experienced tutelage. Furthermore, it is argued that Indochinese peoples could not maintain peace among one another without French watchfulness and arbitration. Similarly, the Counsellor of the French embassy in Washington tells the State Department SEA office that 'the Vietnamese were not like us'; they were 'incapable of governing themselves', 'a cruel and vengeful people. The complete withdrawal of the French would be followed by bloodshed and possible anarchy and at least by the crushing of the Laotians and Cambodian peoples'.[23] In sum, the Indochinese needed France to stave off a descent into barbaric bloodbath.

Britain

In the period between late 1948 and September 1947 British diplomatic understanding of the conflict saw dramatic change. The key change, promoted by Foreign Secretary Bevin, was to consider ongoing conflicts in Southeast Asia as part of a regional communist offensive. Foreign Office files suggest this change in understanding the First Vietnam War was spurred by the explosion of a communist insurgency in Malaya in the summer of 1948, to which it was sometimes compared. This led British policymakers to seek US assistance for apparently similar British and French anticommunist struggles in Southeast Asia. At this time, representation of the conflict as partly spurred by French colonial intransigence shifted to a consideration that the new Bao Dai solution represented some progress towards satisfying nationalism. Meanwhile representation of Vietminh changed considerably, from a nationalist 'left wing' rebel alliance willing to negotiate peace, to a communist stooge.

By 1949 The UK was providing major diplomatic assistance to France, including intercession to secure US assistance. In the second half of 1949, the Foreign Office was making significant moves on behalf of France. In late 1949, they lobbied the State Department to recognize the State of Vietnam created as part of the Bao Dai solution. The UK's Commissioner-General in Southeast Asia visited Indochina – previously avoided to eschew association with French colonialism.[24] Military and intelligence collaboration was established,[25] and the Office even acceded to 'put Bao Dai in as favourable a light as possible with the Indians' and 'convince Nehru that Ho Chi Minh is a Communist'.[26] Earlier, in late 1948, British diplomats had pressured US policymakers to grant assistance to France in Indochina. The understanding of the political context that sustained these actions gestated and solidified over 1948. By late 1948 Southeast Asian communism was represented as a monolithic offensive from China to the Philippines spearheaded by the CCP. To contain the threat of communist expansion in British Southeast Asia it was to be fought on all fronts, including Malaya and Indochina.[27]

If we backtrack to 1948, we find this policy was an expansion of anticommunist policy for Europe. Mandated by the Cabinet, this transposition of European policy to Asia was informed by the same understanding of communism as a Soviet-directed offensive, its response based on containment by a united Western front.[28] A March 1948 memorandum by Foreign Secretary Ernest Bevin titled 'The Threat to Western Civilisation', one of the guidelines for British relations 1948–50, laid out the representations that informed policy. Communism is represented as a monolithic conspiracy designed to 'achieve dictatorship' over 'the whole of Europe'. Bevin suggested that after the coup in Czechoslovakia 'measures are in process of being taken to bring Finland and Hungary more directly under the control of Moscow'. To survive, a 'really united front' against communism was needed, 'and if the necessary economic means are made available by those who have them, the danger of war is, in my opinion, not imminent'. Diplomacy could help obtain such assistance 'by continuing to warn the [US] Administration of the danger of delay'.[29] The memorandum extended understanding of Soviet aggression in Europe to 'control of the whole World Island'. Events in China and Korea suggested 'Soviet policy in the Far East is developing, though not perhaps with as rapid tempo as in Europe';[30] an offensive that presented 'a considerable threat to the territories of South-East Asia'.[31] As in Europe, defensive strategy included involving the US.[32] The Cabinet rarely discussed French Indochina, almost not at all, and no specific decisions about the conflict were taken by the Cabinet. Rather, supporting France against Vietminh was the result of broader British policy to contain communism in Southeast Asia. We are back to the power of representations in diplomacy: if Vietminh was seen as part of the global Communist offensive, policy would be addressed against it.

Diplomats strived to find proof of the Soviet offensive in Southeast Asia. For instance, Siamese–Soviet relations became the subject of much reporting when a Soviet legation was established in Bangkok in March 1948.[33] Belief that with a CCP victory communism in Southeast Asia 'will be increased and the contacts between communists in these countries will be facilitated' added urgency.[34] However, concrete evidence of a Soviet plan was lacking. A desperate drive for evidence produced an improbably large and detailed report investigating Soviet film distribution networks in Asia led by a 'suspected Soviet agent'. Complete with diagrams of film retail networks, the report, though absurd, suggests very real concerns about Soviet plans in Asia and pressure on diplomats to substantiate it. In the context of policy positing that 'the frontiers of Malaya are on the MEKONG' and the need 'to establish a bastion against Communism in this area',[35] Indochina came to be written about as a front in the anticommunist struggle and Vietminh a communist stooge. On this basis, in late 1948 Britain helped France persuade the US to grant assistance. After having considered it a left-wing nationalist group for years, how did British diplomats come to subsume Vietminh into an international communist conspiracy?

Substantiating 'Communist control' of 'the rebel movement' entailed relying on French-supplied intelligence, which British diplomats had previously treated with extreme scepticism.[36] Considering their previous high standards this is a strange situation. Drawing on French reports, approximation became evidence: 'it is not definitely known that Ho Chi Minh has direct contact Moscow, but he has a permanent representative in Bangkok who is presumably in contact with the Russian Legation there'. Sometimes simple assertion that Vietminh sought 'an eventual communist state in Indochina' sufficed.[37] The sudden late 1948 willingness to accredit French reports and the plight of desperate diplomats resorting to investigating networks of commercial film distribution raise the question of why they went to such unusual extremes.

Late 1948 Foreign Office communications to diplomats in Indochina provide clues. Foreign Secretary Bevin responded with alarm to rumours that 'the French are considering a plan to evacuate Tonkin and North Annam [...] if Chinese Communists reach the northern frontier',[38] as 'this would mean a very powerful accession of strength to Viet Minh'.[39] Certainty (rather than the suspicion) that Vietminh was a Soviet stooge came from the very top: Foreign Secretary Bevin regularly classed the war in Indochina as part of a broader Communist offensive. A September 1948 report on communism outside of Europe ordered by him defines Vietminh as penetrated and 'controlled' by a small number of powerful communists.[40] In January 1948 he informed the Cabinet that a Soviet 'attack against the Western democracies is levelled against the United Kingdom in Pakistan-India, Burma and British colonial possessions, against the Dutch in the Netherlands East Indies, against the French in Indo-China' using 'Asiatic races'.[41] This was a fallacy; there was no such connection, no Soviet coordination of Indonesian and Vietnamese nationalists, Burmese communists and syndicalist communist rebels in Malaya. It is likely that the unusual sudden faith of British diplomats in French evidence was the result of attempts to substantiate the Secretary's assertions of Vietminh links to Moscow.

The crossover to British diplomacy of the French representation of Vietminh communism was enabled by the possibility of a link to Chinese communism. From mid-1948 it reflected Britain's greatest Southeast Asian policy concern: the 'Malayan Emergency'. After two years of rolling labour strikes by minority Malayan Communist Party supporters, mostly ethnic Chinese landless farmers and mining labourers, in June 1948 violence escalated into insurgency.[42] In this context parallels between France's Vietminh problem and Britain's own Malayan insurgency took vast policy significance. The diplomatic evidence suggests that it was not proof that was convincing, but rather the risk and contingency that the war in Indochina was related. The contorted Vietminh–CCP link suggested by French intelligence posited that the Chinese diaspora provided an ideological and command link as it was thought had occurred in Malaya.[43] French intelligence sometimes scratched the barrel for evidence such as 'several tracts printed in Chinese', 'concerned with British policy in Malaya [signed] "the Democratic League of Chinese Emigrés of Hanoi"' deploring repression of Chinese emigrés in Malaya by 'English imperialists' and, tenuously linked to Indochina 'by French and Dutch invaders'.[44]

The key to representing this link was race, drawing on the presence of ethnic Chinese in Indochina and Malaya. This was a powerful linkage to make considering the Malayan Communist Party was based on the CCP, including flags, organization and slogans. For Vietminh, however, it remained but suggestive speculation. Despite the firm belief of the Foreign Secretary in an Asian Stalinist conspiracy, many British diplomats remained sceptical. The Joint Intelligence Committee Far East at Singapore found reports of Vietminh–CCP pacts were 'a

K.M.T. fabrication, connived or sponsored by the French' and the alignment suggested by propaganda and ideological similarity in some propaganda 'rather woolly and insufficiently specific' and of 'little consistency'.[45] Even as late as August 1949 Foreign Office analysts concluded that similarities in Vietminh–CCP 'propaganda provides the most obvious evidence of the Communist alignment of Viet Minh but this information by itself would not be sufficient to provide proof of active collaboration'.[46] Between the instructions of the Foreign Secretary and diplomats' scepticism, what representation of Vietminh did British diplomacy produce?

In this context, a May 1948 review of the conflict became one of the most important texts in Britain's role in the conflict. Produced by the Saigon consulate, it elaborates on Vietminh's anti-Japanese efforts, its 'first democratic government', and castigates the French policy 'to disregard the presence of the Viet-Minh resistance'. Vietminh is repeatedly qualified as a 'Communist-inspired but very real Nationalist independence movement'. The cable argues that 'there is little prospect of peace being restored unless representatives of the Ho-Chi-Minh Government are approached or can be persuaded to attend a round-table conference'. Vietminh communism is bluntly asserted: '[a]lthough [the DRV Government] includes only five Communists, it is undoubtedly dominated by the Central Committee (Tong-Bo) which works behind the scenes'.[47] This is the first time the Saigon consulate made unsubstantiated statements on Vietminh communism such as 'VIET MINH, or Communist Party of Indochina'. French intelligence regularly confused the Tong Bo, Vietminh's leadership committee, with the defunct 1930s Standing Bureau of the ICP.[48] Incorporating this mistaken information demonstrates willingness to believe French reports and relay their contents without qualification.

The situation review responded to an urgent request from London. The Foreign Office had been asked for opinion and advice by the State Department, an extraordinary opportunity to directly inform US policymaking. The Americans wondered 'whether anything can be done about ['the potential dangers of the situation'] (though they think not) and have asked us for our views [...] and if there is a solution, whether there is anything positive we and/or the Americans might do to encourage it'. The situation review from Saigon was a key part of the British response and was sent to Washington for discussion with State Department officials. Crucially, the Foreign Office request for the review strictly framed the terms of the answer. Firstly, it imposed the assumption of 'growing Communist ascendancy in Indochina' – Vietminh communism. Secondly, the impossibility of negotiating with Vietminh is imposed by reference to the risk of UN Security Council involvement 'on the analogy of Indonesia.' UN-mandated peace talks between Sukarno's Republic of Indonesia and the Netherlands had been mandated by Security Council Resolution 27, in practice implying mutual recognition. The Foreign Office reporting request thus frames Vietminh as communist and forecloses negotiation.[49]

The London-mandated assumption of a communist link made it appear on text. With it, the French policy to negotiate only with a Vietnamese government of their own creation entered British policy. This move depended on a chain of linked representations – some true some not, whence the value of analysing representations. The Bao Dai solution was the only feasible option; this was a consequence of Vietminh intractability; itself contingent on Vietminh communism; in turn predicated on links to the communist international. Representation of Vietminh as a communist stooge was not absorbed from French diplomatic text but mandated by the Foreign Office, possibly by Ernest Bevin. This allowed the rest of the linked representations of Vietminh and the conflict promoted by France to cross into British diplomatic reporting and inform policy – despite serious misgivings by many diplomats. We have followed this process from its consequences in 1949 to the crossover, the moment of persuasion by French diplomacy in April 1948.

This entire representation was communicated to the Americans as per their request. Discourse analysis reveals that this is the exact articulation of representation we find in the September 1948 US Policy Statement – see the detailed analysis in Part II, Chapter 11. This is one of its discursive sources and origins. We know because both representations of the conflict include the same elements interlocked and functioning in the same manner. That is, in the context of a communist offensive in Southeast Asia, the nationalist movement Vietminh has been 'penetrated' by communism and is no longer a possible negotiating partner, while French colonial intransigence aggravates the need to allay nationalist sentiment by adopting a progressive solution. This analysis determines that the crucial policy-defining representation informing US policy in September 1948 came partly from British diplomacy.

Before April 1948 Vietminh was considered a left-leaning party seeking independence, not a communist stooge. A frequently quoted Foreign Office Research Department paper analysing Indochina 1939–48 is representative of British understanding of Vietminh before the communist shift. It rejects claims of Japanese collaboration, explaining that Vietminh is 'a left-wing party' that included communist survivors of the suppressed 1940 anti-French uprising. It expounds that '[t]he <u>Communist Party</u> was closely connected with the <u>Viet</u>

<u>Minh</u>, and in fact Ho Chi Minh, who was then known as Nguyen Ai Quoc (his real name is Nguyen Van Thanh), was leader of both groups, but on the whole its policy differed from that of Viet Minh'. In other words, Vietminh sought independence, not communism. A related paper covered Vietnamese history from Antiquity to 1939. Though its premodern history is ridiculously ethnic, focus on early twentieth-century Vietnamese nationalist movements highlights how nationalists drew on Sun Yat-sen's thinking. '[T]he French, however, with some astuteness, were disposed to label all Nationalist movements "Communist" by way of placating world opinion, and especially American opinion, when they undertook repression.'[50]

British diplomacy was consistently sceptical of French willingness to concede colonial reform.[51] Even as late as December 1948, after accepting Vietminh communism and the Bao Dai solution, it was believed that French intransigence incited anticolonial extremism. Cabinet concluded that containing communism in Asia 'was seriously complicated by the hostility provoked throughout Asia by the recent activities of the French in Indo-China'.[52] This hostility furthered communism since 'anti-communist elements exist within Viet Nam but are silent and ineffectual since they are anxious not to split resistance to the French'. Even ultra-nationalists, Catholics, and a revived Dai Viet party, 'led by Catholic leader NGO-DINH-DIEM' would 'make demands even more uncompromising than the Viet-Minh'.[53] British diplomats were exasperated by the absence of 'any signs on the part of the French to accord any form of sovereignty' and argued that 'so long as the French use the Central Government as mere puppets there will be no peace, and more Vietnamese will go over to the Viet Minh [...] It is consequently also true to say that the French are creating more and more Communists'.[54] Bad faith on the part of d'Argenlieu back in 1946 was seen as part of a systemic problem in which the 'French public has been constantly misled'.[55] Though anticommunism remained, satisfying nationalist demands remained crucial.

The only French attempt to satisfy Vietnamese nationalism, the Bao Dai solution, was castigated as insufficient and fraudulent. Consul Hanoi felt it was 'very much going to be a puppet government with about twenty ministers many of whom [...] can only be described as political nonentities carrying no weight at all with the vast majority of the people of the country'.[56] It was considered unlikely that its Prime Minister 'General Xuan will succeed in winning the support of the militant nationalists'.[57] Early in the development of the solution, British diplomats 'bemoan' not having sufficient information on the new status of the State of Vietnam.[58] The consul in Saigon was excoriating, finding that 'there is little likelihood of any satisfactory settlement being reached unless the

French are prepared to come to terms with the Ho Chi Minh Government', and damning the entire scheme to a farce and Xuan as a 'stooge'.[59] In late 1947, before the "new" Bao Dai solution had been floated, criticism was ever harder. The Paris embassy informed that 'the French Government could not agree to bargaining', and Bollaert's September 1947 offers 'appear to represent a step back from the principles on which the agreement with the Viet Nam Government of 6 March 1946, was based'.[60] Considering the consistency of the criticism of French colonial policy and its unwillingness to dialogue, support for France was clearly never predicated on the belief of their willingness to reform.

In this period US–UK relations came to be significantly dependent on anticommunist collaboration and the extent of British collaboration. A widely distributed analysis of US foreign policy in 1947 focuses on reactions to communism and consequences for the UK. In the context of the Truman Doctrine, the British 'decision to withdraw from Greece, our "retreat" in India, difficulties with Egypt, and the expectation that we should shortly relinquish our zone in Germany were all interpreted as the results of military decay. Obituaries for the Empire were written, often sorrowful and kindly, sometimes replete with *Schadenfreude*'. Furthermore, Americans were concerned that British 'socialistic policies must have precipitated the apparent *debacle*, and confidence in our reliability was undermined.' However, '[t]he stronger line adopted by His Majesty's Government *vis-à-vis* the Soviet Union has also diminished mistrust in the political field'. As the USSR 'is now treated as a direct antagonist of the United States' 'we are now seen to be firmly aligned on the side of the democracies.'[61] British diplomatic reporting in this period amusingly represented America as deprecated by anticommunist paranoia as '[a]lmost every day some new report of Communist machinations appears in the press'.[62]

US

Containing communism dominated American diplomacy in this period. The ideational context of this representation was a global communist offensive that from Indochina to America worked by infiltrating legitimate organizations. US diplomacy was tasked with investigating communist penetration throughout the globe. French claims that Vietminh were benefitting from Soviet assistance stoked such preoccupation that in July 1947 we find Secretary of State George Marshall ordering diplomats and spies to hunt down eight 'Soviet advisors' travelling through China. Disappointingly, they turned out to be seven Russian tramps. This comical episode highlights lingering uncertainty about French claims and the need to substantiate them as well as the role of identity in diplomatic information processes. This is vital, for by early 1948 this need for proof disappeared; US diplomacy ceased to support negotiation with Vietminh and began to consider a non-communist nationalist Third Force. As in earlier periods, US policy in the Philippines (granted independence in 1946) was proposed as a more enlightened course of action.

There were concerns that brutal French colonial practices and Soviet infiltration might create '600 million Communists'. Consequently, by 1948 US diplomacy was heavily invested in uncovering communist agitation throughout the French Empire. Diplomats went to extremes dissecting communist activity, collecting exhaustive biographical information on communists and fellow travellers, offering predictions, researching communist support and the feasibility of takeovers. They concentrated on individual agitators. In Martinique the consulate produced an extensive report on renowned poet, teacher and anticolonial activist Aimé Césaire.[63] The report concluded that communism was unlikely to spread to the Caribbean from Martinique, but fails to mention that Césaire was renowned for his poetry – which focused on colonialism.[64] Such glaring omissions demonstrate that American reporting on communism was tightly framed by directives prioritizing information on communist 'penetration', 'expansion', and agents. Similarly, reports arrived from New Caledonia concerning strikes by indentured Vietnamese workers and the socialist reading habits and acquaintances of a local gasoline distributor,[65] while the Pondicherry mission reported on socialist students and asylum granted to Indian communists.[66]

In Indochina the crucial difference was reliance on French-supplied intelligence. Despite the failure of the Hanoi and Saigon consulates to secure convincing independent substantiation, by mid-1948 such evidence was no longer deemed necessary. Rather, ideological approximation proved the communist takeover of Vietminh. This is evident in the late 1948 consternation at Defence Minister Ramadier's comment that 'the French are considering a plan to evacuate Tonkin and North Annam [...] if Chinese Communists reach the northern frontier.'[67] Such concern shows American diplomats represented the conflict in the very terms promoted by French diplomacy, as a war against international communism. Backtracking to February 1948 we find the link that made proof in Indochina less necessary. Drawing on French intelligence, the Naval attaché and First Secretary of the Bangkok embassy reported that the conflict 'can be exploited by the Soviets' 'to slowly but surely bring Viet Nam and all of Indo-China under Communist domination.' The report, read by almost every office at the State Department and copied to missions in Europe and Asia, appeared to prove a regional communist offensive – though the only concrete evidence was that a Soviet diplomatic post had opened in Bangkok.[68] This confirmation was key to Franco–American rapprochement based on Vietminh becoming 'complicated by Communism'.[69] This articulation of proof, based on approximation to Southeast Asian communism, crossed from French to American diplomacy in early 1948, substantiating American concerns about Vietminh's part in a Soviet offensive.

Before early 1948 American diplomacy demanded verified evidence. Diplomatic reporting was dominated by a never-ending saga of inconclusive 'observations on Vietminh political methods'. A ridiculous intelligence and diplomatic manhunt for 'Russian agents' found only seven homeless conmen 'leaving a trail of bad debt'.[70] It had been requested two months earlier by Secretary Marshall, who sought to confirm French reports of 'eight Russians now on Indochina border' to 'reorganise Vietnam military forces'.[71] That the most influential diplomat on Earth was so concerned with these seven vagabonds showcases the extent to which it was felt necessary to substantiate Vietminh–Soviet links. The only alternative was sheer speculation or approximation. For instance, the Paris embassy pointed to a speech by Soviet leader Andrei Junnov in which Vietminh is included in the 'anti-imperialist camp'.[72] The ambassador in Paris, it should be noted, was an enthusiastic proponent of Vietminh's links to international communism and defended French-led containment 'if Indochina is to be kept out of the hands of the Communists'.[73] The missions in Hanoi and Saigon were far more sceptical. A report suggested Vietminh was not Soviet since they did not collectivize land and farming.[74] Summarizing an Haut Commissariat report, Consul-General Saigon comments that, though 'undue emphasis has been given to the matter for propaganda purposes, Indochina is a fertile ground for the spread of Communism', Vietminh is 'symptomatic of a communist movement',[75] and 'weight must be given to the Communism background of President Ho'.[76] Ho's own background, though emphasized by French diplomats since 1946, remained the only solid evidence. However, this intelligence appealed to the State Department's biographic approach to uncovering communist subversion and was widely distributed.

Representation of the Bao Dai solution as the ideal Third Force was as important to obtaining US assistance as proving Vietminh–Soviet links. It took until November 1948 for US diplomats to be persuaded of the Bao Dai solution, which had been revamped by new Haut Commissaire Léon Pignon in October 1948. As seen above, this move was encouraged by British reports of French progress in developing a just solution. The "new" Bao Dai solution promised sovereign statehood, self-government and concessions on racial equality – just as the September 1948 US Policy Statement had required.[77] Although Pignon had finalized and stabilized diplomatic representation of a solution amenable to the Americans, we find this had been underway since late 1947 in increasingly more stable articulations.[78] This was important, for until late 1948, representation of France as anticommunist and progressive was significantly destabilized by its relentless colonialism. Until this element in the articulation of French representation was removed, any claims to progressive concessions would not stick and only highlight Vietminh anticolonialism.

The scale of Vietnamese nationalism was clear to US diplomats, as was the need for any US-supported French solution to rally the non-communist nationalist majority. By late 1947 the CIA estimated that without US assistance France could not triumph by force of arms alone.[79] While American diplomats had finally agreed that it was impossible to talk to Vietminh,[80] they were concerned that an insufficiently nationalist solution would lack support.[81] Among examples of the extent to which nationalist sentiment had been captured by Vietminh, in May to August 1948 consul Hanoi recounts the saga of a little island in Hoàn Kiếm lake in central Hanoi. On a May night a 'Viet Minh flag [was] placed on island of small lake in center Hanoi during night'. The island was symbolic, featuring a temple dedicated to General Tran Hung, a nationalist hero who in the thirteenth century defeated a Chinese invasion.[82] The perseverance of Vietminh 'agents' in replacing the flag eventually drove the French to destroy the island. Likewise, consul Saigon suggests that photographs delivered to the consulate by hand of a Vietminh attack on a French convoy near Saigon demonstrated anti-French determination and Vietminh success in controlling the countryside.[83] As described by American diplomats throughout 1947, this passion, support and commitment stood against determined French reticence to make any concessions. Before the resuscitation of the Bao Dai solution in 1948, Bollaert's September 1947 offers are considered 'less than March 6' and 'show little inclination go much beyond pre-war status'.[84] US diplomacy was clearly concerned that French reticence to make concessions might turn the Vietnamese against the West 'and would ensure irretrievable orientation intellectuals and people towards communism and Moscow'.[85]

Consequently, throughout 1947 US diplomats represented Vietnam as torn between the extremes of communism and colonialism.[86] US diplomats questioned whether Bao Dai was yet another 'French stooge',[87] as suggested by Prime Minister Xuan's failure to garner support,[88] and sought Vietnamese opinions on whether the Bao Dai solution could capture nationalist sentiment. The responses were discouraging.[89] Former Prime Minister Ngo Dinh Diem, already considered a key nationalist voice by US diplomats, emphasized that Vietminh would triumph until nationalist demands were not met, for French offers fell 'far short of real independence, which is the ultimate desire of his people' who were 'turning to Communism' in despair.[90] This conversation was very widely circulated and quoted. Concurrently, over a hundred cables produced over only two weeks discussing 'farsweeping independence promises to Bao Dai' demonstrate huge interest as to whether the Bao Dai solution might outflank Vietminh.[91] During Bao Dai's late 1947 visit to France American diplomats exhaustively reported on Bao Dai's every move, even those of his wife,[92] particularly since the French appeared at times to be willing to grant more autonomy to a Vietnam under Bao Dai.[93] Although still considered insufficient, by 1947 the groundwork had been laid for US diplomats to seriously consider the Bao Dai solution. In late 1947 the crossover of the Bao Dai solution from French to American diplomatic knowledge production was only beginning.

Vietminh

In this period Vietminh is intentionally isolated by other actors and contact is minimal and unilateral. When contact is made, Vietminh diplomacy represents the conflict in the same terms found in previous periods. Vietminh's key goal is the reunification and emancipation of Vietnam from French imperialism. They continue to emphasize that Vietminh is not a stooge of Russian or Japanese interests, but rather a league for independence. There are, however, two crucial and related changes to Vietminh representation of the conflict. From early 1948, peaceful self-determination as per UN principles is dropped, as are appeals to the US as a champion and an example to subject peoples seeking emancipation.

There was no contact with France and Britain. With the US it was ever rarer. In October 1947, photographs of a Vietminh attack on French forces are delivered by hand to the US consulate in Saigon, showing how rudimentary US–Vietminh relations had become.[94] This is remarkable considering that less than two years before the head of the State Department's Southeast Asia office had met with Ho Chi Minh in Hanoi. Besides the photographs and a trickle of propaganda leaflets handed to US and British consulates in Hanoi and Saigon in early 1948, the last diplomatic contact I could find in this period occurred as far back as September 1947 when the US embassy in Bangkok received a Vietminh demarche from Dr

Pham Ngoc Thach 'who describes himself as Under Secretary of State at the Vietnam Government'. It was Vietminh's last request for US assistance. It was written as a questionnaire with exactly the same format and structure used by US diplomats to establish their interlocutor's positions when contacting Vietminh in their previous exchange in May 1947 (cited and discussed at the end of Part II, Chapter 5). I could not find a reply on file.

The text of this last communication, in French, makes specific requests for US assistance for the DRV including a loan for basic foodstuffs, medical material, transport and non-military equipment. Furthermore, it enquires whether the US would mediate in the conflict or allow the case of Vietnam to be heard at the UN. The letter frames the conflict in strictly colonial terms, one in which 'a people fight for their freedom', independence and unity. It represents the 1945 Vietminh takeover and subsequent anti-French struggle as the 'expression of the immense majority of the people', a principle that it highlights is enthusiastically espoused by the US. This is pitted against French 'policy of force', 'imperialism', 'exploitation', which is defended with every possible means, even American lend-lease material and 'employing Nazi troops'.[95]

These communications were entirely unable to shift US thinking about Vietminh or its cause and they are not relayed within US diplomatic analysis. It was too late for Vietminh to seek to promote its representation of the conflict, its actors and reasons. As shown in this chapter, in French and subsequently in British and US diplomacy, Vietminh had come to be represented as too communist to engage with.

13

August 1947–September 1946: French intransigence and Anglo-Saxon antipathy

Reversing to the period between August 1947 and September 1946 we find a very different set of dominant representations and context. As in mid-1947 the war in Indochina slowly ground to a stalemate, French diplomats resented what they described as concerted 'Anglo-Saxon' hostility towards France and her right to 'liberate' its colony. As evidenced by American and British reticence to provide increased military and economic assistance, this was not a period of powerfully persuasive representations like those studied in the previous chapter. The foundations of those representations, however, were established in this period as French diplomacy began a slow shift from representing the conflict as a hangover of the Second World War, with Vietminh as fascist Japanese terrorists fighting liberation, to representing it as a Cold War front pitting Vietminh-Soviet stooges against the reforming and progressive Union Française.[1]

French representation of the conflict was in fact only catching up with rapid changes in an international context increasingly marked by concerns about Soviet expansionism. US concerns over communism had led to the proclamation of the Truman Doctrine in March 1947. American anticommunist policy remained focused on Europe, however. Southeast Asia was not yet described as a communist target; Indonesia was still at war with its Dutch colonial master, setting a poor example of the consequences of colonial intransigence that informed the representation of events in Indochina. In contrast, following Indian independence British diplomats joined their American colleagues in congratulating themselves for their postcolonial enlightenment and recommending that France and the Netherlands follow suit.

D'Argenlieu and the Haut Commissariat resisted. Their staunchly Gaullist and colonial patron in Paris, Foreign Minister Bidault, who also served as prime minister between 24 June and 28 November 1946, allowed d'Argenlieu's administration to shape French policy on Indochina. This freedom of action led to the breakout of war after d'Argenlieu scuppered the Fontainebleau talks in the summer of 1946 when he created the puppet Republic of Cochinchina and provoked Vietminh with a series of military ultimatums, including the one that provoked the Haiphong Incident. The Cochinchinese Republic was such an ignominious failure among the Vietnamese public that Dr Nguyễn Văn Thinh, d'Argenlieu's puppet President of Cochinchina from 26 March 1946, committed suicide on 10 November 1946. In March 1947 d'Argenlieu was replaced with Émile Bollaert. Initially seen as more moderate, he nevertheless defended the policy that France should only negotiate after full control had been restored.

The beginning of hostilities unleashed torrents of Franco–Vietminh diplomatic accusations, which for this book is precious evidence of how they represented one another and especially whether and how they succeeded in persuading any international partners. As illustrated in Fig. 13, formal and informal contacts between the French and Vietminh were common until the very breakout of war. When the war began communication between France and Vietminh was reduced to a trickle at the tactical military level. However, communication with third parties increased sharply as each sought to communicate their version of events.

Figure 13 Giap reviews troops with Leclerc and Sainteny in late 1946. Archive Sainteny.

France

This was a period of momentous change in how French diplomacy represented the conflict to America and Britain. We see a gradual move away from the Gaullist argument that ongoing imperial conflicts were simply efforts to complete the liberation of France and the Empire from Axis powers and their supporters. Crucially, this meant Vietminh were ever more rarely described as Annamite Japanese agents seeking to subjugate weaker Indochinese nations. The entire French Empire is reinvented as the Union Française, a more enlightened post-imperial community that, though described in the language of the British Commonwealth, brought no practical difference to colonial rule. The normative reasoning for French colonialism remained immutably represented as a necessary œuvre civilisatrice, a benevolent sharing of French progress, culture and liberty that contrasted sharply with Vietminh 'terrorism'.

This period saw the final struggle and death of d'Argenlieu's representation of Vietnam as a Vietminh invention designed to subjugate other Indochinese races whom it was France's duty to protect. As seen in the previous chapter, it would take until the very end of 1947 for this representation to be replaced by an understanding that Vietnam exists and should be allowed to reunite under French sovereignty. The most important representation in the diplomacy of this conflict, Vietminh as a Soviet stooge in Asia, began to emerge hesitantly and inconsistently. Not least because of contradictions with other coexisting representations, it would take two years for this representation to gather steam.

French representation of Vietminh as Soviet agents is the most important change observed in this period. It is particularly fascinating not only because for nearly two years this representation met stiff Anglo-American scepticism, but also because French representation of Vietminh as Stalinist agents appeared suddenly in late September 1946. As seen in the previous chapter, it would continue to develop until it was finally accepted later in 1947–48. By August 1947, Haut Commissaire Bollaert, who replaced d'Argenlieu in March 1947, consistently tells foreign diplomats that 'to treat with Ho [...] is to deliver Vietnam into hands totalitarian regime'.[2] This was a continuation of d'Argenlieu's communications strategy to secure American assistance for the conflict and acquiescence of his refusal to negotiate with Vietminh. It involved representing Vietminh as an unacceptably communist and terrorist actor while contemporarily proposing a more progressive unilateral French solution that 'Chinese and American governments would probably support', a solution involving Bao Dai.[3]

This strategy was resisted in Paris as well as London and Washington. Between November 1946 and his dismissal in March 1947, d'Argenlieu waged a two-front diplomatic communication campaign to persuade his government in Paris as well as Britain and America. Even though he was dismissed in March 1947, his strategy remained in place for years. In February 1947 he made the case to the COMINDO that Vietminh 'cannot be considered a partner for peace talks' because 'Ho Chi Minh is without a doubt inspired by Communists' for 'the Indochinese conflict is, in reality, another battlefield in the struggle between Western democracies and international Marxism', adding that 'he is struck by the bizarre fact that the American press supports Vietnamese communism in Indochina, while this press strongly opposes Communist influence in other regions of the world'. At the end of the telegram he reveals that he expounded this argument to American journalists before submitting it to Paris. With this manoeuvre – for which he was reprimanded – d'Argenlieu skilfully locked French policy into an accept-or-reverse situation.[4] He was so impatient with the COMINDO due to their lack of reply to a Memorandum advocating 'the official announcement that [France] will not deal with the Ho Chi Minh government'.[5] By this point d'Argenlieu had no choice but to press the French government to adopt this communication strategy, for he had himself been enacting it from September 1946. For instance, he told the US ambassador that France had no intention to resolve the problem 'by reconquest' but 'we must face the fact' that Vietminh is Communist and represented only a 'very small part of the population of Indochina'.[6] In his determination to enact this strategy, d'Argenlieu had been quietly helped by diehard Gaullist and colonialist Foreign Ministry personnel and by Foreign Minister Bidault.

D'Argenlieu's impatience and institutional struggles in early 1947 are explained by his previous freedom to dictate French Indochina policy. While Bidault was prime minister from 24 June to 28 November 1946, d'Argenlieu could draw on the vast resources and support of French diplomacy and the Presidency. For instance, in November 1946 'a high Foreign Ministry official' told the American ambassador in Paris there was 'positive proof that Ho Chi Minh is in direct contact with Moscow and is receiving advice and instructions from the Soviets'.[7] Contemporarily, the President's cabinet leaked an intelligence report purporting to document a Soviet plot to take over all of Southeast Asia that was led and executed by Vietminh.[8] The d'Argenlieu–Bidault diplomatic era inaugurated the practice of leaking and handing over large volumes of French intelligence documenting alleged Vietminh communist links to US and British diplomats. These reports usually consisted of files on Chinese communists and 'much Communist propaganda' in the colony.[9] As seen in the previous chapter, this practice begun in 1946 became a staple of French diplomacy 1947–49.

Even with this support, d'Argenlieu and his government in Saigon were exasperated by the lack of sufficient backing from Paris. In a very Gaullist critique of French foreign policy, the admiral felt that parliamentary debate precluded decisive action in Indochina. He actively misled public and political opinion in France by retaining some reports while promoting Haut Commissariat accounts of Vietminh atrocities ad nauseam, and at one point directly deceiving his superiors. This is corroborated by a French Presidential Office investigation that found evidence that d'Argenlieu purposefully delayed transmission of Vietnamese communications to the COMINDO to prevent Franco–Vietnamese negotiations.[10] Though reprimanded, he was protected by Bidault from further repercussions.

The sudden appearance of the communist thesis in French diplomacy in September 1946 did not go unnoticed. As many American diplomats highlighted, this is firstly because it was so sudden (it began on 22 September 1946), which made it appear cynically instrumental.[11] Secondly, the representation was suspicious due to irreconcilable contradictions in French representation of Vietminh, for the communist thesis overlapped with the previous Second World War representation of Vietminh as a fascist Japanese agent. As evidence for the latter, French diplomats argued that Vietminh's goal of reuniting Vietnam's three Kys was a racist Japanese-like expansionist project. This was difficult to reconcile with communism. The French government only dropped representation of Vietminh as a fascist Annamite racial expansion project – and therefore opposition to reunification – in March 1947 when it announced to foreign policymakers that 'France has no objection to the reunification of the three Kys' as long as it is the will of the people and not of Vietnamese imperialism'. When 'peace and democratic order' have been achieved, France would not only hold a referendum in Cochinchina, but also in 'Annam south of the 16th Parallel'.[12]

Even greater inconsistencies arose *within* representations of Vietminh as communist agents. They were always partial (few members were proven communists) and relied on approximation – similarities with Soviet or Chinese organizations for instance. Such an unstable early French representation of Vietminh communism is analysed in detail in Part II, Chapter 7, where it is found that communist allegations were directed more at defending the legitimacy of French sovereignty and undermine Vietminh's than proving Vietminh communism. As analysed in the previous chapter, a very specific set of political, discursive and contextual circumstances as well as the Malaya Emergency would be needed for this representation to gain believable coherence.

Contemporarily, d'Argenlieu and French diplomats were working to represent France as willing to reform its colonial practices and make concessions to nationalism. D'Argenlieu proposed to revive the very same arrangement used in Vietnam since the 1860s and only briefly interrupted by the Second World War: a Vietnamese emperor under French 'tutelage', the Bao Dai solution. In March 1947 we find a circular sent in the clear to all French diplomats for promulgation with the entire text of the Bao Dai solution. It explains that as part of the restoration of the Vietnamese state under Bao Dai – reunification subject to referendum – the French military is 'responsible for the restoration of peace to allow for the free expression of the will of the peoples of the French Union', and that the latter will 'protect ethnic minorities against the Annamite attempts at absorption' and even 'native and French workers'. The French Union is 'not a reestablishment of the Empire of the past' but a 'good will free association of nations'. The document additionally confirms that France will no longer negotiate with 'the Viet Minh Party'.[13] The diplomatic push to publicize this apotheosis of colonial enlightenment had been prepared on 14 March 1947 with the dismissal of d'Argenlieu as Haut Commissaire, replaced by the "liberal" Émile Bollaert – who, however, kept d'Argenlieu's approach and his advisers.[14]

D'Argenlieu's allies had been floating the idea to foreign diplomats for some time. In December 1946 Lacoste, minister of the French embassy in DC, discussed with the State Department's SEA Office a 'possible solution' involving 'the displacement of Ho Chi Minh and other communist extremists with more reasonable, moderate Vietnamese leaders'.[15] The same month d'Argenlieu and Léon Pignon, author of the late-1947 "new" Bao Dai solution and Political Counsellor to the Haut Commissaire, had the same discussion with the British consul in Saigon, arguing that 'any form of Annamite Republic Government must necessarily either be Marxist or fascist and if they wanted to introduce any form of democratic government it could only be done through a monarchy'.[16] These approaches met with very little success in 1946, for British and US diplomats felt France should negotiate with Vietminh in order to allay nationalist sentiments and address key grievances.

Meanwhile, colonial officials worked hard to understand how American policymakers understood colonialism. The research they carried out in 1946 reveals one of the sources of French success in resuscitating the Bao Dai solution in late 1948. As analysed in the previous chapter, the 1948 Bao Dai solution was contingent on the impossibility of negotiating with Vietminh and on making credible concessions to a Vietnam led by Bao Dai. In the files of the Diplomatic and Political Counsellors of the Haut Commissariat for 1946 we find documents hitherto unconsidered in the study of this conflict.[17] They reveal that French consul in Manila Gaston Willoquet, Haut Commissariat Political Counsellor Léon Pignon, Diplomatic Counsellor Achille Clarac and Documentation Bureau Chief Étienne Schulumberger gathered an inordinate volume of documentation and analysis on the 1946 US grant of independence to the Philippines and assistance against the Hukbalahap (Huk) Rebellion. We find extensive documentation, including speeches given at independence, intelligence reports, and fierce criticism of American anticolonialism. This extensive research into US relations with the Philippines in 1946 is the last missing piece of the puzzle of Pignon's successful 1948 "new" Bao Dai solution.

Pignon's research focused primarily on American assistance to the new Philippine Republic in fighting the Huk Rebellion. Reports highlight that the Huk are

'a violent insurgent movement that has presented a number of parallels with the Indochinese and Indonesian uprisings. Fomented by a group of political parties of communist tendencies, the Hukbalahaps, or "Huka", this movement has been vigorously repressed. This repression was enterprised by order of an autochthonous government, which has left the Americans, who have taken part, leaving a good impression in world opinion.'

Crucially, '[t]he revolt is of a form analogous to that of the Viet-Minh movement in Cochinchina' since the 'Hukbalahaps currently comprise several political parties of which the most important is the P.K.M, or National Peasant Union of clear communist tendencies.'[18] As in Indochina, the Huk Rebellion could not be directly linked to Moscow and intelligence reports could only speculate – in fact the Philippine Communist Party (PKP) only joined the rebellion in 1948. French documents focused extensively on transfers of American military material to the Philippines worth 'six hundred forty million dollars'.[19] Pignon and his colleagues therefore knew that the threat of communism and the postcolonial legitimacy of a native government's request for assistance were key to how the Philippines obtained assistance from the US in 1946. It is no coincidence that Pignon's 1948 plan for the Bao Dai solution envisaged a Vietnamese request for French Union assistance against Vietminh.

French files on the Philippines offer a fascinating precedent for the Bao Dai solution's diplomatic representation. An earlier report on American colonialism in the Philippines scrutinizes how the US planned to grant independence to the islands and chastises the American idea of 'enlightened colonialism' for dropping the 'sacred burden of the white man'.[20] Authored by Pignon or Clarac, it keenly individuates the normative basis of American decolonialization: a period of self-government to 'inculcate in [indigenous peoples] the ideals of the law, liberty and democracy' before independence, noting that the American logic of tutelage is not necessarily too distant from the French colonial ethos. It concludes that Philippine independence brings serious 'difficulties for England, France and Holland that seem to conceive the problem of the autonomy of their Asian possessions as a more evolutionary process' and wonders whether 'will we shortly need to enthusiastically follow the suggestions of the parable of the fox that cut its own tail?'.[21] Though these reports were not widely circulated, their lessons on American decolonialization resurface in how – and especially with what language – Pignon sought US assistance to defeat Vietminh in 1948. This is particularly evident in the linguistic and ideational similarity between this report's exploration of American 'enlightened colonialism' and the 1948 Bao Dai solution explored at the beginning of the previous chapter, particularly Pignon's written and oral declarations in October and November 1948.[22]

In this period of American hostility to French colonialism, diplomats worked overtime to defend French rule in Indochina. This defence was based on two opposing representations: Vietminh as an uncontrolled terrorist group thriving on ideological fanaticism pitted against France, an advanced power willing to make concessions to colonial subjects. Both representations were sustained by the traditional colonial discourse of France as a paternal trustee ensuring peace.

In April 1947 we find French diplomats combating 'foul factoids' in the American press and 'circulated' among policymakers. The COMINDO provides diplomats with documentation figures to counter anticolonial recriminations. Despite repeated US requests for information on corveé labour (forced upon colonial subjects by the nineteenth-century Code de l'Indigénat), recruitment of former Wehrmacht German soldiers (tens of thousands had been recruited into the Foreign Legion in 1945–46) or that France trades in opium ('otherwise addicts would have to resort to harmful contraband opium'[23]) are never addressed in public and only rarely in diplomatic communication.[24] In late 1946 we find French officials in Hanoi desperately trying to persuade the American consul that he had not in fact heard hundreds of soldiers singing loudly in German.[25] In 1947 the Foreign Ministry launched a concerted drive to encourage (and pay for) American press articles praising the 'œuvre coloniale' to 'correct misinformation'.[26] It was emphasized that France understood 'American sympathy for the ideal of national independence, but the American public cannot fully appreciate the Marxist influence in the Vietnamese movement'.[27]

French colonialism was represented as progressive. In February 1947 Bidault explains that 'the day of colonial empires in the nineteenth century sense of the word is a thing of the past' and that 'you may assure your government that we are more than anxious to find a peaceable liberal solution'.[28] Rather, the continuation of empire is warranted by the nature of colonial subjects. For instance, State Department SEA Chief Moffat and d'Argenlieu agreed only on one thing: the Vietnamese were politically unready; it was necessary to 'stop the Asiatic masses from slipping into a political formula he felt was worrying'.[29] That is, without Western oversight the 'Asiatic masses' would readily slip into bloody extremism. Colonies Minster Moutet tells the US ambassador that despite his 'well known advanced views as well as his life-long activities on behalf of native inhabitants', the terrorism he witnessed during a visit justified continued French rule, for 'France does not oppose aspirations of Vietnam people but merely methods of force being used'.[30]

Representing French rule as necessary therefore focused on Vietminh extremism, terrorism and illegitimacy. Terrorism was then, like now, a normatively powerful representation. As Moutet told foreign diplomats, it is 'France's firm intention not to be ousted out of Indo-China by terrorism'.[31] A report prepared for foreign diplomats observes that Vietnamese elections in 1946 were a fraud, since 'they completely controlled the population'.[32] Furthermore, Vietminh are fanatical ideologues, 'racist' 'annexationists' who rely on 'fanaticising individuals' and ultimately 'a few hundred' who illegitimately 'claim to speak for all Annamese'.[33] Vietminh terrorism contrasts with French responses of 'the strictest pulchritude'. Countering charges that Vietminh attempted to present at the UN, French diplomats reiterated that France committed no atrocities and did not rely on ex-Nazi and colonial troops – although some French diplomats were aware the charges were true.[34] The counter-report for the UN rewrites history: Vietminh did not fight the Japanese and remains their 'creature'.[35] D'Argenlieu was evidently obsessed by this Second World War representation, for the same frame and terminology (a Vietnamese 'renewal of Pearl Harbor') can be found in a personal letter to President Bidault complete with handwritten 'hommages a madame Bidault'.[36]

Backtracking in the diplomatic communication, we find that this tempering in representation of French colonialism originated in a late 1946 French diplomatic panic that the US might consider referring the conflict to the UN. In an effort to stop the Americans, an extensive seven-page cable details the attitudes of anticolonial officials, politicians, and the arguments that would preserve French freedom of action in Indochina. It suggests diplomats emphatically use words like 'caretaking', 'eventual emancipation', 'development', 'paternal protection' while highlighting the risk to colonial populations should France withdraw.[37] The next two sections explore why British and American diplomats did not find this convincing.

Britain

British understanding of the conflict August 1947 to September 1946 was very different from later years. Though between late 1947 and 1948 it would accept the French argument that Vietminh was spearheading a Soviet conquest of Southeast Asia, in the 1947–46 period the war was not seen as a Cold War conflict. Rather, British diplomacy saw it as a French attempt to restore its war-torn international 'grandeur', while Vietminh was considered a standard anticolonial nationalist party pushed into extremism by French unwillingness to negotiate meaningfully. There was an understanding that Vietminh was amenable to a negotiated peace for, although socialist, it was not under Soviet control. During this period Britain sought to avoid intervening. Shy of being seen to assist France in repressing the rebellion, it pressed France for concessions similar to those made to the British Dominions. This surprisingly un-imperial approach was informed by the impending independence of India (15 August 1947) and, it should be noted, a hitherto unconsidered level of pressure from Nehru's government. As seen in the previous chapter covering late 1947–48, only later did anticommunism became a British foreign policy priority in Southeast Asia.

British diplomacy followed in minute detail the growth of concerns about communism in US policymaking. A widely circulated report from the Washington embassy observed that anticommunist concerns were vital in positioning Anglo–American relations since the 'United States necessarily relies on the assistance of Great Britain because it feels unable to man all the bastions alone.' Helping in the struggle against the Red had practical diplomatic consequences: '[i]f we are to obtain further American economic assistance for the rehabilitation of the British economy and for the renaissance of the United Kingdom as a leading world Power, it is axiomatic that we should so comport ourselves as to convince the American public, and more particularly Congress, that the costly game is worth the candle.' Consequently, 'to bar the way to further Soviet expansionism Great Britain is likely to retain a favoured position in calling upon the United States for material assistance.'[38] This was not only true of Anglo–American relations; reports make it clear that American foreign policy now saw the world through a Cold War lens: 'on the developments in colonial areas as on virtually all other international problems,

American opinion sees all roads leading to Moscow', a key 'development in international relations, not only for America but probably for the whole world'.[39] While this shift was useful for the UK, there was growing awareness in this period that anticommunism was becoming paranoia, with concerning developments such as 'loyalty tests for government employees'[40] and, as the House Committee on Un-American Activities increased its activities, 'indications that this country is on the verge of an anti-Communist drive'.[41]

British diplomats reported sardonically on France's intransigent colonial policy and were completely unconvinced by claims of liberal progress. The recalcitrance to negotiate or make concessions observed in French government and parliamentary circles was seen as the result of material gain and especially French post-Second World War inferiority complex.[42] The Union Française that replaced the Empire gave 'the impression of having been created rather for effect than to last' and brought no improvements, as '[n]early all the French overseas territories are at grips with some form of nationalism movement'.[43] While plans for a French Union envisaged a loosening of the French Empire, 'these various proposals did not, however, proceed much beyond the enunciation of general principles'. The Vietnamese conflict, where d'Argenlieu preferred to resort 'to force and manipulation rather than negotiating', only confirmed that French colonialism had undergone no substantial change,[44] since they 'have no intention of entering into negotiation with HO CHI MINH'.[45] Diplomats observed with concern that French colonial policy was in fact becoming *more* intransigent during this period, as shown by the outbreak of the Madagascar rebellion in early 1947;[46] the appointment of General Juin, a notorious imperialist, as governor of Morocco; and the arrest of all three Madagascan native Assemblée Nationale deputies and of seventy-eight of the eighty deputies of the Madagascan Assembly.[47] It is not surprising that in this context British policymakers could not heed claims of a new liberal and progressive approach to colonialism.

French intransigence in Indochina had become an embarrassment for British diplomacy. The UK Special Commissioner for Southeast Asia, responsible for coordinating Franco–British collaboration in that part of the world, warned that 'we must be extremely careful to avoid any false impression of a policy of "South East Asia for Europeans". So long as there is no agreement between the French and Asiatics in Indo China we must put each foot down very warily'.[48] This reflected a policy that limited Franco–British cooperation in Asia, 'leaving out political matters for the time being', which was framed as part 'of a regional system rather than a bilateral Anglo-French agreement' and further limited to 'questions such as health'.[49] This was due to awareness that anticolonial sentiment was growing, irreversible and that Britain's policy of gradual decolonization was having a positive impact on diplomatic relations. In Thailand, for example, the ambassador warns that 'our enemies may seize upon the result of [French Prime Minster] M. Blum's recent visit to London to allege that we are sympathetic towards the French policy of repression in Indo-China'.[50] But shame at association with French colonialism was not only the result of the postwar Labour government's anticolonialism.

India had a key role to play in British diplomacy and policy on Vietnam in this period. Jawaharlal Nehru and the Indian National Congress Party had dominated Indian politics in a broadly peaceful anticolonial struggle since the 1930s and led the Interim Government of India from 2 September 1946 and independent India since 15 August 1947. After the collapse of Franco–Vietnamese negotiations in late 1946, they had been supportive of Vietminh efforts to achieve Vietnamese independence. Under Indian pressure British diplomats resist – with incredible politeness – French attempts to obtain assistance or arms. Just weeks before Indian independence the question came to a head when the Government of India informed the Foreign Office that

> '[i]t is understood that His Majesty's Government have sold surplus military vehicles from stocks in India to the French in Indo China. Government of India are in considerable difficulty in this matter as they have previously declared that they will not assist the French in any way to pursue hostilities in Indo-China. Requests that the sale of the vehicles be cancelled.'[51]

The Foreign Office considered the French proposal to sell the hardware from stocks in Singapore, but there too, like in India and Ceylon, local nationalists were extremely unhappy. When Nehru's Indian Congress was joined by dockworkers from ports in all three territories threatening to boycott French shipping, the Foreign Office reconsidered.[52] The French insisted, but discussions at the Foreign Office and Cabinet concluded that 'it is a little difficult to answer this French request' 'we should get into acute difficulties with Indian authorities if we did so' due to the 'Government of India's objections to supplying French Indo-China on political grounds'.[53] In April 1947 the French embassy in London requested intelligence on Vietminh representatives active in India.[54] Considering that 'it would be unwise to ask [Indian Intelligence] for any information on this point in view of the attitude of the Government of India towards VIET NAM', the Foreign Office consoles the French with a useless MI5 report.[55] Keeping India as a close postcolonial ally meant condemning the Franco–British colonial solidarity that had allowed the French return to Indochina in 1945.

Britain's approach to the Indochinese conflict in this period was also influenced by the ungainly brutality of French behaviour in Indochina. Assisting France had become diplomatic suicide.[56] This was not only due to pressure from Nehru's India, but also to mounting American concerns about French policy and military conduct. While one might expect atrocities against Vietnamese civilians to have taken centre stage, views of French policy were plagued by Eurocentric matters such as contrast with British and American decolonization (particularly the refusal to negotiate) or the mass recruitment of German Second World War veterans into the Foreign Legion to fight in Vietnam. The question of German Légionnaires in particular and the mass conscription of Algerians and Senegalese returns constantly in the diplomacy of all actors studied, reinforcing the view of French colonial radicalism.[57] British diplomats reported that in the US '[m]uch attention has been paid to the outbreak of fighting in Indo-China and [despite Ho's communism] regarded as a notorious example of colonial misrule and the French government accused of never having shown the capability to deal wisely with the legitimate demands of the natives'.[58] The UK consul in Saigon likewise reported that the recently appointed Commissaire for Tonkin, General Morlière, 'was of the old die-hard school' and concluded that 'a workable agreement will only be possible if the French adopt a more conciliatory policy'.[59]

The diplomatic deadlock with Britain and the US could only be broken when France made a progressive solution appear credible, as it finally managed to do in 1948. In 1947, however, the first incarnation of the Bao Dai solution to establish a friendly 'Annamite Government' is qualified as 'the formation of a puppet Government in Hanoi on similar lines to the original Government in Cochin-China'. Conversely, diplomats found evidence that Vietminh was very willing to negotiate, particularly if future independence was on the table, as 'the partial elimination of the more extreme elements in the Viet Nam government might be taken as an attempt to smooth the way towards the forthcoming negotiation'.[60] Against French claims that few totalitarian extremists wanted independence, British diplomats reported on a clear Vietnamese consensus: 'there is no doubt that all the political parties, as well as those who are directly associated with HO CHI MINH, will accept nothing short of complete independence'.[61] The language used by British diplomacy in mid-1947 to late 1946 suggests that they took Vietminh's nationalist claims at face value, referring to them as 'nationalists', 'rebels' and 'rebel alliance' of 'communist proclivities'.[62] Crucially, in December 1946 British diplomats begin using demonyms ('Viet Namians' 'Viet Namese') that refer to Vietnam rather than colonial Annam.[63]

This is not to say that British diplomacy was not concerned about communism. Reports contain infinitesimal details as to Soviet intentions in Southeast Asia. For instance, we find much reporting and speculation on the establishment of a Soviet diplomatic mission in Bangkok,[64] as well as concerns that the Chinese community might import Maoism to Siam.[65] Discussion as to whether Vietminh were part of a Soviet drive in Asia centred on two key markers. Firstly, evidence as to whether Ho's past Soviet links remained active. As no evidence of such links emerged throughout this period, this often degenerated into speculation involving Ho's past and similarities between Vietminh and the Chinese and Soviet communist parties. Secondly, and more convincing for policymakers throughout this period, is the attitude of Soviet and French communists to the conflict. This produces sometimes amusing and convoluted explanations such as '[m]anoeuvering of this kind does not usually cause much strain upon a party less troubled by the claims of consistency than most'.[66]

Despite near-permanent discussion as to their communist links, British diplomacy represented Vietminh largely outside the Cold War frame. It was qualified as a socialist, Marxist, revolutionary, but primarily nationalist movement. Most importantly for the key analysis of this book, it was not considered a Soviet ally. The report from Saigon analysed in detail in Part II, Chapter 9 of this book is a key document in British understanding of the conflict and the role of Vietminh's communism therein. It was very widely distributed by the Foreign Office and cited for over a year as the British "view" of Vietminh in early 1947. It warns that though 'the danger of Communist infiltration undoubtedly exists and will require careful watching. I feel that the sudden raising of the Communist Bogey by the Haut Commissaire [...] was part of the plan to discredit the Viet Nam Government and to obtain support, or at least non-interference, from the United States'. British analysis found that French-supplied intelligence substantiating Vietminh 'collusion with Foreign Communists' did not amount to 'clear evidence of outside control of the Communist movement'.[67] Backtracking to the origins of this report on Vietminh communism, the Foreign Office felt the allegations warranted investigation into 'the seriousness of the communist menace and the accuracy or otherwise of these views [expressed by d'Argenlieu]'.[68] This effort went into incredible detail including 'manifestation of Communist tendencies' in village life and labour strikes – crucially, these observations never substantiated links to the USSR or CCP.[69] British analysis at this time, however, attached greater importance to reports from Moscow. They suggested that the Soviet establishment did not care about the Indochinese conflict, for it was not mentioned in official circles or the press besides 'short comments' hoping that French imperialism will be thwarted by 'the young Republic'.[70] This analysis reveals not only that British investigations into Vietminh revealed no Soviet links, but also that at this time they treated French-supplied evidence with extreme caution.

In this period British diplomats faced French attempts to tar Vietminh with the brush of Second World War enemies and terrorism. These efforts backfired spectacularly. In February 1947 the consul in Hanoi was made privy to a French investigation into the 'Japanese Special Services, and have obtained at last the proof of the existence of an underground net-work in South East Asia' that stayed behind after the Armistice to foment rebellions, which 'has borne fruit in South East Asia' as 'revolutionary movements with nationalists, religious, or racial backgrounds have swept the East'.[71] British analysis did not give credence to the thesis that all Asian nationalist discontent was the fruit of Japanese plots. In December 1946 the Saigon consulate saw a copy of a document purporting to be 'confidential instructions issued by HO CHI MINH to his "key-men"' that included drawing on 'the help of German and Japanese technicians now manufacturing members of war in Viet Nam'; 'a chain of strikes is to be organised in French industrial concerns'; threatening 'letters' and 'assassination'; the sabotage of the Fontainebleau conference; 'to ban all French books'; and, most concerning for British interests, 'a general boycott directed against the colonising European Powers. Burma, Malaya, Siam, India'. Because of the 'violence of the views expressed and the reference to assistance from Germany and Japan' the consul sought confirmation. He was only able to find 'Monsieur LEGREZE, a [former Vichy] French official' who yet left the consul still 'unable to vouch for the authority of these "instructions"'.[72] It is little wonder that, after such absurd and fantastic allegations British diplomats treated French allegations and intelligence documents, especially those dealing with communism, with extreme scepticism.

Though British diplomacy treated French claims with scepticism, this was not because of the inverse amount of credence which was accorded to Vietnamese sources. Diplomatic analysis remained deeply Eurocentric and orientalist. This is evident in the extent to which diplomats preferred to confirm Vietminh's non-alignment via lack of attention from their supposed masters in Moscow or the understanding that French diplomacy was scraping the barrel with ever less believable fabrications. 'A Tour of the Laos' by the British Consul in Saigon reads like an ethnological colonial adventure: Laotians are 'an indolent though happy race' 'completely unpolitically minded'. The cable reflects a French understanding of the ethnic "characters" of their subject populations, which worked well with

British orientalist discourses that classified the various subject peoples through assessment of ethnic qualities.[73] The representation of 'indolent' and 'unpolitically minded' Asians was crucial to 'the rather academic question (in this backward oriental country) of the popular support which may be enjoyed by Ho Chi Minh'. This is why it was assumed that communism must necessarily be a foreign import. It is sadly fascinating to see that the political support of Asian subjects, not unlike the love of a Vietnamese woman (as described by Greene, analysed in Part I, Chapter 2), is qualified as normatively different, less real and less sincere in this orientalist racialization of politics.[74]

US

American diplomacy, meanwhile, wrote about the conflict as a colonial struggle with unconvincing Cold War hues. In this period communism took centre stage in US foreign policy. Containment became policy with the proclamation of the Truman Doctrine to Congress on 12 March 1947 leading to assistance to Greece and Turkey. American diplomacy, analysis and policymaking, however, did not believe French allegations that Vietminh was spearheading a communist offensive in Southeast Asia. While US diplomacy was concerned about potential Soviet plans to hijack nationalist movements in the colonies to spread communism, they did not yet believe that Vietminh was a communist movement, rather considering it as an extremist reaction to French intransigence.

Backtracking to August 1947 to September 1946 reveals that without a credible liberal progressive French proposal, the conflict's representation in US diplomacy tilted towards attributing the conflict to French intransigence. This position was informed by hostility to European imperialism and a self-congratulatory view of decolonization that posited US 'tutelage' of the Philippines as the ideal example to follow. This conspired to make French allegations appear self-serving and instrumental, highlighting the ruthlessness of French colonialism and the refusal to negotiate with the Vietnamese. This understanding led to a policy to avoid entanglement and encourage both parties to negotiate.

French representation of Vietminh communism was too contradictory for American diplomats to believe outright. In July 1947, the consul in Hanoi remarked that 'it remains curious that French discovered no Communist menace in Ho Chi Minh Govt until after September 1946, when it became apparent VN Govt would not bow to French'.[75] Concern about the global expansion of communism, however, meant that French allegations could not be dismissed.

Like their British colleagues, American diplomats sought to punctiliously verify and triangulate information. The State Department constantly requests verification of all and any communist links that might substantiate 'whether influence Communists in present coalition GOVT [...] would be sufficient put Vietnam in Soviet Camp'.[76] The archival evidence reveals that this concern came from the highest levels of US diplomacy. Secretary Marshall feared Vietnam was but a small part of a broader Soviet 'long range colonial strategy' to turn '600 million dependent people' to communism. Marshall's response to this conspiratorial concern was to urge France to 'be most generous attempt find early solution'. Meanwhile, his diplomats were tasked with finding proof of these Soviet plans.[77] This is why a year later (as seen in the previous chapter) we find US spies and diplomats desperately looking for evidence of this Soviet plan throughout the French Empire, including hunting down Russian tramps in China, a poet in Martinique and a gasoline dealer in Nouméa.

Despite concerns about communism, American diplomats feared being manipulated.[78] In February 1947 the consul in Saigon notes that communist concerns appear to be reserved for US diplomats 'it is note-worthy that Communism is nowhere mentioned' in internal French deliberations. This added to suspicions by State officials that French diplomats sought to manipulate US policy by leveraging concerns about communism.[79] Some found 'some truth in charge by Marxist press that Haut Commissaire plays up Communism to cover deficiencies French policy' and argued that Vietminh's appeal was nationalist and Ho was the 'real representative of people'.[80] This was supported by lack of evidence of Vietminh links to Chinese and Soviet communism. For instance, major efforts were made to find whether 'Gunpung', whom the French accused of being a CCP agent, was responsible for Vietminh's military successes.[81] No proof was forthcoming, however. The only solid evidence of Vietminh–Soviet links found by the State Department in this period was a supportive 'anti-imperialist' seven-line telegram from the Soviet Youth Congress addressed to the Vietnamese youth.

Backtracking to January 1947 we find the origin of Marshall's disproportionate concern about Soviet plans for the French Empire. French reports alleged that 'the Indo-Chinese problem is not an isolated one' but concerned the whole 'French empire, where the Communists are busily encouraging the Nationalists, especially in North Africa.'[82] However, this was tempered by the total abandonment of Vietminh by French and Soviet communist parties, which was widely reported by US diplomats.[83] As a result, in late 1946 State Department analysis suggested that while Vietminh might use 'Communist party techniques and discipline with which they are familiar', 'attempts to communize their country are secondary and would await successful operation of a nationalist state'.

In this period communism and anticolonialism contended as rival explanations for the war. This is illustrated in a December 1946 cable where the consul in Hanoi speculates that the conflict was either the '[r]esult orders from Moscow' to 'upset Southeast Asia' or an anticolonial strategy to force France to grant a settlement.[84] For most of this period the latter thesis was dominant, with little credence that Vietminh anticolonialism was a cover for communist expansion. In a more nuanced assessment, Abbot Low Moffat, head of the State Department's SEA Department, warned that French policy 'such as the apparent reneging on the March 6 agreement' might result in anti-Western feeling that in time 'might open the door for development of strong Communist influence in SEA'.[85] The suggestion that France might be to blame for the conflict further decreased the believability of French accusations and increased the need for independent verification.

French colonial and military policy in this period did not recommend itself. American diplomats found it so regressive and violent that it legitimized Vietminh's nationalist demands. They consequently pressed the French foreign and colonial ministries for a negotiated solution involving Vietminh. Specifically, US diplomats found the first Bao Dai solution to be yet another 'puppet government'.[86] American diplomats were so suspicious of French colonial officials that in February 1947 the consul in Hanoi requested intelligence on Sainteny's financial interests in Indochina,[87] and feared that French forces were using chemical weapons.[88] The consul in Hanoi was scandalized by evidence that Vietminh had sent a messenger to establish a dialogue with Colonies minister Marius Moutet but that 'Viet Namese state messenger bearing letter of invitation for Moutet disappeared'.[89] French military and diplomatic intransigence was confirmed by the French siege of Hanoi witnessed by the US consul. In December 1946, he reported that 'French have made pillaging military policy' in Haiphong where 'Vietnamese quarter MASHED by artillery fire' and 'burning some villages vicinity'.[90] This contrasted with Vietminh conduct of the war in which Vietminh 'tried to protect other foreigners – one American caught in battle area was even given turkey for Christmas'.[91] Reports from this period conclude that French actions 'can only be interpreted as expressing a desire to employ force to bring the Vietnamese to accept the French will' while French accusations of Vietminh terrorism were dismissed.[92] This is why American acceptance of French arguments in 1948 necessitated a convincing progressive development of French colonial policy.

Conversely, American diplomats found evidence that the Vietminh rebel alliance was representative of Vietnamese 'nationalist sentiment' and grievances.[93] The presence and continuous emergence of many political parties sharing Vietminh's platform made it clear that Vietnamese independence and unification was not, as d'Argenlieu claimed, the result of communist or fascist extremism.[94] Vietnamese contacts confirmed strong 'adherence to Ho and unabated anti-French feeling, especially towards High Commissioner and [...] colonialists'.[95] Even Catholics and monarchists, previously supportive of French rule, were quickly 'drifting toward break with French'.[96] French arguments about Vietminh extremism were further undermined by evidence suggesting wider discontent with French colonialism. In November 1946, for instance, Navy intelligence obtained a copy of a petition by the 'Free Laos Government' asking Chiang Kai-shek to support Laotian independence.[97]

Recognition of Vietminh anticolonial grievances was, however, informed by contemporary attitudes to Asian colonial subjects. While diplomats deplored French actions and sympathized with Vietnamese nationalism, they doubted 'whether they are capable of running an independent state' and point to the fact that 'the Philippines after 40 odd years of benevolent tutelage, in which the advantages of education and instruction were available to all, are still not a model of good government'. In other words, they reasoned that if the Philippines were still facing major challenges despite enlightened American colonialism, the Vietnamese would be even less prepared for independence and 'without Occidental check or control the result would be chaos –and in that chaos either the Soviets or the Chinese would find their opportunity'.[98] The fear that anti-Western hatred fuelled by French actions might expel 'Occidental check or control' and enable communism informed a policy of mediated negotiation that would keep an independent Vietnam close to Western interests. The solution offered by American diplomats and personally favoured by Secretary Byrne in late 1946 was US mediation. Secretary Byrne himself sounded out French diplomats about this option but was energetically rebuffed.[99]

Vietminh

Vietminh diplomacy sought the same goals as in other periods studied in this book: reunification of colonially divided Vietnam and independence. Vietminh representation of the conflict focused on French colonialism, which was historicized as unjust, exploitative, racist and detrimental to the Vietnamese.

Conversely, Vietminh represented themselves as a nationalist rebel alliance motivated by grievances legitimized by the post-Second World War San Francisco UN Conference and Charter. In this period Vietminh sought to directly confront French allegations that it was a Soviet or Japanese stooge, arguing that an independent Vietnam would look to the UN, the West and particularly the US for assistance, guidance and advice on domestic and international policy. In a testament to the influence and work of large and experienced diplomatic establishments, despite being in contact with French, American and British diplomats, Vietminh diplomacy was far smaller in volume and number of contacts.

In this period Vietminh leaders still held hopes for a solution based on the internationalist liberal principles of the post-Second World War settlement. They appealed to the principles of self-determination and human rights enshrined in the Atlantic and San Francisco Charters, arguing that as subject peoples they were entitled to break free from French rule. Even after the outbreak of hostilities in November 1946, they argued for a peacefully negotiated end to colonialism such as that granted to the Philippines by the US. Crucially, they seemed to believe that, as per Roosevelt's declarations about French colonialism in Indochina, America might champion the cause of subject peoples. Their hopes for an internationally mediated end to the conflict are revealed in two large-scale diplomatic efforts to bring an end to the conflict by involving the UN or a mediating third power.

In April 1947 Pham Ngoc Thach appeared at the US embassy in Bangkok to deliver a large file concerning Vietminh, its goals and the war. Though solemnly titled 'DRV Undersecretary for Foreign Affairs', Thach was, perhaps more impressively, a special envoy who frequently travelled large distances risking capture, torture and assassination by the French Sûreté and other French agents to communicate with foreign and particularly American diplomats. This extraordinary file included seventy individual documents and many supporting French documents. The file's accompanying cover letter requested that the US put the case of Vietnam before the UN or, at least, offer mediation.[100]

The documents accompanying the April 1947 mediation request reveal how Vietminh sought to portray itself and the conflict. The core argument concerned colonialism, which explained the need and logic of Vietminh's own existence and the nature of the conflict. This representation was nuanced by awareness that only a segment of the French population and political spectrum wanted war in Indochina. Besides the by-now-familiar descriptions of Indochina's wealth being plundered for private interests using cheap or forced native labour, it argued that racism and a 'right to rule' disposition led to unprecedented colonial terror and cruelty in efforts to quash the rebellion. The rebellion, always referred to as the 'Vietnamese Revolution' was represented as the actualization of self-evident and humane Vietnamese wishes for Vietnamese reunification, independence that retained a non-sovereign link to the French Union, and rights equal to those afforded to French citizens. These demands were squarely framed by the language of the rights afforded to dependent peoples under the Atlantic Charter willed by the 'missed former President Franklin D. Roosevelt'.[101]

Backtracking to the beginning of the war, in February 1947 DRV Foreign Minister Hoang Minh Giam addressed a memorandum to French Foreign Minister Bidault concerning the outbreak of hostilities. It blamed French officials, particularly d'Argenlieu and the military, for provoking the outbreak of war, atrocities and criminal abuse. Although the cable purported to inform the French government about its wayward colonial officials, Giam might not have appreciated the influence of the 1944 Gaullist colonial consensus, of which both d'Argenlieu and Bidault were key components. It is also clear, however, that Vietminh did not have much hope for this correspondence. Considering that Vietminh sent American diplomats three copies via the missions in Saigon, Hanoi and Paris, it was probably designed to demonstrate that Vietminh was trying to reach an amicable resolution.[102] This diplomatic strategy would be repeated on at least three other occasions, though unbeknownst to Vietminh, the US ambassador in Paris forwarded copies to Bidault.[103] Vietminh willingness to negotiate an end to the conflict was not only a ploy. Throughout this period Ho consistently told all foreign diplomats that he was available for peace talks.[104]

In December 1946 Vietminh prepared an extensive 'Memorandum concerning the origin of the Franco-Vietnamese conflict'.[105] This earlier diplomatic drive to obtain third-power or UN mediation represented the conflict as one pitting rapacious colonialists against freedom fighters. This is framed historically, as the culmination of a century of Vietnamese efforts to combat unjust foreign domination. It uses poignant examples of racist injustice, for instance explaining that the murder of a French citizen by a Vietnamese is punishable by death, while the opposite garners only a suspended sentence of four months. French actions at the beginning of the conflict are explained as a symptom of this incurable colonial abuse, which explains subsequent military brutality and executions. The legitimacy of Vietminh's cause is constituted in universal terms: firstly, through the binary of 'freedom' against 'subjugation', and secondly through the experience of the Second World War in which Vietminh assisted the Allies against the Japanese – unlike the French who surrendered the colony without a shot.[106]

The December 1946 memorandum was the culmination of efforts led by Giam to keep the Americans abreast of events from a Vietminh perspective.[107] In December 1946, the American consulate in Hanoi received a very elaborate English-language booklet titled 'Factual records of the Vietnam August revolution'. Although Consul O'Sullivan reports that none of its contents were new, the description of the 1945 Vietminh uprising is crucial. It is described as an explosion of pent-up Vietnamese desire for liberation fuelled by grievances and injustices and expressed through numerous nationalist rebellions, particularly in the early twentieth century. It is noteworthy that it treats Nguyen Ai Quoc and Ho Chi Minh as two separate people, perhaps as O'Sullivan notes, to dissociate Vietminh from communism. The Vietminh-led DRV government that emerged in 1945 is described as led by 'a national congress' democratically elected and an ally validated by anti-Japanese resistance.[108]

Even as the war was becoming more violent, Vietminh made very public attempts to demonstrate a desire for peace with France. This was very much a Ho initiative against the wishes of leading Vietminh leaders including Giam and Giap. An open letter 'to the French National Assembly and Government' deplored the violations of the 14 September 1946 Modus Vivendi, the only outcome of Fontainebleau, but suggested that only 'a number of Frenchmen in Indochina have and continue to act against these accords'. Furthermore, since they 'have a monopoly of information, they report falsely' back to France, misleading public and political opinion. This is corroborated by a French Presidency investigation that found evidence that d'Argenlieu purposefully delayed transmission of Vietnamese communications to the COMINDO.[109] The letter requested that the Assembly compel colonial officers to adhere to the Modus Vivendi. Though an accurate assessment of d'Argenlieu's approach to informing France and to violations of agreements, the appeal was ineffective.[110]

At the breakout of war in November 1946, the Vietnamese made efforts to tell their side of the story behind the Haiphong Incident. Giam met with US and British diplomats in Hanoi to hand them a dossier blaming the French military, particularly Generals Valluy and Morlière, for dragging Vietminh forces into a war trap. It explained that the Haiphong massacre began with an ultimatum that had no feasible time to be responded to.[111] Responsibility for the outbreak of war would remain in question until research published in 2010 validated that it was a 'trap' by Morlière and Valluy.[112]

Concurrently, Vietminh diplomats worked hard to dispel any notion that Vietminh was a communist or even Japanese creation. In May 1947, the dependable Thach responded in detail to a US embassy questionnaire (analysed in Part II, p. XX), explaining that Vietnamese communism is entirely devoted to national liberation, emphasizing that the Vietminh programme is based on modern capitalist ideas.[113] In April, Thach pointed out that Vietminh had no support for its anti-imperialist cause from the French Communist Party.[114] Earlier that year, Ho gave a series of interviews to American papers arguing that Vietminh is representative of 'just' Vietnamese ambitions and is an alliance of nationalists, Marxists, democrats and socialists 'not to mention catholics and bouddhists who belong to no party'. Discussing specific policies, Ho argued that 'France and England have pushed nationalisations further than we have'.[115]

Rejection of communist or fascist links required consistent efforts. Earlier in September 1946, Ho told the US ambassador in Paris that 'he had at one time studied Marxism but that he is not a Moscow fellow-traveller'.[116] Back in Hanoi, Ho told State Department SEA Chief Abbot Low Moffat that he had 'admiration for the United States and respect and affection for President Roosevelt' and particularly America's enlightened 'policy toward the Philippines', explaining that his people desired the same. When questioned on communism, Ho highlighted that 'the Communist party as such dissolved itself several months ago' and that the DRV constitution guarantees human rights and 'the right to personal property'.[117] In September 1946, before the outbreak of war, the American consul in Hanoi was given extensive documentation on the 'platform of the Viet-Minh League', which 'promises universal suffrage and democratic liberties', and in a clear move to reject French accusations of Vietnamese ethno-supremacist fascism, full rights and protections for the minorities of Vietnam, including the Tai and Muong.[118] As seen in the study of US representation of Vietminh in the previous section, Vietminh efforts were, to a small degree, successful. However, this was only possible due to American and British representation of French colonial intransigence in this period.

14

August 1946–April 1945: Second World War ghosts and rethinking colonialism

Our reverse genealogy still has a few tasks to complete as the history of some key ideas in this conflict remain unaccounted for. The previous two chapters charted how representation of the conflict and its actors moved British and American policy from rejection between 1946 and 1947 to support of the French war in Indochina from late 1947. However, some of the representations of the conflict and its actors that enabled that complex policy shift stretch back to before the end of the Second World War. These include French representation of the conflict as a continuation of the Allied *libération* of France, and the sometimes perplexing representation of Vietminh as a fascist ethno-nationalist Japanese creation. Perhaps most importantly for the later and more famous Second Vietnam War, it is vital to explore the claim that there was no such entity as a unitary Vietnam. The claim that Vietnamese reunification was a fantasy of an ideologically extremist Vietminh would resurface, though not constructed in the same manner, during US support of South Vietnam.[1] Finally, it is in the last few months of the Second World War and its immediate aftermath that Vietminh's political identity came to be framed in the context of Japanese-led anticolonialism and the broader emergence of anticolonial movements in Asia.[2]

This chapter reverses from August 1946 to the last few months of the Second World War. It continues the hunt for the history of these representations of the conflict and its actors through the texts of diplomatic communication where they emerged, grew and came to surface. This period is deeply marked by the ideational as well as practical exigencies of the still-ongoing World War. While it is tempting to draw the line at VE or VJ-Day, it is important to note that in Southeast Asia, as in other parts of the world outside Western Europe, the conflict did not end upon Japan's surrender in August 1945. Vast Japanese armies and their puppet and allied regimes from Thailand to Manchuria remained active and yet to be disarmed. These meant that the end of the war was slow and drawn out, with Mountbatten's Allied SEAC facing the daunting task of disarming and repatriating enormous Japanese armies, particularly in Burma, Indochina, the Dutch East Indies and Malaya. Furthermore, SEAC was tasked with keeping order in these territories while Dutch, French and British colonial administrators returned. In this international context, all actors drew on the ideational continuities of the Second World War, Allied vs Axis, to locate their political identities and allegiances in a changed world. For any actor, association with the Axis was fatal after 1945.[3]

The situation in Southeast Asia was confusing to outside observers. Amid efforts to discern the 'character' of events, the British Foreign Office filed cuttings from *The Times* that contradictorily described Vietminh as 'a coalition of older Annamese independence movements under Communist control'. This exemplifies how complex the situation appeared to Western observers in 1945. It was not entirely fanciful to speculate about such contradictory political formations. The Japanese had used anticolonial discourse to justify their own imperialism in Asia,[4] and after its capitulation a variety of Japanese collaborators, puppets, as well as enemies like Vietminh and the Indian Congress, sought to overthrow European colonialism. Sukarno for instance had sought in 1945 to prevent the return of colonialism to the Dutch East Indies by force of arms. As in Indochina, British forces acting under SEAC to disarm the Japanese in the East Indies ended up fighting local nationalists – using Japanese troops. This is the complexity that explains the believability of contradictory reports on Vietminh.[5] Telling friend from foe was a complex affair of superposed and contradictory representations: Allies contra Axis, colonials against anticolonials.

Conversely, despite the June 1945 shelving of Roosevelt's Trusteeship plan for Indochina, two key developments kept fuelling hope for Southeast Asian and particularly Vietnamese nationalists. On 14 July 1946, the Philippines acquired independence, peacefully negotiated with the US, setting an ideal model for many nationalists. Furthermore, UK–Indian negotiations progressed and in a transitional concession towards full independence the following year, the colony passed to the administration of a Congress–League coalition Interim Government of India led by Jawaharlal Nehru while negotiations continued between the two Indian parties. Furthermore, a British government increasingly wary of supporting the Dutch reconquest of the East Indies brokered negotiations at the UN for the end of Dutch colonialism in Asia. This context set a tough political challenge for the re-establishment of French colonialism.

France

From 1944, de Gaulle had been concerned with the fate of Indochina. From his wartime base in Algiers, he arranged the dispatch of loyalists led by Admiral d'Argenlieu to 'liberate' Indochina and re-establish French sovereignty. The 1943 Brazzaville Conference Declaration had been the only concession to nationalist aspirations simmering in the French Empire. It was entirely rhetorical. It offered no self-rule of any degree, no improved rights for the indigenous populations who remained subject to racially codified colonial law, nor abolishment of many detested French colonial practices.[6] Such developments were considered unnecessary as French nationalists led by de Gaulle argued that French colonialism was progressive by virtue of French republicanism and enlightenment, a discourse originating in the 1920s reincarnation of the nineteenth-century *mission civilisatrice*.[7] De Gaulle's many speeches on the subject, consistently echoed by diplomats, represented Indochina as a 'loyal' colony awaiting *libération* from the Axis.[8]

On 2 September 1945 Ho Chi Minh unilaterally declared the end of colonialism in Indochina and the establishment of the DRV. De Gaulle and French diplomats immediately declared Vietminh as a scion of Japanese fascism that invented the notion of Vietnam to subjugate other Indochinese races. The same month the first Free French mission, led by Jean Sainteny, arrived in Hanoi to find the colony in anticolonial effervescence. In this period August 1946 to mid-1945 we find that French diplomacy contradictorily represented Vietminh as both fascist and communist. The stakes could not be higher: Roosevelt, who argued that Indochina was an example of colonial misrule and exploitation, had sought to constitute it as a UN Trusteeship after the war.[9] Upon his death in April 1945, Truman made no decision on Trusteeship for Indochina until June 1945, marking a period of febrile activity for French diplomats. They not only sought to avoid US censure and termination of colonialism in Indochina, but furthermore sought American support for French efforts to restore sovereignty over the colony.

In this period representation of Vietminh as communists was very different from that studied in previous chapters. It was so sporadic, French-centric, and contradictory that it is understandable that American and British diplomats ignored it. It was inconsistently framed as a Soviet plot to conquer France with no distinction as to Indochinese, Soviet or French communists.[10] It was predicated on the French domestic context, where Communists had 'saved' France with their wartime resistance to German occupation and were reaping electoral dividends in 1946 to the great anguish of Conservatives, Catholics and Colonialists.[11] These accusations were as contradictory as they were abundant and concerned more the fierce Gaullist–Conservative–Socialist–Communist debates in France than Indochina, with Gaullists tending to accuse detractors – even Americans – of treacherous 'collaborationisme' or 'Communisme'.[12]

French diplomats and agents in Indochina did not attribute the 1945 Vietminh revolution and its unprecedented cross-spectrum support to communism. Rather, they blamed the Chinese occupation of the north 'for facilitating the formation of a national union government' 'when this seemed impossible'.[13] Extensive 1945 reports compiled by Pignon under Sainteny's auspices conclude that Vietminh is a league of many pre-existing parties united by the goal of independence. There was no evidence Vietminh planned to communize the country; communism appeared to Pignon more as a set of techniques for anti-French 'subversion' and a 'historical' Vietminh factor.[14] Rather, Vietminh was reported to be a complex alliance of anti-French groups that included socialists, communists, the ultraconservative Dai Viet party, Catholics, and monarchists 'who have filled Annamite heads with dreams'.[15]

The threat of communism in France, however, provided de Gaulle with significant leverage over US policy. This was desperately needed to reconstruct France and 'regain ground' 'morally and materially'. Furthermore, American and British support were needed to arm and ship to Indochina the Corps Expéditionnaire d'Extrême Orient force led by General Leclerc. Furthermore, diplomatic support was needed to pressure Thailand to return Indochinese territory annexed during the Second World War and quickly end the Chinese occupation of north Indochina.[16] A July 1945 analysis pointed out that French influence in the US, though somewhat enhanced by the Second World War, was limited by 'misunderstanding' of its colonial rule.[17] Between June and December 1945, reports from the French embassy in DC widely distributed and thoroughly analysed at the Quai d'Orsay expounded growing American fears of a communist takeover in France.[18] This was a threat that de Gaulle leveraged frequently when British and American diplomats refused to aid France.[19] In May 1945, for instance, de Gaulle told ambassador Caffery that 'if he could not work with the United States, which he would prefer to do, he would have to work with the Soviet Union in order to survive even temporarily'.[20]

French diplomacy sought to justify the restoration of sovereignty over Indochina as progressive. A July 1946 article in glossy magazine *France Illustration* approved by d'Argenlieu is a good guide to French diplomacy's representation of Indochina and its political, territorial and military context. It is framed around Second World War binaries: the military effort in Indochina is a continuation of the *libération* of France from a Japanese-manufactured terrorist organization left behind by the Japanese.[21] Vietminh's anticolonialism, it specifies, is a xenophobic anti-white leftover of Japanese occupation.[22] Privately, diplomats briefed that Vietminh 'are but puppets in the hands of the Germans and the Japanese' with Ho Chi Minh 'carrying out the war objectives of the Germans and the Japanese, all while plunging his country in ruin'.[23] Analysis from the Foreign Ministry explains that 'China's considerable role in fomenting trouble and sedition should not be forgotten', a role that 'follows old habit' – presumably a reference to Chinese domination of Vietnam fourteen centuries earlier.[24]

D'Argenlieu ardently argued that Vietnam did not exist, even against orders from his superiors. In the summer of 1946, under pretences of a 'broken foot' he missed the Fontainebleau conference – which gave him opportunity to call the Dalat II conference and establish the Cochinchinese Republic even as Franco–DRV talks proceeded in Paris. Despite this major breach of his mandate that scuppered the Fontainebleau agreements, he was reprimanded without further consequence. As analysed in Part II, Chapter 6 (p. XX) of this book, d'Argenlieu argued that "Vietnam" was a creation of fascist extremists bent on regional conquest.[25] On several occasions, d'Argenlieu calls 'genius', the 'idea of reviving the ancient name of Vietnam' and associated Vietminh's goal of reunification with Hitler's revival of 'Germania', repeatedly demanding that the Foreign Ministry 'bans all usage of the term Viet Nam'.[26]

Documents reveal that d'Argenlieu's argument that Vietnam did not exist was not well received by his superiors at the COMINDO or the Americans.[27] To support this argument, the Haut Commissariat produced documents detailing massacres, terrorism, mass executions, abductions and abuses of minorities by Vietminh's 'imperialist' and 'xenophobic' fanaticism.[28] The level of detail is astonishing, with a nineteen-page report devoted solely to the 'destruction of Cochinchinese property' complete with estimated value, dates and names of owners, as well as 'translated Viet-Minh orders for destructive expeditions'.[29] In this representation of Vietminh fascism, Cochinchina needed French protection to survive 'Annamese' imperialism – this would become the core of the policy against Vietnamese reunification. Retracing the history of this initially unpersuasive argument, we find that during Fontainebleau d'Argenlieu made a secret and personal appeal to Prime Minister Bidault arguing that 'to allow the Hanoi government to retake Cochinchina [would form a bloc] that would prepare our eviction, for this bloc will be united <u>against us</u>'.[30]

During this period French diplomacy tied the restoration of French sovereignty to its civilizing *œuvre* and enduring Indochinese loyalty to France. D'Argenlieu, de Gaulle and Bidault were exasperated by Vietminh and American 'diatribes' against the achievements of French colonialism, the *œuvre française*, often arguing that detractors did not appreciate that France brought civilization and progress to Indochina.[31] Earlier, in May 1945, the French Press and Information Service in New York had sent the State Department extensive documentation on 'the present situation in Indochina'. Written in the same language used to describe the struggle for the liberation of France, it constructed a narrative of Japanese occupation fighting Free French Forces including 'Indo-Chinese and French sympathisers in equal proportions' that proved that 'the solidarity of the French and Indo-Chinese people has been maintained and is continually evident'. Crucially, it dismisses independence movements as 'propaganda' and 'brutal interference by the Japanese'.[32]

Anguished by American anticolonialism, the French Cabinet devised a 'diplomatic strategy [. . .] to manage the positive disposition of the American Government through assurances on French intentions concerning the future political and economic status of Indochina'.[33] Reframing colonialism, France promulgated a progressive plan for Indochina that reorganized it as an Indochinese federation of five countries within the 'French Union', making sure that it was widely reported in the British and American press.[34] The plan was billed as the liberal evolution of empire allowing for self-government 'without prejudice of French or natives' 'for the general interest' 'and social and economic development' based on 'liberty of thought, faith, press, association and organisation. The civilisation, race and traditions' of Indochina 'will be respected and guaranteed'.[35]

French diplomacy was extremely concerned by the prospect of US intervention. Until American recognition of French sovereignty in Indochina in June 1945, this was due to Roosevelt's Trusteeship plan. At the San Francisco Conference in June 1945, US diplomats accepted that agreement of the colonial power (if Allied) was required to establish UN Trusteeship. This was not a complete turnaround, however, and following subsequent French overtures to purchase American weapons American diplomats 'made it clear that that they had no intention to help colonial powers re-establish themselves by force'.[36] By November 1945 French diplomats were so concerned about US interference that any sign of 'Annamite-American contact' was investigated and loudly denounced to the State Department.[37] Rumours even circulated that 'the Americans might have facilitated travel to Washington of a representative of the Annamite revolutionary Government carrying many anti-French documents'.[38] This concern was aggravated by early Vietnamese diplomatic efforts in October, which saw a large dossier critical of French colonialism and repression handed to OSS Major Patti to carry to the State Department (where I found it), a communication that raised alarm in French diplomatic circles.[39] Backtracking to the final months of the war, it was evident that French suspicion of American colonialism had begun much earlier. In March 1945, for instance, Paris demanded that the US cease delivering 'weapons to the Annamites or unqualified groups'.[40]

Despite their energetic name-calling, before December 1945 French diplomats knew very little about Vietminh.[41] During the war, the only available reports on Indochina had reached France through the consulate at Kunming, China. Only in December 1945 do they discover that Vietminh includes former political prisoners previously interned at the island prison of Paulo Condor. As reporting became more extensive, the controller of the Sûreté concluded that 'considering our magnificent *œuvre* here' Vietminh must be a 'hidden Communist party' 'heeding Stalin's call' concealed 'under a nationalist label'.[42] More sober assessments of 'anti-French revolutionary' parties describe Vietminh as 'the result of the merger of the Communist party and old nationalist elements, trying to rally a sort of Annamite national front'.[43] Backtracking to September 1945, we see that this lack of intelligence on Vietminh is why five French missions ('M5') commanded by Jean Sainteny were sent into Indochina. The uncertainty felt by these envoys, spies and soldiers about the level of anti-French sentiment is reflected in the report from one of the missions tasked with sailing up a 'dark' river in Annam. It reads like a fearful 1945 adaptation of Joseph Conrad's novel *Heart of Darkness*, complete 'with hostiles surrounding the mission', 'deceitful Annamese' and 'terrified' white colonials.[44]

The initial reports from the Sainteny missions are extremely concerned about a 'nefarious' convergence of Vietnamese nationalists, 'francophobe' American officers 'who flirt with the Annamite government' and Japanese manipulation of natives. It notes that the Vietnamese are assembling a large force 'riddled' with 'Nippons'. As a solution to the Vietminh problem, it suggests that '[i]deally we could obtain that that it be considered by the allies as a "puppet" force and disarmed' by the Allies.[45] This was the beginning of the Japanese stooge argument. Before the Sainteny missions, the Free French knew even less about Vietminh and did not mention it to foreign diplomats other than as a Japanese puppet. A March 1945 report by the French ambassador in China characterizes the 'fusion of different nationalist Annamite parties' as an anti-French 'Japanese initiative'. Perhaps disingenuously, this report and earlier 1944 French depositions to SEAC

confuse the puppet nationalist party created by the Japanese with Vietminh –
though at this point Vietminh was fighting the Japanese.[46]

As de Gaulle, Bidault and d'Argenlieu had often discussed during the Second
World War and would publicly declare in its aftermath, Indochina was key to
symbolizing French global power and prestige.[47] Days after the end of the war,
on 27 August de Gaulle declared that 'it is united to the overseas territories that
she opened up to civilization that France is a great power'.[48] The anxiety to regain
great power status was so evident that it became the talk of diplomatic circles
during the end of the war and at one point de Gaulle caused a major diplomatic
incident over whether Roosevelt had called the General a 'prima donna'. The
drive to restore *grandeur* was such that France was willing to 'take on the allies
[. . .] whenever a shred of French pride was at stake'.[49] French policy in the
postwar period sought to reclaim 'its place amongst the nations charged with
directing the world'.[50] Bidault even fought for French to be an official language at
the San Francisco Conference by threatening to block its inauguration, to
strident applause from de Gaulle and the press.[51] Even as early as February 1945,
the US ambassador in Chungking and the First Counsellor of the French
embassy discussed France's 'new inferiority complex' and de Gaulle's frustration
at not having an equal position to the Big Three in the Dumbarton Oakes, Yalta
and San Francisco conferences.[52] The US ambassador in Paris kindly qualified
this sentiment and its resulting diplomatic drive as 'post-liberation neurosis'.[53]

Britain

British diplomacy in this period was still in wartime mode but struggling to
reframe its global commitments. Reflecting military and economic exhaustion,
colonial policy shifted to peaceful disengagement beginning with India. The
election of a Labour government under Clement Attlee in July 1945 refocused
British politics to economic reconstruction and domestic services and welfare.
Military ventures became less politically feasible, as exemplified by the
withdrawal from Greece in March 1946. The reporting, intelligence-gathering
and analysis of the Foreign Office, however, remained that of a great empire. Vast
worldwide networks of information gathering and contacts remained intact and
basked in the prestige of victory. It is remarkable that during 1945–46 the British
had far more extensive and detailed information on Indochina than the French.

In late 1945 Mountbatten's SEAC occupied the south of the colony to disarm
Japanese forces. British Indian Army colonial officer General Douglas Gracey

immediately engaged in an anti-Vietminh campaign, taking control of Saigon and rearming French troops. SEAC did not approve. Mountbatten ordered immediate disengagement and ordered Gracey to limit himself to disarming and repatriating Japanese troops. Gracey's actions were an act of European colonial solidarity and were particularly awkward for having been executed using Indian troops. French troops and civilians carried out acts of retribution against the Vietnamese, particularly in Saigon, and suppression of Vietminh in the environs. By February 1946 Britain had completely withdrawn.[54] During this period British diplomats reported that a French 'inferiority complex is very much in evidence', a fixation with restoring *grandeur*.[55] The late 1945 belief in French willingness to make progressive colonial reforms had collapsed entirely by March 1946. At the same time, their conception of Vietminh shifted from that of a Japanese puppet (or at least ally like Sukarno), to a 'left-wing' though not Soviet nationalist rebel alliance.

By May 1946 it had become evident to British diplomats that France had no desire to liberalize the Empire. French diplomats and officials were increasingly unwilling to accept criticism of colonial practices, at one point demanding an investigation into the 'impartiality' of All India Radio's Indochina reporting.[56] Foreign Office analysis briefings concluded that protestations about Annamese imperialism were designed to 'maintain French influence there', particularly 'French settlers' and 'business interests'.[57] It also became clear that the conciliatory Ho–Sainteny 6 March agreement was not a basis for further negotiation, but a ploy to force the Vietminh-supporting KMT Chinese to withdraw from Indochina.[58] Furthermore, British diplomats were shocked by the violence and reprisals they witnessed during the French reoccupation of Saigon. On 2 March 1946 French settlers and troops broke into the house of the French editor of a Saigon newspaper, injuring him and destroying presses while 'neither the Military nor the Civil authorities appear to have made any attempt to stop the rioting'.[59] Later that day, a French woman who had signed a petition supporting Vietminh had her head shaved and was paraded naked through the streets.[60] In fact, for two months the consul in Saigon had feared that French diplomatic expressions of colonial progressivism were designed to gain time so that the French military might 'present a virtual fait accompli'.[61] Colonial intransigence and brutality killed British diplomatic goodwill.

This had not formerly been the case. Between mid-1946 and the last months of the Second World War British diplomats were far more sympathetic to remonstrations of French desire for a progressive colonial policy. In this period the French government often made reference to the Indian solution of self-government followed by independence, frequently requesting detailed information on British plans for India.[62] On the issue of Vietnam's diplomatic representation, the French Colonial Ministry Head of the Asiatic Department even declared that he envisaged 'something more on the lines of the representation of British India in Washington'.[63] The British and Indian governments, then negotiating independence the following year, happily explained that India was 'an international "person" capable of concluding treaties and conventions with foreign powers separately from the United Kingdom' and a member of the UN.[64] The issue did not reappear in French diplomacy until the second Bao Dai solution in mid-1948. The Foreign Office keenly researched the 'reforms now promised', highlighting that the infamous 'régime de l'indigenat' was to be abolished.[65]

British diplomats, not without self-congratulation, compared French reforms with their own solution in India. Backtracking to March 1946, evidence shows they cautiously welcomed the 6 March agreement whose terms appeared 'more liberal than was generally expected' but decided that its implementation remained to be seen.[66] However, doubting whether the reforms were as extensive as claimed, analysis concluded that 'the aim of the new Constitution is not Dominion status but full membership of the French Union'.[67] In this period French diplomats assiduously communicated with British, American and Chinese colleagues in Indochina, London, Paris and Chungking about their progressive policies for Indochina, often calling conferences in Saigon to expound 'very optimistic' plans.[68] In the second half of 1945, the highest levels of British policymaking sympathized with French and Dutch proclamations of new self-government progressive colonial models, believing that if they matched British reforms in Malaya Southeast Asia might be stabilized.[69] In November 1945, they expressed hope that the French government had learned from British thinking about India, which reflected unwillingness to impose British rule by violence.[70]

Despite d'Argenlieu's claim of 'Annamese' extremism, British reporting found Vietminh amenable to a negotiated peace. Communications with Vietminh in March 1946 suggested that Vietminh was willing to delay independence under an arrangement like that of India or the Philippines,[71] and to make major concessions such as the return of French military forces to north Indochina. Conversely, they noted that while Ho appeared keen to implement the agreement,[72] Leclerc and d'Argenlieu were delaying.[73] As soon as the 6 March agreement was signed Vietminh attempted to establish diplomatic relations with the UK, with Ho sending a telegram to the prime minister via the Saigon consulate (see the Vietminh section below, p. 184). The Foreign Office decided not to reply in writing to avoid 'offence' to the French. Rather, it verbally replied that the UK would await the outcome of the Fontainebleau negotiations' settlement of Vietnam's diplomatic status.[74] In all, analysts had reason to believe that Vietminh willingness to make peace need only be matched to provide a peaceful settlement.

British diplomatic reporting on Vietminh was strikingly detailed and extensive. A March 1946 Foreign Office Memorandum (analysed in detail in Part II, Chapter 8, p. XX) carefully placed Vietminh in a historical context of permanent anti-French resistance. 'On the collapse of Japan the principal Annamite nationalist party (Viet-Minh) seized actual power'. It was 'the most important party but others exist. Of these, the next is importance is the Viet-Nam Quoc Dang Dang (VNQDD), a traditionalist party, as opposed to the left-wing trend of the Viet-Minh'. This document was widely distributed via Confidential Print and would have been read by all officials dealing with Southeast Asia, in effect making it Britain's official understanding of Vietminh.[75] In this representation, Vietminh was defined as a 'left-wing' nationalist movement that included 'a strong Communist element'.[76]

French officials like Haut Commissariat Political Counsellor Clarac argued that 'there would be much difficulty in treating with Ho Shi-ming, who was a fanatic and Moscow-trained'.[77] Likewise, reports passed to the British consulate posited that all of Vietminh 'holds a decidedly communist observance [obéisance]. Founded in 1941 with, it would seem, the support of the U.S.S.R'.[78] The British consul in Saigon, however, believed it was possible to negotiate with Ho since 'the nationalist element have no person of any standing or ability compared with Ho Chi Minh',[79] who is most often simply described as 'the most prominent Annamite nationalist leader'.[80] The Foreign Office understood that Vietminh was an alliance of parties enjoying unprecedentedly broad support among the Vietnamese population.[81] A series of January 1946 reports from Hanoi do not even mention communism. Rather, their chief concern was Chinese influence on Viet Nam Dong Minh (the Vietnamese KMT) part of the Vietminh governing coalition.[82] An important factor in reducing the importance of Vietminh communism was silence from Moscow. When the Moscow embassy was asked for a report on Soviet attitudes to Vietnam, a cable noted that 'no comment or even news has been published here, in spite of the obvious similarity to the situation in Indonesia which is the subject of almost daily hostile comment'.[83]

British concerns about Vietminh's international links focused on the possibility that, if war broke out with the French, 'the effect of resistance by a united nationalist movement will lead to its activities receiving the same publicity in the world press as has been achieved by the Javanese nationalists'. Analysis suggested that war with the 'Annamite opposition' was far from justified by socialist connections that were, at most, unproven and of limited significance.[84] The significance of these connections was further challenged by numerous reports proving that Vietminh not only included various non-socialist parties, but that it was working with several more (at least two, four at one point) including monarchists and ultraconservatives, in a 'coalition likely to strengthen the attitude of the anti-French element' and which enjoyed mass support.[85] A follow-up report confirmed that the various parties had formed a 'new Coalition'.[86]

Backtracking to the last weeks of 1945 and early 1946 we find Vietminh described as Axis collaborators. A statement by the Foreign Secretary to the House of Commons explained that '[i]n Indo-China as in Java the Japanese followed a policy of encouraging the growth of nationalism and with Japanese backing and arms nationalist groups were able in August last to establish what has become known as the Viet Nam Republic'. British troops were fighting the Vietnamese because 'General Gracey found himself obliged to contend with continual looting and attacks by Annamite armed bands'. Despite Gracey's actions, there was very little colonial solidarity in London, as Attlee had earlier declared: 'His Majesty's Government do not desire to be unnecessarily involved in administration or in the political affairs of non-British territories, and their objective is to withdraw British troops as soon as circumstances permit'.[87]

Of the many representations deployed by French diplomats, racially framed descriptions resonated particularly well. A Foreign Office research memorandum posited intra-Indochinese relations as a racial struggle for survival: 'The Lao are a weaker race than the Annamites, whom they fear, and they have in the past relied on French support to withstand Annamite oppression'. As we saw in Part II, Chapter 6 (p. XX), this is d'Argenlieu's argument that 'Annamites' should be contained by French power for the good of all Indochina. This argument is unproblematically absorbed into British diplomacy, proving the success of racial representations in convincing British diplomats.[88] Postwar Hanoi, under Vietminh rule and Chinese occupation, greatly anguished Western observers, for this was the first time since the 1880s that 'Asiatics' ruled over Europeans. The British Military Mission representative (later consul) in Hanoi was concerned that 'not only are the Chinese police incapable of protecting the French population but what is more serious, they tolerate any acts against white people, and sometimes encourage them'.[89] In another twist of ethno-strategic geopolitical thinking and Sinophobia, the consul in Hanoi appears convinced by French speculation that 'ex-Chinese soldiers are either deserting by arrangement or being demobilised on the spot [...] to form the nucleus of a strong Chinese minority which may become active when the French return'. He does not report again on the matter, probably having decided that the argument was silly.[90]

US

American diplomacy in Indochina was significantly behind. Its local, historical, linguistic and cultural knowledge were minimal, with the notable exception of State Department SEA Division chief Abbot Low Moffat. Reporting in this period reflected these difficulties in its lack of background knowledge, depth, detail and occasional contradictions. Reporting on Indochina consistently represented the conflict as the result of exploitative European imperialism and posited the need to negotiate with Vietminh, which they did not consider a Muscovite agent. They particularly encouraged French diplomats to consider US treatment of the Philippines as an ideal model. American concerns about communism emerged with Soviet–American hostilities in Europe and were projected globally, obscuring and confusing understanding of communist movements in Asia – particularly in anticolonial political contexts. Awareness that colonialism stoked anti-Western hostility fuelled fears that it generated the conditions for a communist drive in the French Empire. Diplomatic reporting responded with efforts to garner more detailed information on communist advances throughout the French Empire, while encouraging French politicians and officials to grant a progressive settlement.

Vietminh is not seen as a communist movement in this period due to contradictory French claims and absence of evidence. The first factor undermined trust in French reporting and claims, while the second constantly led to requests for more information on 'Tonkinese political parties',[91] 'to learn the extent and degree of any anti-French sentiment'.[92] A May 1946 dispatch from Paris, based on a 'Chinese official source', inconclusively reported that 'it is not entirely certain that Ho Chi Minh has remained "100 percent" Stalinist since he may prove to be more "Nationalist"'.[93] Reporting from Indochina painted a complex picture, with Vietminh formed of three parties: the former CPI, and two nationalist parties. They did not have Catholic support, which had not been 'captured' by any faction, not even France.[94]

Rather, concerns about communism focused on France. To growing American consternation, the Communist Party won 26 per cent of the vote (the largest party) in the October 1945 general election and in June 1946 held on to 25.9 per cent. An April 1946 cable by George Kennan, then Counsellor at the Moscow embassy, focused on the dangerous possibility of the Soviet Union gaining control of France, not even mentioning Vietminh or Indochina.[95] In this period the State Department considered communism in the French colonies in the context of Soviet exploitation of anticolonial grievances.[96] This growing concern is the origin of Secretary Marshall's September 1946 order (analysed in the previous chapter's US section) to investigate communism throughout the French Empire in case of a 'long range colonial strategy' to turn '600 million dependent people' into communists.[97]

Not without sympathy, US diplomacy unambiguously described Vietminh as a nationalist party and its cause logical. A 1946 policy statement explains that France has been 'castigating' the 'Annamite nationalists' as 'rebels', deploring French 'hardening policy reflected in personnel shifts in Indochina', a reference to the removal of the moderate Gaullist Leclerc with the fiercely nationalist Valluy as military commander.[98] Reports do not question Vietminh's representativeness, estimating that 'all Annamese [are] strongly united in opposing French resumption of sovereignty', and noting that Vietminh claimed to have won '8 or 9 million voters' in elections for the DRV 'Provisional Government'.[99] Early intelligence reports on 'the Indo-China Revolutionary Party' describe its leader Nguyen Ai Quoc as 'fully fledged Communist', but points out that his actions since 'being educated in Moscow as a Communist', including revolts in the 1920s, 1930s and during the Second World War, point to nationalist aspirations.[100] Despite French arguments, there is no assumption that Ho Chi Minh was controlled from Moscow.

Hostility to French colonialism was important in informing American representations of Vietminh and its cause. Reports from 1946 explain that 'while the Viet Minh League may be disliked, the French are hated',[101] while French negotiating efforts are described as a series of false commitments designed to facilitate military changes on the ground,[102] since 'old Indo China hands' are 'intolerably opposed giving more than modicum to natives'.[103] Upon the elevation of Cochinchina to a 'Republic within the Indochinese Federation' reports warned that this was extremely unpopular throughout the country and endangered negotiations.[104] Furthermore, reports confirmed that the puppet Cochinchina government had no significant native support.[105] The 6 March agreement caused much interest and optimism among American diplomats, policymakers and analysts, and the subsequent betrayal of the agreement caused great disappointment. Vitally, it scuppered hope of progressive developments, creating a firm scepticism that would last until 1948.[106] On the ground, near-daily reports of retaliations against Vietnamese, including 'wholesale arrests and burning houses',[107] showed a failure 'to take the opportunity to make friends among natives'.[108] Analysis made a strategic case for progressive reform, for 'unless policies ['of democratic self-government'] are followed in southeastern Asia', 'there will be substantial and increasing social and political unrest and possibly armed conflict'.[109] The economic and humanitarian case for reform was, of course, overwhelming. A March 1945 analysis of colonialism in Indochina concluded that 'French Indochina in its political, economic, and social development was the least progressive dependency in Southeast Asia'.[110]

Earlier, in November 1945 OSS officers and diplomats returning from Indochina and China provided the earliest reports about Vietminh. The report of a diplomat (analysed in Part II, Chapter 10, p. XX) who visited Tonkin in October described Vietminh as 'radical Annamese opponents of both France and Japan': an alliance of several political parties united by Vietnamese nationalism.[111] These officers criticized French colonial administration for causing the 1945 famine by withholding rice stores (even the Japanese were less cruel, wrote Major Archimedes Patti), and obstructed OSS during the Second World War, unlike Vietminh who 'feel strongly pro-American'.[112] General Philip Gallagher detailed that Vietminh 'nationalists' were numerous, well-led and enjoyed mass support throughout Vietnam. He specified that Vietminh 'should not be labelled full-fledged doctrinaire communist', and that there were other 'definitely Communist' groups like Cao Dai (Cao Dai was in fact a religious sect).[113] Nor was Vietminh the only group seeking independence: a memorandum from OSS director General William Donovan mentions 'the Annamite Kuomintang', a 'Free Annamite organisation' who do not want the return of French rule and who request assistance or even 'a US protectorate'.[114] Earlier, in response to a State Department request for information prompted by French accusations, the US SEAC military mission in Colombo found 'no reliable evidence' that Vietnamese nationalists are 'under Japanese, Chinese, Communist or any other foreign influence'.[115] Further reports clarified that the rebellion of 'the League' (Vietminh) was the latest in a long history of anti-French uprisings.[116] In balance, American hostility to colonialism in Indochina and total absence of evidence to the contrary came to support the representation of Vietminh as genuine nationalists.

However, sympathy with Vietminh anticolonialism did not translate into support. Reporting on Indochina competed for policymaking attention with European concerns, and the State Department's European Office was adamant that Indochina should impair relations with France. It clashed with the Far East Office and Moffat's Southeast Asia Division in a war over policy memoranda.[117] The Asianists lost, and advice to President Truman made Trusteeship 'voluntary' by drawing an improbable assumption from an unrelated statement made Yalta.[118] This was a fudge. Secretary of State Edward Stettinius told Bidault that 'the record is entirely innocent of any official statement of this government questioning, even by implication, French sovereignty over Indo-China.'[119] This was untrue, but in practice, keeping France friendly had won the day, rather than Indochinese matters having lost.

Internecine conflict at the State Department and the strategic prevalence of Europe were not the only reasons for dropping Trusteeship.[120] Firstly, the volume and relevance of reporting concerning Indochina was far smaller than that concerning Europe and the postwar role of France since the Truman administration prioritized Europe over colonial issues. Secondly, following the progress of this reporting within the State Department shows that Indochina almost never made it to President Truman's desk.[121] If we treat policy urgency as a representation, as a perception so to speak, Indochina was not urgent because it did not resonate with dominant policy concerns of that moment, which prioritized keeping France on the friendliest terms possible. Indochina fell out of the reporting chain on its way up to top policymakers, filtered out as a detail irrelevant to dominant policy concerns. As examined in previous chapters, it only made it there when communism did and, crucially, when French diplomacy had managed to persuade that Vietminh was communist. As we saw with Marshall's request to find communists in the most unlikely places and Bevin's orders that his global assumptions be substantiated, policymakers can influence diplomatic reporting, bending it to fit their priorities but prejudicing how policy discussion is informed.

Filtering and simplifying diplomatic issues was particularly frequent during the transition from Roosevelt to Truman. The archival evidence makes it clear that Roosevelt's concentration of Second World War information flows and decision-making upon himself kept the Vice-President in the dark about vital diplomatic and military issues – including Trusteeship. Truman had to catch up very quickly. A month after his inauguration, we find Truman, Acting Secretary Grew and Assistant Secretary Acheson directing US diplomacy in near-daily meetings. Overlapping aspects of US policy on Southeast Asia required urgent decisions: how to liberate Southeast Asia, whether to pursue Roosevelt's rather vague anticolonial policy, whether to ship French troops to fight the Japanese in Indochina, and how to prevent further breakdown in Franco–American relations. Truman knew alarmingly little about these issues and had to be briefed on the most basic aspects of each, making it ever more necessary for Grew and Acheson to prioritize.[122] The need to quickly inform Truman made filtering information ever more radical and less nuanced, helping the Indochina issue fall out of information processes on the way to his desk. The decision to drop the Trusteeship policy was thus more an accident resulting from the urgency to resolve European and Japanese policy than a decision on Indochina per se.

Despite being wartime allies, Franco–American relations were very poor, and French goodwill for a postwar settlement was not guaranteed. After dropping Trusteeship, France requested assistance to re-establish sovereignty over Indochina, which was turned down by an exasperated State Department.[123] American diplomats were unimpressed by de Gaulle's demands in Europe, which included annexing Aosta, the Saarland, the Rhineland, as well as an occupation zone in Germany.[124] Rejecting most of these demands made relations worse. Mid-1945 saw a low point in Franco–American relations, with French complaints on insufficient arms were being supplied to the French military, lack of supplies for civilians, and even that German prisoners were being treated too well. American diplomats described this 'paranoia' as stemming from postwar weakness, but clearly they were not as able to soothe these tensions as their British counterparts.[125] In March 1945, a ridiculous diplomatic altercation arose when de Gaulle refused an invitation to the United States and communication with Roosevelt following allegations that the latter had privately accused the French President of behaving like 'a prima donna'. Considering de Gaulle's behaviour, it would have been understandable if he had. To soothe relations US diplomats categorically denied the allegations.[126]

American solutions to Indochina were consistently Eurocentric. A September 1945 memorandum for Undersecretary Acheson recommends that the French be encouraged to negotiate with the Vietnamese, if necessary establishing a joint US, French and British commission. It argues that offence caused to France by 'intervention in a problem which they consider strictly French' is 'far less dangerous to the position of France and of all Western powers' than 'a further explosion of Annamese nationalism and French resort to military force'.[127] This option is delayed indefinitely, pending approval of the French.[128] However, the discussion illustrates deep concern at the prospect of an all-out war that would turn Asia against the West – possibly into Soviet hands or Japanese-like radicalism. Despite sympathy with the plight of colonial subjects, the Vietnamese, like almost all non-Western subjects, were considered unready for independence because an independent Vietnam would be too vulnerable to resist foreign influence. This is why their ideal settlement necessarily included protracted self-rule under French – or UN – protection and sovereignty.[129]

Vietminh

The Vietminh rebel alliance was keen to collaborate with the Allies. Since its founding in 1941, it quickly garnered broad Vietnamese support on a radical anti-Japanese and anti-French platform. During the Second World War it worked enthusiastically with the American military in Kunming, passing intelligence to the OSS and carrying out anti-Japanese military activities including sabotage, rescuing US airmen, and larger guerrilla operations. Crucially, amid this collaboration it sought to present its version of events in Indochina, particularly French colonialism. Towards the end of the war, Ho Chi Minh even acted as an OSS agent under the code name Lucius.[130] In OSS reports, diplomatic communication, and articles in the Vietminh newsletter *Độc Lập*, Ho consistently expressed hope that the US might support Vietnamese independence.[131] This hope was justified, he reasoned, because America was itself a revolutionary postcolonial state that had overthrown European rule, a state that prided itself in not being colonialist.[132]

In this period Vietminh communicated with foreign diplomats with surprising ease. On the one hand, until their military return to north Indochina in mid-1946, French authorities had no means of blocking telegraphic and postal communications from Hanoi. On the other, while Vietminh held on to Hanoi until the French siege of December 1946, DRV officials had access to the British, American and Chinese consuls, with whom they socialized with incredible regularity and kept minutely informed. Furthermore, the French government kept Sainteny and other officials in Hanoi to maintain communications. Vietminh was straightforward and consistent in how it represented itself and its cause. The party was a league, an alliance of parties united by the drive to reunite the three colonial Kys and achieve independence – Độc Lập, a term repeated with staggering assiduity. Evidently, they categorically denied being Japanese or Soviet agents. France was represented as an exploitative, cruel and racist colonial overlord, while Vietnamese self-determination was a self-evident right consistent with the new Atlantic and San Francisco Charters.

Following the signature of the 6 March agreement, Vietminh attempted to extend diplomatic relations. One of the first attempts was the telegram to the British prime minster discussed in the British section of this chapter. It is worth citing in full as it is representative of how Vietminh articulated the case for Vietnamese statehood in the context of the emerging postwar multilateral international compact.

> Hochiminh President of Vietnam Democratic Republic of Hanoi to Prime Minister of Great Britain, London.
>
> I beg to inform Your Excellency that on March 6th 1946 a preliminary agreement has been signed between representatives of France and Vietnam. In this agreement France recognises the Democratic Republic of Vietnam as a free state. Friendly and sincere negotiations began immediately after the signature of the agreement. On behalf of the Vietnam people and Government I respectfully request the Government of Great Britain to recognise the Democratic Republic of Vietnam as a free state. We are firmly convinced that acknowledgement by your government of our Republic will be an important step towards the materialisation of Atlantic and San Francisco Charters and will be highly contribute to the maintenance of world security while it will open a new era of co-operation between the British Commonwealth and our nation.[133]

It inserted Vietnamese statehood and recognition of its independence into the framework of the postwar compact. Crucially, Vietminh regularly linked its case to US advocacy of these principles. In a February 1946 interview with a Vietnamese newspaper Ho framed the independence of Vietnam in terms of 'Truman's 12 points' of November 1945. He quoted their precepts of self-determination of dependent peoples and adhered to 'the enlightened policy of the USA towards the Philippines and our country has faith in American generosity'.[134] Vietminh supporters also hoped for US support. In September 1945, a commercial-service telegram arrived at the Department of State from Kunming signed by the 'Annamese in China' supporting the bid 'by their brethern at home and abroad for the independence of Annam' (sic). It celebrates that 'freedom and human felicity shall henceforth be preserved' and asks that the 'Allied Constitution be therefore put into effect' to 'let the oriental nations stand on their own feet and govern themselves' and 'let Annam be emancipated and independent'.[135] It is a testament to Vietminh's capacity to capture Vietnamese sentiment that such messages arrived from the Vietnamese diaspora in Southeast Asia, Paris and China.[136]

Vietminh represented Độc Lập as a goal to be attained peacefully following the Philippine precedent. Furthermore, and this is vital for the 'lost opportunity' school of Vietnam War research, in this period Vietminh repeatedly declared that an independent DRV would follow America's foreign policy lead and seek advice from US policymakers, telling diplomats that '[Ho] would pay great attention to any suggestions made by [State] Dept'.[137] DRV officials at the summer 1946 Fontainebleau talks sent frequent updates to the US Secretary of State, probably hoping that US oversight might keep negotiations on a multilateral basis and thus ensure outcomes.

Just before the outbreak of war in late 1946, Vietminh made strenuous efforts to appear conciliatory to French officials and civilians. It was clear to them, as Ho repeatedly suggested to British and American diplomats, that any provocation might be used by colonial hardliners to scupper a negotiated settlement. In August 1946 he publicly ordered party members and the population to let celebrations for the first anniversary of Vietnamese independence pass 'without any unamicable character in regards to France so that its representatives might participate'.[138] He repeatedly sent spectacularly polite and affable messages to French politicians, including parliamentarians, the president, and prime minister, promising 'to do what I can' to help keep peace and prevent anti-French demonstrations.[139]

Reunification was of even greater immediate importance than independence. Described as a reversal of the 1880s colonial 'mutilation' of the Empire of Vietnam conceived to divide and conquer, it was to be achieved before independence. When reunification of the three "Kys" of Vietnam was discussed at d'Argenlieu's Dalat conference in May 1946, the Vietnamese delegation made the case for 'geographic, racial, historical, linguistic unity', arguing that 'union of three Kys life or death question for Vietnam although only a matter of pride for France'.[140] This, however, remained d'Argenlieu's main points of contention throughout his tenure – and in many ways his longest-lasting legacy besides the war itself, perpetuated into the 1970s by continued Vietnamese desire for reunification and the Franco–American creation of South Vietnam. An extensive Vietminh Memorandum concerning 'Nam Bo' ('Southern Region') advanced evidence of longstanding historical, linguistic, racial, cultural, gastronomic, political and even rice-farming unity. By July 1946, however, DRV officials realized that the strongest argument they could bring to bear on the case was a French one: the Franco–Vietnamese treaties of 1862 and 1874 detailed that Nam Bo, though ceded to French 'protectorate', 'was part of the Vietnamese Empire', showing that 'France itself has undeniably recognised that Nam Bo is an integral part of Vietnamese territory'.[141]

Độc Lập was Vietminh's central goal, though it is clear that it was willing to negotiate its timing. After all, Độc Lập was in the very name of the League. Independence was conceived as a self-evident right, a human right older than the rights enshrined in the postwar Allied Charters. In this context, their priority concerned more making the case for immediate self-governing statehood – even if remaining within the French Union. This is also how Vietminh defended itself from French accusations of Soviet control in this period. For instance, when a visiting British colonel asked Ho about it, 'he denied that he was a Communist, saying that he was only as much a Communist as Sun Yat-sen was when he founded the Chinese Republic.'[142] This is an important reference, Sun Yat-sen's nationalism being key to the emergence of anticolonialism in Asia. Likewise, when State Department SEA Division chief Moffat asked him the same question, Ho replied that 'independence that was enough for his lifetime'.[143] Backtracking to August 1945, Vietminh garnered legitimacy in Indochina and beyond by claiming continuity from the millennial Vietnamese Empire and the emperor acting as a French puppet. In August 1945 Emperor Bao Dai abdicated 'for the good of the Fatherland', recognizing Vietminh's August Revolution as the long-awaited emancipation from France and ceding the emperor's sovereignty to the DRV.[144] This text was widely distributed in Vietnam and forwarded to foreign powers.

Enshrining Vietnam's right to exist in Western terms, Vietminh framed independence as a human right articulated in classical Enlightenment terms, equivalent to those conquered by the French Revolution and the Allied and Free French Second World War effort against the Axis. When French forces reoccupied Saigon amid bloody retaliations against the Vietnamese, Ho wrote to the Secretary of State calling for US and UN 'immediate interference' (this text is analysed in Part II, Chapter 5, p. XX). Recalling that Vietminh fought the Japanese before establishing the DRV, it appeals to the Atlantic Charter's provision for self-determination before arguing that French colonials in Indochina betrayed the Allies, whereas Vietnam seeks peace in the terms of the 'noble principles' of UN declarations.[145] The right to determine their future was a relentlessly reiterated part of Vietminh's representation of its cause. Conversely, the experience of colonial rule was used as historical proof that no such rights were possible under French domination. Sainteny, meeting with Ho in September 1945, describes that though behaving 'very correctly with shade of cordiality', Ho 'embarrassed us with the principles of [17]89 and Free France'.[146] He was not wrong, the contradiction between the democratic republic and its colonial practices was embarrassing.

Simple Enlightenment and democratic ideas were at the heart of Ho's declaration of independence. It began by quoting the preamble of the American Declaration of Independence and the 1892 French Declaration of the Rights of Man, contrasting their provision and protection of inalienable rights with the French denial of these rights to the people of Vietnam:

"All men are created equal. They are endowed by their Creator with certain inalienable rights, among them are Life, Liberty, and the pursuit of Happiness."

This immortal statement was made in the Declaration of Independence of the United States of America in 1776. In a broader sense, this means: All the peoples on the earth are equal from birth, all the peoples have a right to live, to be happy and free.

The Declaration of the French Revolution made in 1791 on the Rights of Man and the Citizen also states: "All men are born free and with equal rights, and must always remain free and have equal rights."

Those are undeniable truths.

Nevertheless, for more than eighty years, the French imperialists, abusing the standard of Liberty, Equality, and Fraternity, have violated our Fatherland and oppressed our fellow-citizens. They have acted contrary to the ideals of humanity and justice.

Vietnam's right to self-determination is self-evident, an argument that Vietminh's diplomatic and public discourse would not reframe again or represent in any other articulation. The end of the declaration of independence, however, exemplified another key pillar of Vietminh's articulation of the right to independence: Second World War service.

Figure 14 Ba Đình Square (then Rond-point Puginier), on 2 September 1945 as Ho Chi Minh declares Vietnamese independence. Archive Sainteny.

A people who have courageously opposed French domination for more than eighty years, a people who have fought side by side with the Allies against the fascists during these last years, such a people must be free and independent!

For these reasons, we, the members of the Provisional Government of the Democratic Republic of Vietnam, solemnly declare to the world that:

Vietnam has the right to be a free and independent country –and in fact it is so already.[147]

This is not a claim to compensation for having fought with the Allies against the Axis. Rather, it linked Vietminh to the principles that animated the Allies, principles enshrined in the Allied Charters and which included the right of self-determination for dependent peoples. Backtracking to the last months of the war, we find the same articulation of Vietnam's right to independence in a July 1945 'Letter to the San Francisco Conference from the Indochinese "Annamese" people'. With passion and lyricism, the Churchillian and Rooseveltian wording of this little booklet makes a liberal appeal to the values of the French Revolution, the US constitution, and the Dumbarton Oakes and San Francisco conferences.[148] Vietnam's 'right to be a free and independent country', as pictured in Fig. 14, is what the crowd was celebrating on 2 September 1945.

Epilogue: onto war made unavoidable

This war began as a dispute about Vietnam's independence, Độc Lập. French refusal to recognize the claim to independence, let alone the declaration of 2 September 1945, inaugurated diplomatic efforts to besmirch Vietnamese nationalism and reinvade the colony. We have now arrived at the end of our history of how the diplomacy of the actors in this conflict produced understanding of the war itself, its participants and their motives. Genealogical analysis has traced the development of the representations that informed policy. Though unconventional, researching this development in reverse chronology has yielded a history of changes in representations, the circumstances in which these shifts occurred and their effects. By pinpointing the instances when specific representations were absorbed by the diplomacy of other actors, we determined when they were believed.

It has been a difficult exercise but determining when persuasion of a version of events occurs is an analytical challenge. I apologize to my readers for the difficulty, complexity and sometimes extreme detail of this exercise. If you have made it here, I have dragged you through over six thousand items of diplomatic reporting, advice, memoranda, analysis as well as the occasional nonsense. An added difficulty for my heroic reader has been the extreme level of textual detail, the sometimes strange textuality of those cables from myriad individuals from so many places, so very many quotes, so many citations of archival sources. Worst of all, writing and reading history in reverse chronological order is very unnatural. Not until I began research of this type did I realize the extent to which language is designed to build narratives that go only from past to present. I apologize for the inevitably clumsy efforts to write history backwards, backtracking, reversing in time and through the documentary evidence, but not for the revelations made by thus dismantling history.

The power and historical constitution of language does not only affect the efforts of historians. Language is implicated in constituting causality, in building time, subjects, space; everything we know about the world. As we have seen with our diplomats posted in Indochina, their colleagues back at the ministries receiving their dispatches and reports, the analysists making sense of this information; they too had to make do with the tools of language to express what they found and what they thought it meant. Language, descriptions and narrative in text had the very real power to constitute who Vietminh and France were, why they fought, why they deserved American assistance. This is why the investigation of this book tracked the power of these efforts through the texts where these crucial acts of informing policy occurred.

This chapter closes off our enterprise. The first section takes a step back from the minute detail in which we have followed the history of the representations of actors and their political contexts and identities. To determine more clearly how they informed and shaped policy, it synthesizes the history of these representations and how they led to gradual American involvement in Vietnam. The second section takes another step back to discuss the significance of these findings for contemporary diplomacy and the policymaking practices that depend upon it.

Learning from the history of representations in Vietnam War diplomacy

We have studied diplomatic reporting, analysis and its input into policymaking in extreme detail. Taking a step back from the textual and documentary detail of the diplomatic papers analysed, it is possible to discuss the dynamics observed in the diplomatic knowledge production practices of the First Vietnam War. I refer to the dynamics governing the practices of reporting, representation of observations and information, analysis, advice and opinion. In other words, the trends that become visible when studying the processes that make, build, pass on, and filter or reject information on its way from the diplomats on the ground to policymakers.

Reporting and analysis from diplomats on the ground was the most consistent. This is particularly true of the American and British consuls in Hanoi, whose terms of reference, descriptions and general representations change little over time. Their reporting was incremental, with cables building on previous reporting while focusing on questions mandated by their superiors. Diplomats on the ground responded particularly well to long-term enquiries, producing frequent and informative updates as we saw with the American consul in Saigon, James O'Sullivan, who developed considerable expertise on Vietnamese politics and produced exceptionally insightful reports. Likewise, the reports of Jean Sainteny, the first Free French intelligence officer and diplomat to reach Hanoi, were consistent over a long period. For instance, his only intimation of Vietminh fascism appears in a recommendation from September 1945 that if it were possible to obtain that the Allies categorized Vietminh as Japanese puppets, SEAC would resolve the problem for France. Because it was incremental and detailed, reporting from diplomats on the ground was extremely context-dependent. This included previous cables and understanding of local history, language and local politics.

A key qualifier of the validity of information was the reliability of sources. Though Consul O'Sullivan tried hard to rate his sources for the benefit of his superiors, they tended to recognize organizations rather than names. By ignoring the detailed context, his superiors often preferred minor officers over the informed sources the consul encountered in a bomb shelter or even an opium den. The difference between reporting from the ground and higher levels of diplomatic knowledge production is especially evident when it is compared against changes in representation mandated from above. A good example is d'Argenlieu's 1946–late 1945 drive to qualify Vietminh as fascists bent on racial domination. Back at the ministry, information from the ground was filtered, prioritized, summarized, and some would eventually contribute to policy briefs. It could not be otherwise – no minister could read that many cables. Furthermore, without expertise, summarizing and analysis, their import is of limited usefulness.

Information filtering processes were vital. The British Foreign Office filtered according to long-term concerns and the resulting briefs benefitted from years of accumulated knowledge and analysis. When policymakers such as Bevin requested information, civil servants drew on extensive reserves of expertise and previous reports. The greatest exception was Bevin's request that diplomats quickly substantiate the 'growing Communist ascendancy in Indochina'. Because there was no proof, diplomats on the ground gathered the little speculative work they had on that 'ascendancy', which in turn was rewritten as certainty.[1] The Quai d'Orsay was, conversely, surprisingly inflexible in its reporting, but far more goal-driven. This meant that sometimes information gathering privileged quantity over quality, as exemplified by the stultifying 400-page draft response to the dossier Vietminh sought to submit to the UN concerning French war crimes (analysed in Part III, Chapter 12). The State Department was far more reactive in its approach to managing reporting and analysis, sometimes lacking long-term reporting strategies but responding quickly and efficiently to information requests.

The rationale governing information management emerges as a vitally influential factor. In the four diplomatic institutions studied, choosing what information was analysed and briefed to leaders and perhaps investigated further was determined by policy priority. For Vietminh, multilateral support for their bid for independence took absolute precedence; for France, the opposite. However, for the US and Britain the Second World War and then communism dominated information management. Dominant policy concerns severely affected diplomatic reporting, analysis and prioritization, refocusing efforts and channelling information flows. This is logical, of course: policymakers need to be given the most relevant briefings. In the diplomacy studied, however, some information was prioritized only thanks to tenuous links of identity. Frequently, the consequences were downright ridiculous. This is how Marshall's order of extensive reporting on communism throughout the French Empire ended up producing speculation on the imagined conspiracies of a poet in Martinique and a gasoline dealer in Nouméa. Short-term fixation with dominant policy concerns can at times mean that policymakers see only what they want to see – and force diplomatic knowledge production to do the same.

This is where identity comes into its greatest power in diplomacy. If a report concerned the identity worried about – fascism, communism – it would be greatly prioritized. This is how American diplomats and spies in China found themselves hunting down eight Soviet advisors who turned out to be seven Russian tramps. While such humorous examples are harmless, they point to a problematic waste of time. Worse, due to these dynamics valuable information never made it to the Secretary of State: the finer detail of Vietminh itself, the French 'trap' to provoke Vietminh into war in 1946, or the colonial grievances that explained Vietminh's militancy. Representations of identity in diplomacy have the power to link and subsume issues and information – sometimes replacing information with temptingly simple strategic assumptions, as was the case with Vietminh's insertion into global communism in 1947–48.

In the First Vietnam War, this book demonstrates, political identity can act as a dangerous shortcut to knowing whom we are talking to, as occurred to Vietminh. Because evidence was entirely lacking, recognizing its political identity came to depend on estimated appraisals that relied on alignment – that is, the appearance of being similar. This was supported by existing assumptions: a Stalinist conspiracy bent on global conquest and strategic thinking that treated every global conflict as a West–Soviet struggle. That made it inconceivable that Vietminh might do and want so much on its own. This was reinforced by racist assumptions that made it impossible to conceive of the Vietnamese as politicized enough to organize a rebellion on such a scale. This is a dark lesson: the hunt for the seven Russian tramps demonstrates the assumption that Vietminh could not have succeeded militarily against France without being in fact tools of Soviet conquest. Tragically, the reporting from the ground was sufficiently detailed and contextualized for this self-misinformation to have been avoided.

There is nothing American policymakers could have done in 1945 to avoid the outbreak of the Franco–Vietnamese war. Imposing UN Trusteeship over Indochina was difficult considering the centrality of the Franco–American alliance. Once Truman had abandoned Trusteeship in June 1945 it would have been impossible to prevent France from launching its invasion of the territory. In France, de Gaulle's political platform had staked too much on the reconstruction of *grandeur* upon the colonies. This self-same political drive to retain the colonies would later drag France into further colonial wars in Madagascar and Algeria.

However, US policy did not need to support the reconquest of Indochina as it did from 1948. The Roosevelt and Truman administrations had refused to support and endorse de Gaulle's demands in Europe – including the annexation of Aosta, Saarland and Rhineland. In hindsight, these demands were scandalous and had they been acceded to, the vicious loop of Franco–German *revanchisme* would have continued ad nauseam. In 1948 American policymakers could have chosen to do nothing and the French military effort would have floundered in the face of Vietminh determination sooner. Like the Algerian War, it would not have become a Cold War conflict, the US would have remained uninvolved and history would have remembered it as the Vietnamese War of Independence.

Besides achieving American involvement in Vietnam, the diplomacy studied in this book left a legacy of ideas, assumptions and representations. Many of the ideas that drove US involvement in Vietnam in 1948 and which propelled continued involvement until 1975 originated 1945–47 with d'Argenlieu and Pignon. The first is Vietminh communism – which became a tragic self-fulfilling prophecy when in 1949 a desperate Vietminh finally sought out Chinese and Soviet assistance. Secondly, the idea that Vietnam did not exist in the unified form that Vietminh claimed. It is no coincidence that from 1954 South Vietnam would occupy the area that d'Argenlieu disputed from DRV and which he fought to retain.[2] Thirdly, the racially framed assumption of Vietminh's lack of agency and its control by an international communist conspiracy was key to US defence of South Vietnam.

Diplomacy emerged as a battlefield where representations were promoted and fought over. By 1947 diplomacy constituted the representation of Vietnam that made it a Cold War conflict rather than a colonial one. It came to deliver a representation of Vietminh constituted around binaries of global politics (communism against the West), political identity (red menaces contra freedom fighters), and subjects (well-advised colonial subjects contra Stalinist stooges). American involvement was unavoidable once this understanding had crossed into US diplomatic knowledge production, for Vietminh had become part of the red enemy. To a very great extent, the US, France and Britain chose to see Vietminh as a global enemy.

We can now reconstruct the final act of the American diplomatic road to Vietnam. Between 1948 and 1947 representation of Vietminh as a communist stooge and France as a progressive ally won the conflict over representations of identity in diplomacy. This is how by mid-1948 US involvement in Vietnam had become inevitable. Analysis of how French, British, US and Vietminh diplomacy represented the conflict, its actors and context in the period between late 1947 and the end of 1948 uncovered two key shifts in the production of understanding of the conflict.

Firstly, the key to Washington's policymaking lay in Whitehall. The State Department's April 1948 request for British assistance meant British representation of the conflict quickly came to frame American reporting on the issue. British representation of the Vietnam War as a Cold War conflict rather than a nationalist struggle was recent and, at the instigation of Foreign Secretary Bevin, went against the analysis offered by UK diplomats in Vietnam and Whitehall. In other words, Secretary Bevin had imposed his understanding of *all* conflicts in Southeast Asia onto the Vietnamese conflict. This was not a policy decision by the British Cabinet on Indochina. Rather, inserting Indochina into the global Communist problem enveloped it into the existing policy of containment. This was informed by developments in Malaya and by the policy to draw on US assistance for British anticommunist efforts. Once Britain came to represent the Vietnam War as a Cold War struggle, comparisons between Vietnam and Malaya by French diplomats were convincing and allowed for a joint Franco–British position in seeking US assistance.

Secondly, acceptance of the Bao Dai solution as progressive was also British-led. Like representation of Vietminh as a Stalinist stooge, British representation of France as colonially progressive only appeared in diplomatic reporting in April 1948. Until then British representation of the conflict was dominated by criticism of French colonial policy and intransigence. Responding to American requests for British opinion on the conflict in 1948, British diplomats described the Bao Dai solution as progress towards self-determination and self-government. British diplomats made this vital condition for US assistance look progressive and in 1949 lobbied US policymakers to recognize and support it. In both moves, persuading secretary Bevin of Vietminh communism led to significant British assistance to France in lobbying American policymakers. British collaboration jump-started the stalled French bid to convince American policymakers that France was reforming and Vietminh should not be negotiated with, crucial conditions for US assistance.

1947 was truly the year in which Vietnam became a Stalinist domino. While some limited US trust in French progressiveness only emerged in 1948, the groundwork for representation of Vietminh as a dangerous communist stooge had been laid the previous year. In 1947 communism became a more pressing global concern. Following Stalin's manoeuvres in Eastern Europe and the civil war in Greece, it was enshrined as a policy priority by the Truman Doctrine and the British policy of containment. As a consequence, diplomacy was tasked with finding and prioritizing everything communist, sometimes with absurd consequences. This was a good time for French diplomats to claim that Vietminh military successes were impossible without Soviet assistance.

Thanks to this ideational situation, events in the second half of 1948 made the communist representation of Vietminh suddenly convincing. This was not because new evidence substantiated of its part in global communism – none did. Diplomats were still struggling to find evidence and were scrambling to interpret scraps of French-provided speculation or locate at least a single Soviet advisor or communication with the CCP and the USSR. British and American understanding of the conflict suddenly, if begrudgingly, believed Vietminh's communism because in the context of Berlin, Malaya, the Philippines and China, it seemed like communism was advancing globally. The insertion of Vietminh into global communism therefore depended entirely on the incorrect assumption that communism was a single global monolith.

US policymakers quickly dropped the need to talk to Vietminh, allowing the preferred French solution, a puppet, to become the only solution. At this point in 1948, Pignon's reinvention of the Bao Dai solution was immensely successful. It was written in the exact language of American policy on postwar colonialism and appeared to implement the suggestions of American and British colleagues. Pignon's resuscitated Bao Dai solution, propelled by the need to have a plausible non-communist solution in Indochina, placated the discursive and analytical currents in British and American diplomacy critical of French colonial intransigence. Pignon managed to rewrite a ninety-year-old puppet-government arrangement so successfully because of his in-depth understanding and analytical experience of the 1945–46 US solution in the Philippines. Pignon has been credited as the author of the 'reinvention' of the Bao Dai solution in Indochina.[3] The diplomatic communication studied in this book substantiates that he drew on the language and structure of the US policy that in 1946 he had hoped France would never have had to follow.

The role of Britain was greater than hitherto estimated. British scepticism of French intelligence, particularly that originating in the Sûreté 2nd Bureau, which never came supplied with hard evidence, was suddenly swept away in April 1948. French intelligence that until then was qualified by serious caveats was suddenly copied directly into British reporting, particularly the assertions that promoted Tang Bo Viet Minh (Vietminh's Central Committee) to shadow communist takeover of the Vietminh party. With their influence on American diplomacy, analysis and policymakers who consulted the Foreign Office on this question, this shift in British representation of the conflict, its actors and its broader political circumstances enabled the French representation of Vietminh to finally flourish in American analysis and policymaking.[4]

India was vital to shaping the British position on Indochina. In the first instance, it informed and framed British reticence to supporting French efforts to re-establish colonialism in Vietnam by force. Moreover, in 1947, Nehru refused to allow for British Indian arms to be sold to the French for operations in Indochina, while in an act of anticolonial solidarity dockworkers in Indian ports refused to service or load French ships. Until Vietminh's communism was believed in 1948, India prevented the UK from showing more than a modicum of colonial solidarity. Secondly, India's peacefully negotiated independence sparked hope throughout Southeast Asia.[5] The Indian precedent furthermore provided a comparison for different responses that paled against its legitimacy and, in turn, legitimized the aspirations of nationalists in Asia.

This book has substantiated how racism affected policymaking. Racism enabled key parts of the understanding of the conflict, its actors and motives that dragged the US into Vietnam. Assumptions of colonial unpreparedness made Vietminh's claim to independence undesirable for American policymakers who felt the Vietnamese could not run and defend a state. Assumptions of oriental political 'indolence' raised doubts about Vietnamese political agency, meaning that Vietminh's militant drive to independence and its military success in late 1947 were attributed to a non-oriental power: the USSR. This was also true of how Mao's communist party was represented in Western diplomacy, a notion that would only be truly disabused in the late 1970s with US–PRC rapprochement and ultimately with the Sino–Vietnamese war of 1979 which proved that communism was very far from monolithic. Racism permeated what was known about the conflict and its actors, feeding the assumption that political agency was the exclusive attribute of developed nations.

This book has one final tragic lesson to bring to the study of the Vietnam Wars. The study of how information was produced, from the envoys abroad to policymakers, shows that reporting from diplomats on the ground, though raw and difficult to use, was frequently accurate and deeply contextual. British and American diplomats in Hanoi and Saigon, as well as those that explored in person like the State Department's SEA chief, did "go native" and lose perspective in unjustifiable bouts of sympathy for those they were reporting on in Hanoi. They were immensely critical of Vietminh, particularly their haste to achieve independence, organizational limitations, and cavalier approach to elections. However, they also made it clear that communism played a very limited role in a rebel alliance that was not only named after independence, Độc Lập, but was truly dedicated to overthrowing an atrocious colonial regime. They also made it clear that the US and UK could influence and guide the nascent Vietnamese state, which desperately sought such relations. If the analysis and advice of James O'Sullivan in Hanoi and Reid in Saigon had been heeded more closely, no American would have had to observe that '[i]n Indochina we have allied ourselves to the desperate efforts of the French regime to hang on to the remnants of an empire'.[6]

On the power of diplomacy and identity

This was the consequence of the power of diplomacy in the First Vietnam War. The soldier in the photograph below (Fig. 15) is a Foreign Légionnaire, most probably a German "volunteer". He is armed with an M1-Garand Rifle and is followed by an M24-Chaffee tank, both the fruits of American assistance. What this book has considered is not a finer detail of diplomatic practice, some obscure theory or an ivory-tower "academic" question. In that photo alone, several tons of steel stand as hard proof of the power of diplomacy.

It turns out that in diplomacy too, the devil is in the detail. The key to understanding the slow path to US involvement in Vietnam 1944–48 lies in how the conflict and its political actors were represented – a question of language, articulation, simplification, aesthetics and fear.

The diplomatic road to the Vietnam War bears lessons for contemporary diplomacy and policymaking. The manner in which policymakers address policy concerns and set their diplomats to work on policy issues is key. A short-term or

Figure 15 Foreign Légionnaire in Vietnam, 1954. Wikimedia Commons.

rushed responsive approach to diplomatic information gathering can result in details falling out, with potentially disastrous consequences. Prioritization is vital to diplomacy's role in helping achieve policy goals in foreign affairs, of course. However, it can also destroy the very diplomatic usefulness they set out to achieve. Simplified, overzealous or dogmatic prioritization of some concerns, as was the case with communism in the late 1940s, opens the door for other international actors to abuse the policy. France abused US concerns with communism to drag the US into paying for the reconquest of the colony. My research on diplomacy in North Africa during the War on Terror showed that in the 2000s Morocco and Mali were extremely successful in abusing US

Counterterrorism policy to fight and repress their own enemies – who were not terrorists. There too, the nuanced and detailed work of diplomats on the ground was ignored because it did not report what policymakers wanted to see.

Narrow policy priorities can have another perverse effect. They shape reporting, sometimes in a self-confirmation bias loop. Some outcomes are unproblematic and amusing, like the reports from the US consul in French New Caledonia speculating on the socialist leanings of a local gasoline dealer. Others, however, were highly problematic, like Foreign Secretary Bevin's orders to find communists, which had them found where he wanted to see them. We have seen this in Iraq, where the same dogmatic drive to find evidence of Saddam Hussain's weapons of mass destruction led to catastrophic misuse of intelligence. At the time of writing, the UK is witnessing the ungainly spectacle of the very public humiliation and harassment of diplomats considered not to be sufficiently 'optimistic' about a post-Brexit free-trade agreement with the European Union.[7] There is little use in shooting the diplomatic messenger or compelling them to report what is not there.

This book should also provide a warning on the facile application of military strategic thinking to diplomacy. The diplomatic work studied in this volume shows the deep effects of that strategic thinking of the kind that the Cold War inherited directly from the Second World War. Politicians, rather than diplomats, were keen on global-scale strategic drives such as the Domino Theory or Secretary Marshall's concern about a Soviet 'long-range plan' to create 600 million communists. These spoke more of the Second World War imaginary and Red Scare paranoia than events on the ground. As we have seen, the geopolitical assumptions of such thinking are sometimes wildly divorced from political events and do injustice to the political agency of many international actors. Like excessively simple or narrow focus on dominant policy concerns, this can result in serious mistakes in identifying whom we are talking to.

This research should act as an encouragement to make better use of diplomatic reporting from missions abroad. While many diplomats work hard to report and investigate, their reports are very often not heeded when they do not match or appear to match dominant policy concerns. In the case of the First Vietnam War, the understanding of the situation emerging from the diplomats on the ground would have saved Britain and particularly America from the catastrophic decision to support French colonialism.

Finally, and perhaps most evidently, I would like this book to remind my reader that knowing whom we are talking to is not always obvious. International actors, groups and individuals can rarely be understood in terms of simple global categories. Sometimes it is dangerously misleading to do so. Whom an international actor is should be problematized and investigated, rather than allow policymaking to be informed by simple global assumptions and political identities. In Vietnam, fitting all actors into the neat and Eurocentric camps of Freedom versus communism made policymakers behave as ignorantly and idiotically, if well-meaning, as Graham Greene's quiet American. This volume demonstrates the contribution that approaches studying identity by means of genealogical methods can make to diplomatic history. I would like it to also demonstrate the need for critical and studious policymaking that can avoid mistakes like those that paved the diplomatic road to Vietnam.

Identity matters in diplomacy. In the Syrian Civil War of the 2010s, much of the policymaking debate in the UK and US focused on identifying "moderate" from extremist rebel groups. As in the run-up to the intervention in Libya in 2012, serious mistakes and problematic assumptions about whom was who might have led to catastrophic policymaking mistakes. This corroborates the huge role played by identity, and the capacity of diplomatic knowledge production to inform policy about it. The approach and methods used by this book are not just interesting to substantiate the finer detail of historical diplomacy, but also of ongoing conflicts. Ultimately, it is the very issue of identity, how we come to know it, that emerges as a vastly powerful policymaking and analytical challenge.

History is written in the very words of the identities that frame conflicts. In this case, the language of diplomacy framed the war as a Cold War conflict, that is why we still find it hard to think of this conflict as the Vietnamese War of Independence. However, one last time before I leave my reader, I would like to point to the words used in the very last day of the First Vietnam War.

By late November 1954, despite vast American assistance, the forces of the French Empire were struggling to defeat the Vietminh rebel alliance. Strategists decided that the establishment of a major fortress in the northwest of Vietnam at Điện Biên Phủ would cripple the rebels. It would destabilize and render the struggling state less strategically viable by establishing a base of operations for elite mobile troops in the heart of the north. This would eventually force the rebels into a pitched battle that the Vietnamese could not possibly win. In one last hurrah for the French colonial elite, the commander of the fortress, aristocratic equestrian sportsman Christian de la Croix des Castries, set up fortified positions around an airstrip, allegedly named after his eight lovers. Des Castries and his superior, General Navarre, were sure that the Vietnamese could never manage to place heavy artillery on the surrounding hills, it was a logistical feat too far for these *indigènes* against *les dieux blancs*. The garrison included elite French paratroopers, Foreign Légionnaires as well as Algerian, Moroccan and other Imperial conscripts.

The Vietnamese were led by the experienced Vo Nguyen Giap. He had accompanied Ho Chi Minh into the mountains to found the Vietminh rebel alliance in 1941 and was the commander that had received the ultimatums by General Valluy that began the war in November 1946. Considered an extremist by the French, like many prominent Vietminh leaders he had lost his family to slow torture and execution at the hands of the Sûreté early in the Vietnamese Revolution. This time it was his turn to trap the French.[8] The Vietnamese forces, by now highly organized, trained, disciplined and very motivated, carried out harrying attacks that had the effect to concentrate French forces at the fortress, while leaving the surrounding mountains and valleys free. Against the expectations of the French commanders, Giap's soldiers lifted large numbers of heavy artillery pieces to the steep mountainsides and cliffs surrounding Điện Biên Phủ. They dug battery emplacements high in the cliff sides and on 13 March 1954 began bombarding the fortress.

Commander of French artillery Colonel Charles Piroth, aghast at his inability to fire back at these Vietnamese positions, committed suicide. On 14 March Vietminh bombardment destroyed the airstrip, isolating the fortress which was now entirely dependent on supplies and reinforcements dropped by parachute. France requested US air strikes, but the Americans hesitated and refused. The French refused to surrender and many of the Algerian and colonial troops deserted, as thousands of their comrades had done months before. Many of these would later resurface in the horrific colonial war for Algeria, for the French Empire, it was now proven, could be defeated.

Desperate for assistance and facing France and America alone, Vietnam had turned to communist China for assistance in 1949, launching a process of veritable communistification that remains to this day. Despite this, for the Vietminh rebels the war had not simply turned into a Cold War conflict. After weeks of battle, on 7 May the end approached. Negotiations over the future of Vietnam would begin in Geneva the next day. As thousands of Vietnamese soldiers stormed the last bastion of the French fortress, they were shouting Độc Lập! Independence! Độc Lập! The hill where the French Empire made its last stand is still named Độc Lập Hill. Độc Lập; that is why this war was fought. But diplomacy had by then already made it into a global conflict, international communism fighting freedom, 'a red menace' against 'a soldier of democracy'.[9]

Notes

Notes to the Prelude

1 Graham Greene, *The Quiet American* (London: Heineman, 1955). I remain grateful to this novel for first bringing this question to my attention. As my friend and colleague Filippo Costa-Buranelli once joked, in some ways this book has been co-authored with Graham Greene.

2 Because of the importance this book attaches to how language contributes to constituting the representation of international actors, the analytical choice is made to refer to Vietminh rather than 'the Vietminh'. This is due to the traditional role of articles in English in qualifying the proper names of states as opposed to movements. For instance, 'the Britain', which suggests the name of a movement, as opposed to 'Britain' and in French 'les Vietminh' against 'le Vietnam'. In this linguistic context, to write Vietminh is a compromise: it is important to retain the name Vietminh to stand for the quasi-state or fully fledged Vietnamese state as well as the nationalist movement since no Western diplomats referred to the Democratic Republic of Vietnam (DRV) and the latter choice would feel more alien than an article-less Vietminh. For the purpose of harmonizing the text of this book with the primary documentary material, the most common spelling or arrangement of names is chosen, for instance Vietminh, Vietnam, Southeast Asia.

3 Other publications utilizing this method include Pablo de Orellana, "Struggles over Identity in Diplomacy: 'Commie Terrorists' Contra 'Imperialists' in Western Sahara," *International Relations* 29, no. 4 (1 December 2015): 477–99; "When Diplomacy Identifies Terrorists: Subjects, Identity and Agency in the War On Terror in Mali", in Scott Romaniuk, Francis Grice, and Stewart Webb, eds., *The Palgrave Handbook of Global Counterterrorism Policy* (London: Palgrave Macmillan, 2016).

4 See note 3 above.

Notes to PART I

1. The Road to Vietnam: historical debates, and the question of representation

1 Gravel, ed., *The Pentagon Papers: The Defense Department History of United States Decisionmaking on Vietnam. Vol. 1.* (Boston: Beacon Press, 1971), 72.

2   2.III.A "'Domino Principle' Before Korea", in Gravel, *The Pentagon Papers.*

3   The most detailed and thoroughly documented account of the complex confluence of events that permitted Vietminh's emergence is David G. Marr, *Vietnam 1945: The Quest for Power* (Berkeley: University of California Press, 1995).

4   "Vietnamese Declaration of Independence Speech", in Ho Chi Minh, *The Selected Works of Ho Chi Minh* (New York: Prism Key, 2011).

5   I do not use these words lightly. All actors in the Indochinese conflict sought to bring American postwar economic, diplomatic and material (though not military) might to further their goals and candidly used such words in their diplomatic communication as examined in Part III, Chapters 4 and 6.

6   see 1.V "Ho Chi Minh: Asian Tito", in Gravel, *The Pentagon Papers.*

7   Moffat to State, in Robert M. Blum and United States Congress Senate Committee on Foreign Relations, *The United States and Vietnam, 1944–1947: A Staff Study Based on the Pentagon Papers Prepared for the Use of the United States Senate Committee on Foreign Relations* (U.S. Government Printing Office, 1972), 41.

8   S. Tønnesson, *Vietnam 1946: How the War Began* (Berkeley: University of California Press, 2010), 146.

9   'Policy Statement: Indochina', 711.51G/9-2748, State Department Record Group 59, NARA.

10 In his novel, Graham Greene emphasized the pathetic belief that Pyle, his fictional CIA agent, placed on the "Third Force", one neither colonial nor communist, that the US supported to save Vietnam. In memoriam, I often refer to the "Bao Dai Solution" as the Third Force.

11 Marilyn B. Young and Robert Buzzanco, *A Companion to the Vietnam War* (Hoboken, NJ: John Wiley & Sons, 2008), 132.

12 John J. Sbrega, "'First Catch Your Hare': Anglo-American Perspectives on Indochina during the Second World War," *Journal of Southeast Asian Studies* 14, no. 01 (1983): 63–78; Russell H. Fifield, "The Thirty Years War in Indochina: A Conceptual Framework," *Asian Survey*, 1977, 857–79; Bernard Fall, *Street Without Joy: The French Debacle in Indochina* (Barnsley, UK: Pen and Sword, 2005); *The Two Viet-Nams: A Political and Military Analysis* (New York: Frederick A. Praeger, 1967); Chinh and Fall, *Primer for Revolt: The Communist Takeover in Viet-Nam*, 133 (Cambridge: Cambridge University Press, 1963).

13 Gary R. Hess, "Franklin Roosevelt and Indochina," *The Journal of American History* 59, no. 2 (September 1972): 353–68; "The First American Commitment in Indochina: The Acceptance of the 'Bao Dai Solution', 1950," *Diplomatic History* 2, no. 4 (1978): 331–50; Joseph M. Siracusa, "The United States, Viet-Nam, and the Cold War: A Reappraisal," *Journal of Southeast Asian Studies* 5, no. 1 (1974): 82–101; "Lessons of Viet-Nam and the Future of American Foreign Policy," *Australian Journal of International Affairs* 30, no. 2 (1976): 227–37.

14 A very early but lone warning that this might have been a problem was Harrison E. Salisbury, "Image and Reality in Indochina," *Foreign Aff.* 49 (1970): 381.

15 See for instance Hess, "The First American Commitment in Indochina"; for an early challenge to this approach see W. Macy Marvel, "Drift and Intrigue: United States Relations with the Viet-Minh, 1945," *Millennium: Journal of International Studies*, 1975, 10–27.

16 Walter LaFeber, "Roosevelt, Churchill, and Indochina: 1942–45," *The American Historical Review* 80, no. 5 (1975): 1277–95; George C. Herring, "The Truman Administration and the Restoration of French Sovereignty in Indochina," *Diplomatic History* 1, no. 2 (1977): 97–117; *America's Longest War : The United States and Vietnam, 1950-1975*, Fourth edition (Boston: McGraw-Hill, 2001); for the consequences of the end of Trusteeship on OSS operations on the ground and their feedback see R. Spector, "Allied Intelligence and Indochina, 1943–1945," *The Pacific Historical Review* 51, no. 1 (1982): 23–50.

17 Herring, "The Truman Administration and the Restoration of French Sovereignty in Indochina"; *America's Longest War*, 18.

18 Thierry d'Argenlieu, *Chronique d'Indochine: 1945–1947* (Paris: A. Michel, 1985).

19 A good example is Philippe Franchini, *Les Guerres d'Indochine: De La Bataille de Dien Bien Phu à La Chute de Saigon*, vol. 2 (Pygmalion/G. Watelet, 1988); *Saigon: 1925–1945 : de la Belle Colonie à léclosion révolutionnaire, ou, la fin des dieux blancs* (Paris: Autrement, 1992); *Les Mensonges de La Guerre d'Indochine* (Éd. France loisirs, 2003).

20 I would also add to the best French studies of the war the sociological and ethnographic work pioneered by Mus. See Paul Mus, "The Role of the Village in Vietnamese Politics," *Pacific Affairs* 22, no. 3 (1949): 265–72; Paul Mus, *Viet-Nam: Sociologie d'une Guerre* (Paris: Seuil, 1952); as well as his critique of French colonialism and the counterproductiveness of colonial assummptions in Paul Mus, *Le Destin de l'Union Française de l'Indochine a l'Afrique* (Paris: Éditions du Seuil, 1954).

21 Philippe Devillers, *Histoire Du Viêt-Nam de 1940 à 1952* (Paris: Editions du Seuil, 1952); Philippe Devillers, *End of a War: Indo-China, 1954* (New York: Praeger, 1969); Philippe Devillers, ed., *Paris-Saigon-Hanoi: les archives de la guerre, 1944–1947* (Paris: Gallimard, 1988).

22 Marr, *Vietnam 1945*; David Marr, *Vietnam: State, War, and Revolution* (Berkeley: University of California Press, 2013).

23 Stein Tønnesson, *The Vietnamese Revolution of 1945: Roosevelt, Ho Chi Minh and de Gaulle in World at War* (London: PRIO Sage, 1991), 269.

24 Tønnesson, *Vietnam 1946*.

25 Tønnesson, 165; Marr, *Vietnam*, 183.

26 Tønnesson, *Vietnam 1946*, 224.

27 Chinh and Fall, *Primer for Revolt*; Chinh, *The August Revolution* (Foreign Languages Publishing House, 1958); Tran Van Giau, "The Vietnamese Working Class," 1957.

28 Hot on the heels of new Vietnamese scholarship and newly opened archival sources, see Marr, *Vietnam*.

29 Tuong Vu, "'It's Time for the Indochinese Revolution to Show Its True Colours': The Radical Turn of Vietnamese Politics in 1948," *Journal of Southeast Asian Studies* 40, no. 03 (2009): 519–42; "Triumphs or Tragedies: A New Perspective on the Vietnamese Revolution," *Journal of Southeast Asian Studies* 45, no. 02 (2014): 255.

30 Marr, *Vietnam*.

31 Tuong Vu, *Vietnam's Communist Revolution: The Power and Limits of Ideology* (New York, NY: Cambridge University Press, 2016).

32 see particularly Gravel, *The Pentagon Papers*, pp. 42–52.

33 Mark Philip Bradley, *Imagining Vietnam and America: The Making of Postcolonial Vietnam, 1919–1950* (Chapel Hill: University of North Carolina Press, 2000), 40.

34 Bradley, 19.

35 Bradley, 70.

36 Bradley, 107.

37 This is reflected in the most appalling American history of Vietnam I have ever encountered, which stretches the orientalist comparison to China's "stuck in time" discourse to the title. Joseph Buttinger, *The Smaller Dragon* (New York: Praeger, 1958).

38 Bradley, *Imagining Vietnam and America*, 168.

39 Bradley, 71, 94.

40 Bradley, 171.

41 Mark Atwood Lawrence, *Assuming the Burden: Europe and the American Commitment to War in Vietnam* (Berkeley: University of California Press, 2005), 182; see also Mark Atwood Lawrence, "Transnational Coalition-Building and the Making of the Cold War in Indochina, 1947–1949," *Diplomatic History* 26, no. 3 (2002): 453–80.

42 This early British role in Vietnam was familiar to historians, see for instance Tønnesson, *The Vietnamese Revolution of 1945*.

43 Lawrence, *Assuming the Burden*, 101–14.

44 Lawrence, 218.

45 Lawrence, 10.

46 Peter Busch, "Constructing Vietnam. . .," *Diplomatic History* 31, no. 1 (2007): 155–58.

47 As well as the lack of diplomatic evidence of such links and the archival documentary evidence in this book that French, British and American diplomacy and Intelligence had no such proof either, I would also point to Vu's convincing research that communistification of Vietminh began in late 1948 – not by coincidence when there was no further hope of Western assistance or mediation and the US had begun to openly support France. Vu, "'It's Time for the Indochinese Revolution to Show Its True Colours.'"

2. Reading diplomatic knowledge: analytics and sources

1 Friedrich Wilhelm Nietzsche, *Human, All Too Human: A Book for Free Spirits; Part I*, trans. Alexander Harvey, 2011, 11, http://www.gutenberg.org/ebooks/38145

2 I am, of course, summarizing three decades of philosophical development led by Michel Foucault and Jacques Derrida. See especially Michel Foucault, *The Archaeology of Knowledge* (London: Tavistock Publications, 1972); "The Order of Discourse," in *Language and Politics*, ed. Michael Shapiro (Oxford: Blackwell, 1984); *Discipline and Punish - The Birth of The Prison*, 2nd Vintage Books edn (New York: Random House USA Inc, 1995); *The History of Sexuality Vol.1: The Will to Knowledge*, trans. Robert Hurley, New edition (London: Penguin, 1998); *The Order of Things: An Archaeology of the Human Sciences* (London: Routledge, 2002); *Society Must be Defended* (London: Penguin, 2003); J. Derrida, *Writing and Difference* (London: Routledge, 2001); *La Verite En Peinture* (Paris: Editions Flammarion, 2010); *The Post Card: From Socrates to Freud and Beyond* (Chicago: University of Chicago Press, 1987).

3 Homi K. Bhabha, *The Location of Culture* (New York: Psychology Press, 1994).

4 Michael Shapiro, *Language and Politics* (New York, NY: New York University Press, 1984); *Reading the Postmodern Polity: Political Theory as Textual Practice* (Minneapolis: University of Minnesota Press, 1992); *The Politics of Representation: Writing Practices in Biography, Photography, and Policy Analysis* (Madison, WI: University of Wisconsin Press, 1988); W. E. Connolly, *The Terms of Political Discourse* (Oxford: Blackwell, 1993); "Identity and Difference in Global Politics," in *International/Intertextual Relations* (Lexington, MA: Lexington Books, 1989).

5 Michael J. Shapiro, "Strategic Discourse/Discursive Strategy: The Representation of 'Security Policy' in the Video Age," *International Studies Quarterly*, 1990, 327–40; *The Politics of Representation*.

6 See discussion on identity as key to discourses enabling violence in Vivienne Jabri, *Discourses on Violence: Conflict Analysis Reconsidered* (Manchester: Manchester University Press, 1996).

7 See the groundbreaking collection Shapiro, *Language and Politics*.

8 Shapiro is the pioneer of reference. See Shapiro, "Literary Production as a Politicizing Practice," *Political Theory*, 1984, 387–422; *Reading the Postmodern Polity*.

9 J. Der Derian, *On Diplomacy: A Genealogy of Western Estrangement* (Oxford: Oxford University Press, 1987).

10 See especially chapter 1 in J. Der Derian, *Antidiplomacy: Spies, Terror, Speed, and War* (Cambridge, MA: Blackwell, 1992).

11 Iver B. Neumann, *At Home with the Diplomats: Inside a European Foreign Ministry* (Ithaca, NY: Cornell University Press, 2012), 67.

12 Der Derian's 'Antidiplomacy' became all the means through which international actors constitute threats, forsaking diplomacy as a practice. *Antidiplomacy*.

13 See especially chapters 4 and 5 in C. M. Constantinou, *On the Way to Diplomacy* (Minneapolis: University of Minnesota Press, 1996).

14 4/11/1945, dossier 1, 2, SA.

15 This is the entrance of Constantinou's instance of diplomatic practice into Neumann's 'bureaucratic mode of knowledge production'. See I. B. Neumann, "Returning Practice to the Linguistic Turn: The Case of Diplomacy," *Millennium: Journal of International Studies* 31, no. 3 (2002): 627; Iver B. Neumann, "'A Speech That the Entire Ministry May Stand for,' or: Why Diplomats Never Produce Anything New," *International Political Sociology* 1, no. 2 (1 June 2007): 183–200; Neumann, *At Home with the Diplomats*; Ole Jacob Sending, Vincent Pouliot, and Iver B. Neumann, "Future of Diplomacy, The," *International Journal* 66 (2011 2010): 527; C. M. Constantinou, O. P. Richmond, and A. Watson, *Cultures and Politics of Global Communication: Volume 34, Review of International Studies* (Cambridge: Cambridge University Press, 2008).

16 See Chapter 3 in Pablo de Orellana, "Hand of the Prince: How Diplomacy Writes Subjects, Territory, Time and Conflict" (King's College London, 2015), KCL Library.

17 See Rebecca Adler-Nissen and Vincent Pouliot, "Power in Practice: Negotiating the International Intervention in Libya," *European Journal of International Relations* 20, no. 4 (1 December 2014): 889–911.

18 See Shapiro, *Reading the Postmodern Polity*.

19 One of my favourite examples because of the subtlety of the retrieval of politicization is the essay on "Heart of Darkness" in Edward Said, *Reflections on Exile: And Other Literary and Cultural Essays* (London: Granta Books, 2012).

20 See his spectacular deconstruction and demonstration in R. Barthes, "S/Z," New York: Hill and Wang, 1974.

21 Marcus Tullius Cicero, *De Inventione; De Optimo Genere Oratorum* (Cambridge, MA: Loeb, 1989); Cicero uses them both to quickly raise a normative position or recognize its presence. See Ernst Robert Curtius, *European Literature and the Latin Middle Ages* (Princeton: Princeton University Press, 1953); they are also suggested for CDA in Ruth Wodak and Michael Meyer, eds, *Methods for Critical Discourse Analysis*, Second edition (London: SAGE Publications Ltd, 2009) though the use of it I make is very different, not considering them as "incomplete" or "partial" arguments, but rather as signals referencing (but not themselves constituting) older and larger normative discourses.

22 These dimensions are the result of twenty years of Poststructuralist advances in the analysis of identity-formation. See for instance Vivienne Jabri, *The Postcolonial Subject: Claiming Politics/Governing Others in Late Modernity* (Abingdon: Routledge, 2012); "Michel Foucault's Analytics of War: The Social, the International, and the Racial," *International Political Sociology* 1, no. 1 (2007): 67–81; Edward W. Said,

"Representing the Colonized: Anthropology's Interlocutors," *Critical Inquiry* 15, no. 2 (1 January 1989): 205–25; "Arabesque," *New Statesman and Society* 7 (1990); *Orientalism* (London: Penguin, 2003); *Culture and Imperialism* (New York: Vintage, 1993); Homi Bhabha, "Of Mimicry and Man: The Ambivalence of Colonial Discourse," *October* 28 (1 April 1984): 125–33, https://doi.org/10.2307/778467; *The Location of Culture*; Shapiro, "Literary Production as a Politicizing Practice"; Shapiro and H. R. Alker, *Challenging Boundaries: Global Flows, Territorial Identities* (Minneapolis: University of Minnesota Press, 1996); Connolly, *Identity/Difference: Democratic Negotiations of Political Paradox*

23 Greene, *The Quiet American*, 5.

24 Michel Foucault, "Nietzsche, Genealogy, History," in *The Foucault Reader*, ed. Paul Rabinow (New York: Random House, 1984); Friedrich Wilhelm Nietzsche, "Genealogy of Morals," in *Basic Writings of Nietzsche* (New York: Modern Library, 2000).

25 "Two Lectures," in Michel Foucault, *Power/Knowledge: Selected Interviews and Other Writings, 1972–1977* (New York: Random House USA Inc, 1988), 97.

26 See the revolutionary literary theory developments of Julia Kristeva, *Desire in Language: A Semiotic Approach to Literature and Art*, ed. Leon S. Roudiez and Alice Jardine, trans. Thomas Gora (New York: Columbia University Press, 1980); J. Kristeva, *Black Sun: Depression and Melancholia*, Reprint edition (New York, NY: Columbia University Press, 1992).

27 J. Der Derian, ed., *International/Intertextual Relations: Postmodern Readings of World Politics* (Lexington, MA: Lexington Books, 1989); Michael J. Shapiro, "Representing World Politics: The Sport/War Intertext," in *International/Intertextual Relations*, ed. James Der Derian and Michael J. Shapiro (Lexington, MA: Lexington Books, 1989).

28 Richard K. Ashley, "Living on Border Lines: Man, Poststructuralism, and War," in *International/Intertextual Relations: Postmodern Readings of World Politics*, ed. James Der Derian and Michael J. Shapiro (Lexington, MA: Lexington Books, 1989), 259–321.

29 In a diplomatic demonstration of intertextuality, until the 1960s the British Foreign office reprinted and distributed important cables, reports and analyses in little booklets called Confidential Print.

30 Nietzsche, "Genealogy of Morals."

31 It is extraordinary to note that many of these files were classified as late as 2009.

3. Diplomatic pathways

1 Michel Foucault, "Nietzsche, Genealogy, History," in *Nietzsche*, ed. John Richardson and Brian Leiter (Oxford: Oxford University Press, 2001), 76.

2 'Mission à bord du Fegaf', within Report File 24/9/1945, dossier 2, 1, SA.

3 4/11/1945, dossier 1, 2, SA.

4 Hanoi to Saigon, 27/12/1946, FO959/12, NA.

5 September 1945, dossier 1, 1, SA.

6 In dossier 1, 2, SA.

7 Enclosure to Kunming to State, 24/10/1945, 851G.00, RG59, NARA.

8 See files GF1 and GF2, INDO, ANOM.

9 It is called the Fond "Gouvernement de Fait" (de Facto Government) at the MAE Archive.

10 see Jean-Pierre Gratien, *Marius Moutet: Un socialiste à l'Outre-mer* (Editions L'Harmattan, 2006).

11 Hanoi to Kunming, 27 August 1945, 2, SA.

12 'Instructions du général de Gaulle', cable Paris to Hanoi via Calcutta, 25 August 1945, 2, SA.

13 Cable Kunming to Hanoi, 1 September 1945, 1, SA.

14 Creation of Haut Commissariat in 'Confidentiel: Indochine', London (DIPLOFRANCE headquarters until the liberation of Paris) to Algiers, 13 July 1944, 174Q0.3, Fond EA, MAE. Such powers are unheard of for this post since the nineteenth century.

15 see HAUSSAIRE to PM and COMINDO, 8/11/46 AP 127, 457, AN.

16 Minister of Overseas France to Mr. Tran Ngoc Danh, 26/11/46, AP 127, 457, AN.

17 See chapter 5 in Tønnesson, *Vietnam 1946*, 146.

18 See 'activités "diplomatiques" extérieures du Viet-Minh', 23 July 1947, which reports with a view to prevent Vietminh foreign communications by any means. 174Q0.96, Fond EA, MAE. Fond EA file 96 is entirely dedicated to French surveillance and countering of Vietminh diplomatic efforts, including attempts to arrest, kill and scupper visa applications, particularly for a Vietminh delegation to the UN.

19 See Tilman Remme, "Britain and Regional Cooperation in South-East Asia, 1945–1949." (PhD, London School of Economics and Political Science (United Kingdom), 1990), http://etheses.lse.ac.uk/1138/; Shigeru Akita, Gerold Krozewski, and Shoichi Watanabe, *The Transformation of the International Order of Asia: Decolonization, the Cold War, and the Colombo Plan* (Abingdon: Routledge, 2014); J. Tomaru, *The Postwar Rapprochement of Malaya and Japan 1945–61: The Roles of Britain and Japan in South-East Asia* (New York: Springer, 2000).

20 Bradley argues that Ambassador Caffery's own Francophilic racism was key to this diplomacy though I would argue this is overstated and is best taken as preferential treatment for Paris reports due to embassy status and which, being informed by the French Colonial and Foreign ministries, was inevitably more anti-Vietminh. See Bradley, *Imagining Vietnam and America*, 169.

Notes to PART II

4. The Vietminh rebel alliance: universal rights and self-determination

1 Letter Ho Chi Minh to Secretary of State 22/10/1945, enclosure to Kunming to State 24/10/1945, 851G.00, RG59, NARA.
2 Nguyen Thi My Hanh, "Tributary Trade Activity in Diplomatic Relations between Vietnam & China in the Feudal Period," *Global Journal of Human-Social Science Research* 15, no. 7 (11 September 2015), http://socialscienceresearch.org/index.php/GJHSS/article/view/1521; Nhung Tuyet Tran and Anthony Reid, *Viet Nam: Borderless Histories* (Madison, WI: University of Wisconsin Press, 2006); John K. Whitmore, "Literati Culture and Integration in Dai Viet, c. 1430–c. 1840," *Modern Asian Studies* 31, no. 3 (July 1997): 665–87, https://doi.org/10.1017/S0026749X00017108
3 Antonio Cassese, *Self-Determination of Peoples: A Legal Reappraisal* (Cambridge: Cambridge University Press, 1995), 25.

5. The French Empire strikes back: aggression against Độc Lập

1 Enclosure to Kunming to State, 851G.00, 10-2545, RG59, NARA.
2 Tønnesson, *Vietnam 1946*, 29.
3 Speech. 24/8/1945 in Charles de Gaulle, *Lettres, notes et carnets 8 Mai 1945–18 Juin 1951* (Paris: Plon, 1983); De Gaulle in fact decreed the formation of the Force that would reoccupy Indochina the day after the Japanese surrender. See 17 August 1945 in Charles de Gaulle, *Le salut 1944–1946* (Paris: Pocket, 2010).
4 Andrée Françoise Caroline d' Ardenne de Tizac, Andrée Viollis, and André Malraux, *Indochine S.O.S.* (Gallimard, 1935).
5 The colonial government hoarded vast reserves of rice during the war for surplus military and commerce purposes, contributing to the famine in 1944–45. When the Japanese took over Indochina in March 1945, they gained some popularity by distributing those same rice supplies. See Marr, *Vietnam 1945*, 96.
6 Nguyen Du, *The Tale of Kieu*, trans. Huynh, New edition (New Haven, CT: Yale University Press, 1987).
7 Extract of US embassy paraphrase of Thach's written reply to questions, Bangkok to State, 851G.00/5-1447, RG59, NARA.

6. Vietminh as Fascists: Vietnam does not exist

1 HAUSSAIRE to COMINDO, 26/4/46, AP 127, AN.
2 Tønnesson, *Vietnam 1946*, 61.

3   It is of note that the 1940s Vietnamese name for Cochinchina was 'Nam Bo' ('Southern Province') which not only recalls its history within the Vietnamese Empire, but also includes 'Nam', which means 'south' for the province and in 'Việt Nam'; from the Mandarin 'nan' ('south').

4   The division of Indochina into 'five countries' 'distinguished by civilisation, race and traditions' was the writ of de Gaulle's 24 March declaration on Indochina. See Alfred Georges, *Charles de Gaulle et la guerre d'Indochine* (Nouvelles Editions Latines, 1974), 131.

5   Circulaire 2/47, AP 127, 457, AN.

6   "Georges Thierry D'argenlieu, 1038 Compagnons, Compagnons – Musée de l'Ordre de La Libération," http://www.ordredelaliberation.fr/fr/les-compagnons/946/georges-thierry-d-argenlieu (accessed 16 August 2016).

7   See for instance Alice L. Conklin, *In the Museum of Man: Race, Anthropology, and Empire in France, 1850–1950* (Ithaca, NY: Cornell University Press, 2013).

7. Vietminh as Communists: 'Moscow's interest in Indo-China'

1   Paris to State, 851G.GO/9-2245, RG59.

2   See for instance 'La mauvaise foi du Président Ho Chi Minh', (undated) December 1946, which accuses Vietminh of being a Japanese stooge, in 174Q0.46, Fond EA, MAE.

3   Henri Claudel report, 26/11/1948, film P4713 (Propagande Française aux USA), 91Q0.123, MAE.

8. A 'united front' and 'the left-wing trend of the Viet-Minh'

1   Saigon to FO, 17/3/1946, FO 371/53960.

2   "Decline in Viet Minh influence", *The Times*, 11 March 1946.

3   See file F4100 in FO371/53960, NA.

4   In scholarship, the difference between the nationalist revolution of 1945–46 and the 'communistification' of Vietminh from 1949 would only be satisfactorily retrieved from the fog of anticommunist and communist propaganda six decades later. See Vu, "Triumphs or Tragedies."

9. D'Argenlieu's 'sudden raising of the Communist bogey'

1   'Situation in French indo-china', Saigon to FO 17/1/1947, FO 474/1.

2   Tønnesson, *Vietnam 1946*, 146.

3   Vu, "Triumphs or Tragedies," 243.

4   Saigon to FO, 27/8/1949, FO 371/75972.

5   See Part 4 in Remme, "Britain and Regional Cooperation in South-East Asia, 1945–1949."

10. Meeting 'radical Annamese opponents of both France and Japan'

1   'Voluntary Report by Charles S. Millet', 6/11/1945, 851G.00, RG59, NARA.
2   United States Department of State, *Foreign Service List (Volume 1945)* (Washington, DC: U.S. Government Printing Office, 1945), 2.
3   Bradley, *Imagining Vietnam and America*, 134.
4   Though not always overtly racial, such discourses often held birth and culture as permanent fixtures, amounting to similar differentiation. See particularly Said, "Representing the Colonized."
5   Bradley, *Imagining Vietnam and America*, 45.
6   'Memorandum of Conversation' [Gallagher State Department debrief], 30/1/1946, 851G.00, RG59, NARA. Note the serious mistake concerning Cao Daism, which is a religious organization that was opposed to both French colonialism and socialism.
7   E. Morris, *The Fog of War: Eleven Lessons from the Life of Robert McNamara*, Documentary (Sony Pictures, 2003).

11. Creating Pyle's "Third Force": 'a truly nationalist government'

1   Policy Statement, 27/9/1948, 711.51G, RG59, NARA.
2   Greene, *The Quiet American*.
3   "Transcript of Truman Doctrine Address to Congress (1947)", https://www.ourdocuments.gov/doc.php?doc=81&page=transcript (accessed 29 August 2016).
4   These are what Foucault calls 'planes of emergence'. They are the discursive and practice sites where difference and similarity gain status and relevance as well as where they are individuated. They are discursively delimited normative domains that can coexist and have different, and sometimes superposed, importance. Michel Foucault, *Archaeology of Knowledge* (London: Routledge, 2002), 45.
5   Alistair Cooke, *A Generation on Trial: U.S.A. v. Alger Hiss* (Open Road Media, 2014).
6   Bangkok to State, 'Approach made by Dr. Pham Ngoc Thach', 851G.00/7-947, RG59, NARA.

Notes to PART III

1   'Les Philippines et l'expansionisme americain', 1/1946, Dossier Philippines-6-1946, INDO/HCI/CD/2-4, ANOM.

2   Undated note, 12/1948, FO959/20, NA.

3   'Policy Statement: Indochina', 711.51G/9-2748, RG59, NARA.

4   Gravel, *The Pentagon Papers*, 72.

5   See Lawrence, *Assuming the Burden*, 147.

12. Late 1948–September 1947: the year of the Stalinist domino

1   For the public political reporting of the time, see for instance The Associated Press, "Communists Menace South Asia; Unified Blow at Resources Seen", *New York Times*, 27 June 1948; Mary Spargo, *Post* Reporter, "Mere 14 Million Communists Are Altering Globe", *The Washington Post (1923–1954)*, 23 May 1948; Robert Trumbull, "Cominform Is in Sight for Southeastern Asia", *New York Times*, 18 July 1948; Harry Roskolenko, "Communism in Vietnam: Recent Statements Queried, Role of French in That Country Criticized", *New York Times*, 7 July 1948; "Government Takes Stern Steps To Stop Red Disorder in Malaya", 17 June 1948; "Malayan Police Hold 600 in Anti-Red Raids", *New York Times*, 22 June 1948.

2   Benedict J. Kerkvliet, *The Huk Rebellion: A Study of Peasant Revolt in the Philippines* (Lanham, MD: Rowman & Littlefield, 2002), 218.

3   Saigon to FO, 1/12/1949, FO371/75972, NA.

4   Daniel Varga, "Léon Pignon, l'homme-clé de la solution Bao Dai et de l'implication des États-Unis dans la Guerre d'Indochine," 2009, https://doi.org/10.3406/outre.2009.4426

5   Léon Pignon to UK Ambassador in Paris, Paris to FO, 18/11/1948, FO959/20, NA.

6   In Saigon to FO, 30/11/1948, FO959/20, NA.

7   Foreign Office Memo of conversation Denning-Pignon, to Paris, Saigon, 22/11/1948, FO959/20, NA.

8   Washington to DIPLOFRANCE, 17/3/48, Film P4715, 91QO.125, MAE.

9   Paris to State, 851G.00/5-1548, RG59, NARA.

10 'Rapport sur les évènements d'interêt diplomatique survenues en Asie du Sud-Est au cours du mois de Juillet 1949', HAUSSAIRE to Paris, 20/8/1949, CD2-4/HCI/INDO, ANOM.

11 Henri Claudel report, 26 November 1948, film P4713, 91Q0.123, MAE.

12 Saigon to FO, 29/11/1948, FO959/20, NA.

13 See for instance 851G.00B/3-2947, RG 59 NARA; 'Transmitting Viet Minh documents' (including 'Commie document'), Saigon to State, 851G.00B/12-749, RG59, NARA. There are dozens of such documents from 1949 to 1947 collected on a file on 'subversion' (851G.00B, RG59, NARA).

14 Bonfils report 21 May 1949, included in Saigon to State, 711.51G/6-949, RG59, NARA.

15 'Report on Chinese Communist activities in Tonkin', Hanoi to State, 851G.00B/4-1747, RG 59 NARA.

16 'Communism in Indochina', Saigon to State, 851G.00B/3-747, RG59, NARA.

17 'Étude sur les activités Americaines en Indochine', 11/9/47, HAUSSAIRE, Film 4714, 91QO.124, MAE.

18 26/9/47, HAUSSAIRE to COMINDO, Film 4714, 91QO.124, MAE.

19 Washington to DIPLOFRANCE, 15/10/47, Film 4714, 91QO.124, MAE.

20 Paris to State, 17/10/1947, 851G.00/10-1747, RG59, NARA.

21 'Le Viet Minh est un regime totalitaire qui regne par la terreur et par son organisation policière', 17/12/47, 174Q0.113, Fond EA, MAE.

22 HAUSSAIRE to COMINDO, 7/6/47, 174Q0.46, Fond EA, MAE.

23 SEA memorandum, 12/9/1947, 851G.00/9-1247, RG59, NARA.

24 See entire file, November–December 1949, FO371/75977, NA.

25 War Office-FO correspondence and joint policy paper draft, communication 6/12/1949, FO371/75979, NA.

26 FO comment on Paris to FO, 2/9/1949, FO371/75988, NA.

27 'Outline of Communist strategy in south-east Asia', FO Report, 15/8/1949, FO959/40, NA.

28 See for instance discussions during the Berlin blockade crisis. Cabinet Conclusions, 19/7/1948, CAB/128/13/12, NA.

29 Cabinet Memorandum, 3/3/1948, CAB/129/25/12, NA.

30 Annex IV, Cabinet Memorandum, 3/3/1948, CAB/129/25/12, NA.

31 Cabinet Memorandum, 5/1/1948, CAB/129/23/7, NA.

32 Cabinet Conclusions, 13/12/1948, CAB/128/13/40, NA.

33 See Bangkok to FO, 27/1/1948, FO422/93, NA; 14/1/1948, FO422/93, NA; Bangkok to FO, 21/1/1948, FO422/93, NA; Bangkok to FO Annual Report for 1947, FO422/93, NA.

34 FO Report to Washington, 20/12/1948, FO959/23, NA.

35 Commissioner General of the UK in SEA, Singapore to FO, 4/12/1948, FO959/23, NA.

36 See the substantial file FO371/75972, NA.

37 Saigon to FO, 16/11/1948, FO959/20, NA.

38 Saigon to FO, 29/11/1948, FO959/20, NA.

39 FO to Saigon, 25/11/1948, FO959/20, NA.

40 'Survey of Communism in countries outside the Soviet orbit', 20/9/1948, FO959/23, NA.

41 Cabinet Memorandum, 5/1/1948, CAB/129/23/7, NA.

42 See chapter 2 in Robert Jackson, *The Malayan Emergency: The Commonwealth's Wars 1948–1966* (London: Routledge, Chapman & Hall, Incorporated, 1991).

43 See for instance Saigon to FO 19/7/1949, FO371/75975, NA.

44 Saigon to FO, 16/7/1949, FO371/75975, NA.

45 Chancery of the Commissioner-General in South East Asia, Singapore to Saigon and FO SEA Dept., 2/9/1949, FO371/75975, NA.

46 F11353, Minutes 8/8/1949, FO371/75975, NA.

47 'Review of the situation in French Indochina', 11/5/1948, FO959/19, NA.

48 Tønnesson, *Vietnam 1946*, 27.

49 FO to Saigon, 14/4/48, FO 959/18, NA.

50 'Historical background of French Indo China to 1939', 19/4/1948, FO371/69661, NA.

51 'Historical background of French Indo China to 1939', 19/4/1948, FO371/69661, NA.

52 Cabinet Conclusions, 13/12/1948, CAB/128/13/40, NA.

53 'Communism in the Far East', 22/11/1948, FO959/20, NA; Minutes (Saigon information file), 9/12/1948, FO959/20, NA.

54 Undated note, 12/1948, FO959/20, NA.

55 'Situation in French Indo-China', Saigon to FO, 11/5/1948, FO432/9, NA.

56 Hanoi to Saigon, 31/5/1947.

57 Saigon to FO, 22/5/1948, FO959/19, NA.

58 Saigon to FO, 19/3/1948, FO959/19, NA.

59 'Politico-military situation in French Indochina', Saigon to FO, 5/5/1948, FO959/19, NA; Saigon to FO, 10/8/1948, FO432/9, NA, see /10 for later excoriation of the French solution.

60 Paris to FO, 13/9/1947, FO432/8, NA; Paris to FO, 17/9/1947, FO432/8, NA.

61 'Annual report for 1947', 12/4/1948 (compiled throughout the year, usually delivered in January but delayed to April for this year), FO462/2, NA.

62 Washington to FO, 12/10/1947, FO462/1, NA.

63 See Martinique to State, 16/9/1947, 851D.00/9-1647, RG59, NARA; Research memorandum, 7/7/1948, 851E.00B/7-748, RG59, NARA.

64 See for instance the beautiful Aimé Césaire and André Breton, *Cahier d'un Retour Au Pays Natal* (Bordas Paris, France, 1947).

65 Nouméa to State, 30/8/1945, 851E.5045/8-3045, RG59, NARA.

66 Delhi to State, 8/7/1948, 851F.00/7-848, RG59, NARA.

67 Saigon to FO, 29/11/1948, FO959/20, NA.

68 Bangkok to State, 10/2/1948, 851G.00/2-1048, RG59, NARA.

69 French Chief of Southeast Asian Affairs at MAE with State SEA Department conversation, 24/2/1948, 851G.00/2-2448, RG59, NARA.

70 Hanking to State, 20/9/1947, 851G.00/9-3047, RG59, NARA.

71 State to Nanking, 3/7/1947, 851G.00/7-347, RG59, NARA.

72 Paris to State, 3/11/1947, 851G.00/11-347, RG59, NARA.

73 Paris to State, 1/10/1947, 851G.00/10-147, RG59, NARA.

74 Hanoi to State, 2/12/1947, 851G.00/12-247, RG59, NARA.

75 'Communism in Indochina', Saigon to State, 7/3/1947, 851G.00B/3-747, RG59, NARA.

76 Saigon to State, 7/3/1947, 851G.00B/3-747, RG59, NARA.

77 Without 'too much optimism', Pignon congratulates himself that he has found a political solution satisfying all parties in 'Rapport politique Fevrier-Mars 1949', CP 93/ HCI/INDO, ANOM.

78 Unlike the argument that the "new" solution was a 1949 success in Varga, "Léon Pignon, l'homme-clé de la solution Bao Dai et de l'implication des États-Unis dans la Guerre d'Indochine."

79 CIA memorandum to Secretary of State, 10/11/1947, 851G.00/11-1047, RG59, NARA.

80 This is demonstrated by concern that a (possibly Indian-led) UN intervention might force France into talks with Vietminh. See for instance State Circular, 29/1/1948, 851G.00/1-2948, RG59, NARA.

81 Hanoi to State, 16/2/1948, 851G.00/2-1648, RG59, NARA.

82 Hanoi to State, 21/5/1948, 851G.00/5-2148, RG59, NARA.

83 Saigon to State, 6/10/1947, 851G.00/10-647, RG59, NARA.

84 See State Department SEA Office analysis, 12/9/1947, 851G.01/9-1247, RG59, NARA; and Saigon to State, 15/9/1947, 851G.00/9-1547, RG59, NARA.

85 Hanoi to State, 24/9/1947, 851G.00/9-2447, RG59, NARA.

86 See for instance Saigon to State, 26/9/1947, 851G.00/9-2647, RG59, NARA.

87 Paris to State, 16/1/1948, 851G.00/1-1648, RG59, NARA.

88 Saigon to State, 13/5/1948, 851G.00/5-1348, RG59, NARA; see also Paris to State, 15/5/1948, 851G.00/5-1548, RG59, NARA.

89 Saigon to State, 24/1/1948, 851G.00/1-248, RG59, NARA.

90 Hong Kong to State, 30/12/1948, 851G.00/12-3047, RG59, NARA.

91 Paris to State, 19/12/1947, 851G.00/12-1947, RG59, NARA.

92 See for instance Marseille to State, 3/11/1947, 851G.00/11-347, RG59, NARA.

93 Paris to State, 28/10/1947, 851G.00/10-2847, RG59, NARA.

94 The photographs are stamped with Vietminh seals. Enclosure to Saigon to State, 6/10/1947, 851G.00/10-647, RG59, NARA.

95 Attachment to Bangkok to State, 9/7/1947, 851G.00/7-947, RG59, NARA.

13. August 1947–September 1946: French intransigence and Anglo-Saxon antipathy

1 For the contemporary political context, see "The War In Indo-China", *New York Times*, 23 June 1947; "France in Indo-China", *New York Times*, 30 March 1947; "Full-Scale War Predicted", *New York Times*, 5 January 1947; "Totalitarian Character of Ho's Regime Cited as Evidence – Japanese Are Said to Have Installed Viet Minh as 'Time Bomb'", *New York Times*, 23 January 1947.

2 Saigon to State, 23/5/1947, 851G.00/5-2347, RG59, NARA.

3 Paris to State, 3/6/1947, 851G.00/6-347, RG59, NARA; Saigon to State, 28/2/1947, 851G.00/2-2847.

4 HAUSSAIRE to COMINDO and COMIINDO résponse to HAUSSAIRE, 10/2/1947, AP 128, 457, AN; Associated Press dispatch, Saigon 27/1/1947, AP 128, 457, AN.

5 Letter to MRP deputy and others, 28/1/1947, AP 128, 457, AN.

6 Paris to State, 28/12/1946, 851G.00/12-2846, RG59, NARA; Paris to State, 13/12/1946, 851G.00/12-1346, RG59, NARA.

7 Paris to State, 29/11/1946, 851G.00/11-2946, RG59, NARA.

8 'Le projet d'union sud asiatique', Presidential Office, 6/11/46, 174Q0.46, Fond EA, MAE

9 Saigon to State, 17/9/1946, 851G.00B/9-1746, RG59, NARA.

10 Rapport 28/11/46, AP 127, 457, AN.

11 See for instance how this scuppers French efforts in Hanoi to State, 19/7/1947, 851G.00/7-1947, RG59, NARA.

12 New York to Washington/DIPLOFRANCE, 10/3/47, Film 4714, 91Q0.124, MAE.

13 DIPLOFRANCE Circulaire, 20/3/47, AP 128, 457, AN.

14 Handover report, 14/3/47, AP 128, 457, AN.

15 SEA Memorandum, 16/12/1946, 851G.00/12-1646, RG59, NARA.

16 Saigon to FO, 27/12/1946, FO959/10, NA.

17 Dossier Philippines-6-1946, INDO/HCI/CD/2-4, ANOM.

18 17/12/1946, Dossier Philippines-6-1946, INDO/HCI/CD/2-4, ANOM; November 1946 Report, Dossier Philippines-6-1946, INDO/HCI/CD/2-4, ANOM.

19 Manila to HAUSSAIRE, 12/9/1946, Dossier Philippines-6-1946, INDO/HCI/CD/2-4, ANOM; 2nd Bureau Indochine to Diplomatic Counsellor, 14/9/1946, Dossier Philippines-6-1946, INDO/HCI/CD/2-4, ANOM; Renseignements 20/9/1946, Dossier Philippines-6-1946, INDO/HCI/CD/2-4, ANOM.

20 This is translated as 'colonialisme eclairé', suggesting 'lit' rather than 'enlightened', suggesting the extent to which the authors of the report wished to dissociate it from associations with the Enlightenment.

21 'Philippines et expansionisme americain', 1/1946, Dossier Philippines-6-1946, INDO/HCI/CD/2-4, ANOM. This is a reference to the fable by Jean de La Fontaine about a fox that, having lost its tail, attempted to persuade its brethren to cut theirs off. See La Fontaine, *Recueil 1*, Livre 5, Fable 5.

22 Léon Pignon to UK Ambassador in Paris, Paris to FO, 18/11/1948, FO959/20, NA; Saigon to FO, 30/11/1948, FO959/20, NA.

23 4/4/47, COMINDO to DIPLOFRANCE, Film 4714, 91Q0.124, MAE. The file is to this day labelled 'Propagande aux USA'.

24 See Washington to DIPLOFRANCE, 5/5/47, Film 4714, 91Q0.124, MAE.

25 This occurs on several occasions – see the State Dept. Files for the Hanoi consulate (Hanoi to State and Hanoi to Saigon under classifications 851G.00/xxxx46) for late 1946 and 1947.

26 DIPLOFRANCE to Holy See and Washington, 17/3/47, Film P4713, 91QO.123, MAE

27 New York to Washington/DIPLOFRANCE, 10/3/47, Film 4714, 91QO.124, MAE.

28 Paris to State, 6/2/1947, 851G.00/2-647, RG59, NARA.

29 HAUSSAIRE to DIPLOFRANCE, 11/1/47, Film 4714, 91QO.124, MAE.

30 Paris to State, 15/1/1947, 851G.00/1-1547, RG59, NARA; Paris to State, 16/1/1947, 851G.00/1-1647, RG59, NARA.

31 Saigon to FO, 27/12/46, FO959/10, NA.

32 'Rapport politique', HAUSSAIRE, 2/46, 174QO.18, Fond EA, MAE.

33 Report 'La methode Vietminh' in 'Reponse Francaise au memorandum du Gouvernement Ho Chi Minh', 9/1/47, 174Q0.117, Fond EA, MAE.

34 These are recounted in the file Fond EA/46, MAE, the most difficult file to obtain in this research project.

35 'Reponse Francaise au memorandum du Gouvernement Ho Chi Minh', 9/1/47, 174Q0.117, Fond EA, MAE.

36 7/1/47, AP 128, 457, AN.

37 Washington to DIPLOFRANCE, 20/10/46, 5/12/46, Film 4714, 91QO.124, MAE.

38 'American Attitude towards Britain–Part III', Washington to FO, 23/8/1947, FO462/1, NA.

39 Washington to FO, 2/1/1947, FO462/1, NA.

40 Washington to FO, 12/7/1947, FO462/1, NA.

41 Washington to FO, 8/2/1947, FO462/1, NA.

42 Paris to FO, 1/4/1947, FO432/8, NA.

43 Antananarivo to FO, 14/6/1947, FO432/8, NA.

44 1946 Report for France, FO432/8, NA.

45 FO report, 13/2/1947, FO959/14, NA.

46 Antananarivo to FO, 7/7/1947, FO432/8, NA.

47 Paris to FO, 27/5/1947, FO432/8, NA.

48 UK Special Commissioner SEA Singapore to Saigon, 3/4/1947, FO959/18, NA.

49 FO to UK Special Commissioner SEA Singapore, 20/2/1947, FO959/18, NA.

50 Bangkok to FO, 18/1/1947, FO422/92, NA.

51 India Office to FO, 2/6/1947, FO371/63455, NA.

52 FO to Paris, 21/6/1947, FO371/63455, NA.

53 6–25/8/1947, File with discussion and internal correspondence, FO/Cabinet Office F854, FO371/63455, NA.

54 Jean LeRoy (French Embassy London) to FE Dept. FO, 14/4/1947, FO371/63454, NA.

55 MI5 (Patterson) to FO, 5/5/1947, FO371/63454, NA.

56 See for instance FO to M. Branch, Admiralty, 16/4/1947, FO371/63454, NA.

57 While French diplomats sought to deceive their American counterparts, they once explained to British counterparts that the 'number of Germans in Foreign Legion in

Indochina varies between 25 and 35 per cent'. Paris to FO, 29/5/1947, FO371/63455, NA.

58 Washington to FO, 2/1/1947, FO462/1, NA.

59 Saigon to FO, 25/10/1946, FO959/11, NA.

60 Saigon to FO, 7/8/1947, FO371/63456, NA.

61 Saigon to FO, 7/8/1947, FO371/63456, NA; Hanoi to Saigon, 6/11/1946, FO959/11, NA.

62 See for example Saigon to FO, 22/12/1946, FO959/10, NA and that entire file.

63 Saigon to FO, 17/1/1947, FO 474/1, NA.

64 Moscow to FO, 6/1/1947, FO422/92, NA; Bangkok to FO, 7/1/1947, FO422/92, NA; Bangkok to FO, 5/9/1947, FO422/92, NA.

65 Bangkok to FO, 1/1/1947, FO422/92, NA.

66 Paris to FO, 30/12/1946, FO474/1, NA.

67 Saigon to FO, 17/1/1947, FO 474/1, NA, see detailed analysis of this missive in this book's Part II, Chapter 9.

68 FO to Saigon, 4/12/1946, FO959/14, NA.

69 Saigon to FO, 25/10/1946, FO959/11, NA.

70 Moscow to FO, 19/4/1946, FO371/63454, NA.

71 Undated, in file with 2/1946, FO959/14, NA.

72 Saigon to FO, 11/12/1946, FO959/10, NA.

73 Saigon to FO, 20/12/1946, FO474/1, NA.

74 Saigon to FO, 29/5/1947, FO371/63455, NA.

75 Hanoi to State, 19/7/1947, 851G.00/7-1947, RG59, NARA.

76 State to Saigon, 17/7/1947, 851G.00/7-1747, RG59, NARA. See also Hanoi to State, 14/4/1947, 851G.00/4-147 and State to Hanoi, 14/4/1947, 851G.00/4-147, RG59, NARA.

77 State to Paris and Circular, 13/5/1947, 851G.00/5-1347, RG59, NARA. See also earlier State to Saigon, 17/9/1946, 851G.00B/9-1746, RG59, NARA.

78 Paris to State, 3/6/1947, 851G.00/6-347, RG59, NARA.

79 Saigon to State, 28/2/1947, 851G.00/2-2847, RG59, NARA.

80 Saigon to State, 14/2/1947, 851G.00/2-1447, RG59, NARA.

81 Saigon to State, 27/2/1947, 851G.00/2-2747; and 22/1/1947, 851G.00/1-2247, RG59, NARA.

82 Paris to State, 9/1/1947, 851G.00/1-947, RG59, NARA.

83 SEA memorandum 24/1/1947, 851G.00/1-247; State to Hanoi and HK, 6/1/1947, 851G.00/1-647; Circular, 20/12/1946, 851G.00/12-2046 and Hanoi to State, 851G.00/12-446, RG59, NARA.

84 Hanoi to State, 23/12/1946, 851G.00/12-2346, RG59, NARA.

85 London to State, 25/11/1946, 851G.00/11-2546, RG59, NARA.

86 Paris to State, 22/5/1947, 851G.00/5-2247 and State Circular, 7/1/1947, 851G.00/1-747, RG59, NARA.

87 Hanoi to State, 10/2/1947, 851G.00/2-1047 and reply Memorandum FW State 10/2/1947, 851G.00/2-1047, RG59, NARA.

88 Hanoi to State, 5/2/1947, 851G.00/2-547, RG59, NARA.

89 Hanoi to State, 11/1/1947, 851G.00/1-1147, RG59, NARA.

90 Hanoi to State, 1/12/1946, 851G.00/12-146, RG59, NARA.

91 Hanoi to State, 9/1/1947, 851G.00/1-947, RG59, NARA.

92 Hanoi to State, 1/12/1946, 851G.00/12-146, RG59, NARA.

93 'Information circular', 17/12/1946, 851G.00/12-1746, RG59, NARA.

94 See for example Saigon to State, 28/5/1947, 851G.00/5-2847, RG59, NARA.

95 Saigon to State, 25/2/1947, 851G.00/2-2547, RG59, NARA.

96 Saigon to State, 30/11/1946, 851G.00/11-3046, RG59, NARA.

97 Central Intelligence Group to State, 22/11/1946, 851G.00/11-2246, RG59, NARA.

98 Saigon to State, summary of Indochinese situation 14/6/1947, 851G.00/6-1447, RG59, NARA.

99 See for instance Paris to State, 24/12/1946, 851G.00/12-2446; SEA Memorandum, 16/12/1946, 851G.00/12-1646, RG59, NARA.

100 Bangkok to State, 17/4/1947, 851G.00/4-1747, RG59, NARA.

101 Bangkok to State, 17/4/1947, 851G.00/4-1747, RG59, NARA.

102 Paris to State, 20/2/1947, 851G.00/2-2047, RG59, NARA. The French also handed a copy of this file to the US ambassador in Paris with an even more extensive reply that explained the 'incidents' in extreme military procedural detail.

103 Caffery to Bidault, 1/3/47, AP 128, 457, AN.

104 Hanoi to State, 20/1/1947, 851G.00/1-2047, RG59, NARA.

105 It is important to note that this memorandum was the core of a Vietminh diplomatic move in December 1946. Confusingly, it appears again among the 70 documents submitted to the US embassy in Bangkok in April 1947. It is therefore important to keep in mind that these were two separate efforts to communicate Vietminh's position and requests to US diplomats.

106 'Memorandum concernant l'origine du conflit Franco-Vietnamien', 31/12/46, 174QO.117, Fond EA, MAE.

107 Hanoi to State, 16/12/1946, 851G.00/12-1646, RG59, NARA.

108 Hanoi to State, 6/12/1946, 851G.00/12-646, RG59, NARA.

109 Rapport 28/11/46, AP 127, 457, AN.

110 6/12/46, (COMINDO-filed), 174QO.46, Fond EA, MAE.

111 'Dossier "Incident de Haiphong" du 16.11.1946 au d.12.1946', Enclosure to Hanoi to Saigon, 15/12/1946, FO959/12; Haiphong to Saigon, 28/11/1946, FO959/12, NA.

112 Tønnesson, *Vietnam 1946*, 148.

113 Bangkok to State, 14/5/1947, 851G.00/5-1447, RG59, NARA.

114 Bangkok to State, 7/4/1947, 851G.00/4-747, RG59, NARA.

115 Washington to DIPLOFRANCE, 19/2/47, Film 4714, 91QO.124, MAE.

116 Paris to State, 16/9/1946, 851G.00/9-1646, RG59, NARA.

117 Moffat memorandum, in Paris to State, 12/9/1946, 851G.00/9-1246, RG59, NARA.

118 Hanoi to State, 14/9/1946, 851G.00/9-1446, RG59, NARA.

14. August 1946–April 1945: Second World War ghosts and rethinking colonialism

1 Ngo Dinh Diem would support this thesis, though he predicated division on Catholicism, after his "Jesus goes South" campaign at the end of the Franco–Vietnamese war.

2 For the postwar context in public political discourse see "France's Joining Big Four Envisaged", *New York Times*, 21 March 1945; "Improved Empire Sought by French", *New York Times*, 4 July 1945; "Indo-China to Gain Limited Autonomy: De Gaulle Reveals Post-War Plan-Move Is Regarded as Anticipating Trusteeship", *New York Times*, 24 March 1945; "British Aid Is Seen for French Empire", *New York Times*, 19 August 1945; "U.S. Avoids Stand in Indies Dispute", *New York Times*, 14 November 1945; "Annamese Accept Truce with French", *New York Times*, 3 October 1945; "Annamese Fall Back Southwest of Saigon", *New York Times*, 29 October 1945; "Annamite Revolt Spreads in Saigon", *New York Times*, 27 September 1945; "British Aid French in Annam Uprising: Japanese Troops Are Said to Be Helping Allies Crush Revolt of Indo-China Nationalists", *New York Times*, 26 September 1945; "Colonies in Ferment", *New York Times*, 7 October 1945; "Flare-up in Into-China: Nationalists Active Along Highway Northwest of Saigon", *New York Times*, 21 November 1945; "French Criticize Yalta Vote Plan", *New York Times*, 31 March 1945; "Indo-Chinese Form New Rebel Faction", *New York Times*, 2 October 1945; "To Win the Peace: Charter Takes Shape Foreign Ministers Leave Action Against Aggressors Question of Colonies", *New York Times*, 13 May 1945; "INDO-CHINA RIOTS LAID TO VICHYITES: Disorders Said to Have Been Result of Arrests to Balk Independence Movement", *New York Times*, 4 January 1946; "Indo-China Revolt Fateful to France: Other Empire Areas Watching Outcome of Dissidence in Troubled East Asia", *New York Times*, 25 December 1946; "Blum Aims to End Viet Nam Revolts before Any Parley", *New York Times*, 27 December 1946; "Colonial Problem Growing in France", *New York Times*, 20 December 1946; "New Colony Plan Outlined in Paris: Change in Ministry's Name Symbolic of Program for Creating Empire Union", *New York Times*, 29 January 1946; "French Face All-out Colonial War: Indo-China Is Aflame With Many Incidents", *New York Times*, 29 December 1946; "French to Discuss Indo-Chinese Reds", *New York Times*, 27 November 1946.

3 Though a few non-combatant Axis-aligned states such as Spain, Portugal, Paraguay and others did manage it.

4   The Yūshūkan museum attached to the controversial Yasukuni Shrine, for instance, still celebrates the Japanese "liberation" of Asia.

5   Cutting, TIMES, 11/3/1946 and 20/3/1946, FO371/53960/NA.

6   For an extensive discussion of these preparations, see chapter 2 in Tønnesson, *Vietnam 1946*.

7   For a detailed history of French colonial theories, see Conklin, *In the Museum of Man*.

8   See de Gaulle, *Lettres, notes et carnets 8 Mai 1945–18 Juin 1951*.

9   for an extensive treatment of this specific question see Tønnesson, *The Vietnamese Revolution of 1945*.

10 'La prise du pouvoir par le V.M', 29/8/1946, SA4, SA.

11 Like d'Argenlieu – who was all three as well as a priest and aristocrat.

12 A good example is the Gaullist newspaper *L'Aube*. Gaullist nationalists such as Sarkozy and Fillon still use this language.

13 Sainteny to HAUSSAIRE, Undated, January 1946, SA4, SA.

14 'Physionomie politique de l'Indochine du Nord', October 1945, SA3; Rapport Arnoux, February 1945, SA2, SA.

15 'Rapport B5', 12/45, SA2, SA.

16 Washington to MAE 5/5/46, 2/5/46, 8/4/46, 2/1/46, and 7/12/45; DIPLOFRANCE to Washington 12/1/46; HAUSSAIRE to DIPLOFRANCE 11/1/46, all in Film 4714, 91QO.124, MAE.

17 Rapport Brunschwig, (undated)/7/1945, Film P4713, 91Q0.123, MAE.

18 Washington to DIPLOFRANCE, 9/12/1945, Film P4712, 91Q0.122, MAE.

19 See for instance Paris to State, 11/4/1945, 711.51/4-1145, RG59, NARA.

20 Paris to State, 5/5/1945, 711.51/5-545, RG59, NARA.

21 'La Lutte a l'interieur', 15/12/1945, SA2, SA.

22 Défence Nationale to DIPLOFRANCE, 10-7-46, Film 4714, 91QO.124, MAE.

23 'La mauvaise foi du president Ho Chi Minh' in 'Circulaire secrete', HAUSSAIRE to COMINDO, 8/3/46, 174QO.46, Fond EA, MAE.

24 'L'appui Chinois a l'agitation Annamite anti-Francaise', 3/46, 174QO.20, Fond EA, MAE.

25 HAUSSAIRE to COMINDO and Prime Minister, Memorandum 'Tournant politique en Indochine', both 26/4/46, AP 127, 457, AN.

26 Circulaire Fevrier 1947, AP 127, 457, AN.

27 HAUSSAIRE to COMINDO, 26/7/45, AP 127, 457, and DIPLOFRANCE to HAUSSAIRE, 26/7/46, AP 127, 457, AN.

28 'Terrorisme excercé par le Viet-Minh sur les populations du territoire', in 'Secret circular' HAUSSAIRE to COMINDO, 8/3/1946, 174QO.46, Fond EA, MAE.

29 1946 'Terrorisme' file for COMINDO, in 174QO.46, Fond EA, MAE.

30 Underlined in the original 'note pour M. Georges Bidault', 10/7/46, AP127, 457, AN.

31 See for instance Note Verbale, 7/7/46, AP 127, 457, AN.

32 State, Eastern Hemisphere, 5/5/1945, 851G.00/5-545, RG59, NARA.

33 'Note pour le Ministre', 4/12/45, AP127, 457, AN.

34 For instance, 'Indo-China to Gain Limited Autonomy: De Gaulle Reveals Post-War Plan-Move Is Regarded as Anticipating Trusteeship', *New York Times*, 24 March 1945.

35 'Indochine', 24/3/45, MAE, 174QO.5, Fond EA, MAE. See also 'Note sur la politique qu'entend suivre le Gouvernement Francais en Indochine apres sa liberation', 8/45, AP127, 457, AN.

36 Hague to DIPLOFRANCE, 31/10/45, Film 4714, 91QO.124, MAE.

37 'Activites Americaines', HAUSSAIRE to DIPLOFRNCE, (undated)/1/46, Film 4714, 91QO.124, MAE; SEA memorandum, 23/11/1945, 851G.00/11-2345, RG59, NARA.

38 DIPLOFRANCE to Washington, 27/10/45, Film 4714, 91QO.124, MAE.

39 DIPLOFRANCE to Washington, 17/10/45, Film 4714, 91QO.124, MAE.

40 DIPLOFRANCE to Washington, 15/3/45, Film 4714, 91QO.124, MAE.

41 Reinsegnements n.50/Sec., 25/6/45, SA1, SA.

42 Humbert report, 2/12/45, SA1, SA.

43 HAUSSAIRE to COMINDO, 8/11/45, 174QO.20, Fond EA, MAE.

44 Rapport 'Mission a bord du Fegaf' (Mission onboard the Fegaf ["watch-out"] vessel), 17/8/45, SA1, SA.

45 'Puppet' in English in the original, an official Allied term. Renseignements n.2263, 10/9/45, SA1, SA.

46 Chungking to DIPLOFRANCE, 22/3/1945, 174QO.20, Fond EA and 'Resumé conference 25 Decembre 1944', MAE Memorandum, 174QO.3, Fond EA, MAE.

47 De Gaulle frequently compared Indochina to how India made Britain a great power. See the many private and public addresses and notes to this effect in his various memoirs and document collections, particularly de Gaulle, *Lettres, notes et carnets 8 Mai 1945–18 Juin 1951*; *Lettres, notes et carnets: Tome 2, 1942–mai 1958* (Paris: R. Laffont, 2010); *Le salut 1944–1946*; as well as Georges, *Charles de Gaulle et la guerre d'Indochine*; and Frédéric Turpin, *De Gaulle, Les Gaullistes et l'Indochine: 1940–1956* (Les Indes savantes, 2005).

48 Allocution 27/8/1945 in de Gaulle, *Le salut 1944–1946*.

49 William I. Hitchcock, *France Restored: Cold War Diplomacy and the Quest for Leadership in Europe, 1944–1954* (Chapel Hill, NC: University of North Carolina Press, 1998), 43.

50 *L'Aube*, 18 January, 13 February, 6 March, 23 March and 28 March 1945; see also de Gaulle, *Le salut 1944–1946*, 200–201.

51 *L'Aube*, 28 April 1945 and de Gaulle, *Lettres, notes et carnets 8 Mai 1945–18 Juin 1951* undated [before 25 April 1945]; *Le salut 1944–1946*, 28 April 1945.

52 Chungking to State, 23/2/1945, 711.51/2-2345, RG59, NARA.

53 Paris to State, 3/1/1945, 711.51/1-345, RG59, NARA. For a treatment in broader historical context, see also Brendan Simms, *Europe: The Struggle for Supremacy, from 1453 to the Present* (New York: Basic Books, 2013), 602.

54 See Lawrence, *Assuming the Burden*, 110.

55 20 January Situation Report, Saigon to FO, 23/1/1946, FO371/53959, NA.

56 India Office to FO (SEA Dept.), 26/3/1946, FO371/53961, NA.

57 Andersen brief on Cochinchinese question, 26/4/1946, FO371/53963, NA.

58 Saigon to FO, 27/3/1946, FO371/53961; Saigon to FO, 12/3/46, FO371/53960, NA.

59 Saigon to Hanoi and FO, 2/3/46 (9.35am), FO371/53959, NA.

60 Saigon to Hanoi and FO, 2/3/46 (3.30pm), FO371/53959, NA.

61 Saigon to FO, 21/2/1946, FO371/53959, NA. See also Situation Report 20 January, Saigon to FO, 23/1/1946, FO371/53959, NA.

62 SACSEA to FO, 31/3/1946, FO371/53961, NA.

63 Paris to FO, 3/4/1946, FO371/53962, NA.

64 FO to Saigon, 11/4/1946, FO371/53962, NA.

65 Also known as 'code de l'indigénat' in Algeria. It exposed colonial peoples to collective punishment, expropriation and forced labour; with no recourse and no reciprocal provisions against French civilian violence. It was the subject of Fanon's critique of the total, 'scientific' and 'psychological' subjugation of the colonized.

66 Telegram Saigon to FO, 8/3/46, FO371/53960, NA.

67 'Constitution and administration of Indo-China: comparison of pre-war position with reforms now promised', 28/3/1946, FO371/53961, NA.

68 Saigon to FO, 28/2/46, FO371/53959, NA.

69 Cabinet Memo, 6/10/1945, CAB/129/3/13, NA.

70 Cabinet Memo, 14/11/1945, CAB/129/4/31, NA. A key difference they failed to notice was that Nehru's right to publicly decry British rule in India in speeches did not exist in Indochina. His Vietnamese counterparts were captured by the Sûreté and faced imprisonment in the island prison of Paulo Condor.

71 Saigon to FO, 28/2/46, FO371/53959, NA.

72 Telegram Saigon to FO, 12/3/46, FO371/53960, NA.

73 Saigon to FO, 27/3/1946, FO371/53961, NA.

74 Telegram cited in full in Saigon to FO, 18/3/46 and subsequent documents including FO discussion on response in file FO371/53960, NA.

75 'FO Research Memorandum (Anderson) on French Indo-China', 20/3/1946, FO371/53960, NA.

76 Saigon to FO, 12/3/46, FO371/53960; FO Analysis, 4/3/46, FO371/53959, NA.

77 Chungking to FO (FAO Sterndale Bennett), 25/2/1946, FO371/53960, NA.

78 'Summary Annamese Parties', undated/12/1945, FO959/5, NA. Some telegrams from this period are undated because of a late 1945 shortage of qualified typing and clerical staff – not to mention the gravest stationery crisis in diplomatic history, which also affected their French and American counterparts.

79 Saigon to FO, 28/2/46, FO371/53959, NA.

80 Saigon Consulate to FO, 22/2/46, FO371/53959, NA.

81 Telegram Consulate Saigon to FO, 21/2/1946, FO371/53959, NA.

82 Hanoi to Saigon, 8/2/1946, FO959/5; Hanoi to Saigon, 26/1/1946, FO959/5, NA.

83 Moscow to Paris and FO, 9/4/1946, FO371/53962, NA.

84 Saigon Consulate to FO, 22/2/46, FO371/53959, NA.

85 'Situation Report as of 20 January', Consulate Saigon to FO, 23/1/1946, FO371/53959, NA.

86 Saigon to FO, 23/1/1946, FO959/5, NA.

87 'Statement made by the Secretary of State' and related briefing file, archived 20/2/46, FO371/53960, NA.

88 'FO Research Memorandum (Anderson) on French Indo-China', 20/3/1946, FO371/53960, NA.

89 Hanoi to Saigon, undated/1/1946, FO959/5; see also Saigon to FO, 22/1/1946, Saigon to FO, 23/1/1946, FO959/5, NA.

90 Hanoi to Saigon, 8/2/1946, FO959/5, NA.

91 State to Saigon, 19/7/1946, 851G.00/7-1946, RG59, NARA.

92 State to Chungking, 14/7/1945, 851G.00/7-1445, RG59, NARA.

93 Paris to State, 10/5/1946, 851G.00/5-1046, RG59, NARA.

94 Hanoi to State, 20/5/1946, 851G.00/5-2046, RG59, NARA.

95 Adding that it was surprising that French voters should support the Communist Party since 'Russia, with its primitive and backward conditions, has nothing to offer a complex highly civilised society like that of France'. Moscow to State and Paris, 1/4/1946, 711.51/4-146, RG59, NARA.

96 Mid-1946 request to the Office of Intelligence and Research, referenced in Memorandum 7/7/1948, 851E.00B/7-748, RG59, NARA.

97 State to Saigon, 17/9/1946, 851G.00B/9-1746, RG59, NARA.

98 France Policy Statement, 15/9/1946, 711.51/9-1546, RG59, NARA.

99 Shanghai to State, 19/2/1946, 851G.00/2-1946, RG59, NARA.

100 Intelligence Report, 29/8/1945, 843.00/8-2945, RG59, NARA.

101 Saigon to State, 31/8/1946, 851G.00/8-3146, RG59, NARA.

102 SEA memorandum, 9/8/1946, 851G.00/8-946; Saigon to State, 27/4/1946, 851G.00/4-2746, RG59, NARA.

103 Saigon to State, 30/4/1946, 851G.00/4-3046, RG59, NARA.

104 Saigon to State, 14/6/1946, 851G.00/6-146, RG59, NARA.

105 Saigon to State, 14/7/1945, 851G.00/7-146, RG59, NARA.

106 See Saigon to State, 7/3/1946, 851G.00/3-746, RG59, NARA and subsequent reports and analysis in that file.

107 Saigon to State, 4/5/1946, 851G.00/5-446, RG59, NARA.

108 Saigon to State, Saigon to State, 8/5/1946, 851G.00/5-846, RG59, NARA.

109 SEA Division Memorandum, 28/4/1945, 851G.00/4-2845, RG59, NARA.

110 'The French regime in Indochina prior to 1940' Report, 8/3/1945, 751.51G/3-845, RG59, NARA.

111 'Voluntary Report', 1/12/1945, 851G.00/12-145, RG59, NARA.

112 Major Patti memorandum of conversation, 5/12/1945, 851G.00/12-545, RG59, NARA.

113 Gallagher State Department memorandum of conversation, 30/1/1946, 851G.00/1-3046, RG59, NARA.

114 OSS memo for State Department, 21/8/1945, 851G.00/8-2145, RG59, NARA.

115 Colombo to State, 23/10/1945, 8514G.00/10-2345, RG59, NARA.

116 Chunking to Navy and State, 30/1/1945, 851G.00/1-3045, RG59, NARA.

117 The war over drafts is recorded in exquisite detail in the files for April–June 1945 in 851G.00/1-145 – 7-3046.

118 'Memorandum to the President on Indochina', copy in 9/5/1945, 851G.00/5-945; State to Paris, 9/5/1945, 851G.00/5-945, RG59, NARA.

119 Stettinius UNCIO (San Francisco) to State (Grew), 8/5/1945, 851G.01/5-845, RG59, NARA.

120 The institutional conflict has been explored in some detail before, particularly by S. Tønnesson, "The Longest Wars: Indochina 1945–75," *Journal of Peace Research* 22, no. 1 (1985): 9–29; and *The Vietnamese Revolution of 1945*.

121 Memoranda for the president in files 711.51 for April–June 1945, RG59, NARA.

122 See for instance Memo of conversation Truman–Grew, 17/5/1945, 711.51/5-1745, RG59, NARA.

123 European Affairs to Acheson, 29/9/1945, 851G.00/9-2945, RG59, NARA.

124 Memorandum of conversation Truman–Bidault, 21/5/1945, 711.51/5-2145, RG59, NARA.

125 There is extensive discussion at the State Department about this problem, see files beginning 851G.00/1-145, RG59, NARA.

126 Paris to State, 14/3/1945, 711.51/3-1445, RG59, NARA and subsequent cables that week.

127 'Memorandum on Indochina', 28/9/1945, 851G.00/9-2845, RG59, NARA.

128 European Affairs Office Memorandum, 2/10/1945, 851G.00/10-245, RG59, NARA.

129 FE-SEA joint paper on Indochina (and file), April 1945, 851G.00/4-2545, RG59, NARA.

130 For Ho Chi Minh's OSS reports (1945), see Box 1393, file 16, RG226, NARA.

131 His OSS reports and newsletter articles have been studied in some detail in Tønnesson, *The Vietnamese Revolution of 1945*.

132 This angle is exquisitely analysed in Bradley, *Imagining Vietnam and America*.

133 Cited verbatim in Saigon to FO, 18/3/46, FO371/53960, NA.

134 The French are greatly concerned by this alignment and report on it extensively. See Intelligence report, COMINDO, 1/10/46, 174QO.18, Fond EA, MAE.

135 State record of telegram, 7/9/1945, 851G.00/9-745, RG59, NARA.

136 Paris to State, 23/8/1945, 851G.00/8-2345; State-War-Navy to State, 18/12/1945, 851G.00/12-1845, RG59, NARA.

137 Hanoi to State, 5/6/1946, 851G.00/6-546, RG59, NARA.

138 COMINDO to HAUSSAIRE, 22/8/46, 174QO.46, Fond EA, MAE.

139 Hanoi to Paris, cited COMINDO to HAUSSAIRE, 12/10/46, also 26/10/46, 174QO.46, Fond EA, MAE. For the many (mostly unanswered) letters Ho sent to Bidault, see AP127, 457, AN.

140 Saigon to State, 17/5/1946, 851G.00/5-1746, RG59, NARA.

141 'Problèmes du referendum au Nam Bo', 7/46, AP 127, 457, AN.

142 Undated, unmarked, in file with 8/3/1946, 851G.00/3-846, RG59, NARA.

143 Moffat to State, in Blum and United States Congress Senate Committee on Foreign Relations, *The United States and Vietnam, 1944–1947*, 41.

144 'Acte d'Abdication', 25/8/45, SA2, SA.

145 Enclosure in Kunming to State, 24/10/1945, 851G.00/10-2445, RG59, NARA.

146 In more modern English the phrase might be loosely but more representatively translated as 'threw 89 and Free France in our face'. Sainteny to HAUSSAIRE, 29/9/45, SA1, SA.

147 "Ho Chi Minh Archive", https://www.marxists.org/reference/archive/ho-chi-minh/ (accessed 8 February 2016).

148 Attachment to cable from Consulate Kunming, 851G.00/6-1445.

Notes to the Epilogue: onto war made unavoidable

1 FO to Saigon, 14/4/48, FO 959/18, NA.

2 A good example of the (slow and at first not considered very important) transition across to US policymaking is 10/3/47, New York to Washington/DIPLOFRANCE, Film 4714, 91QO.124, MAE.

3 Varga, "Léon Pignon, l'homme-clé de la solution Bao Dai et de l'implication des États-Unis dans la Guerre d'Indochine."

4 FO to Saigon, 4/5/1948, FO 959/18, NA.

5 This is a key addition to Bradley's estimate of the ideas and drivers informing Vietminh's bid for postwar independence. Bradley, *Imagining Vietnam and America*.

6 John F. Kennedy cited in Gravel, *The Pentagon Papers*, 72.

7 See for instance the front covers, 3/1/2017 of the *Daily Mail*, *The Sun*, the *Daily Telegraph*, and 3/1/2017, BBC News.

8 For an excellent broader account of the last years of the French Empire in Indochina see Devillers, *End of a War*; For the battle see Bernard B. Fall, *Hell in a Very Small Place: The Siege of Dien Bien Phu*, Second edition (New York, NY: Da Capo Press Inc, 2002); and, from the French military perspective Henri Navarre, *Agonie de l'Indochine: (1953–1954)* (Libr. Plon, 1956).

9 Greene, *The Quiet American*, 32.

Bibliography

Archives

Citations of archival documents begin with a brief descriptive name ('Memorandum from D'Argenlieu to COMINDO'), followed by the date (British format: day/month/year) and its original archive reference. All translations from French, Spanish, Italian and Portuguese are my own. The below breakdown of sources includes primarily archival data as well as open-source data obtained by the author.

Archives Diplomatiques du Ministère des Affaires Étrangères, Rue de La Courneuve, Paris (MAE)

    Fonds États Associés (Fond EA)

    Communication avec les États-Unis

Archives Nationales, Pierrefitte-sur-Seine, Paris (AN)

    Bidault Presidential papers collection (AN fond 457AP)

    D'Argenlieu private collection (AN fond 517AP)

Archives Nationales d'Outre-Mer, Aix-en-Provence (ANOM)

    Collection Haut Commissariat d'Indochine, fond HCI

    Archives Gouvernement de Fait, fond GF

Archive Historique Fondation Nationale des Sciences Politiques, Paris (SA)

    Fond Sainteny (aka Archive Sainteny)

    Photos du Fond Sainteny

National Archives and Records Administration (NARA)

    State Department Records – RG59

    Posters and maps archive

    CIA Records Search Tool at the NARA – CREST

National Archives, London, United Kingdom (NA)

    Colonial Office Records – CO

    Cabinet Office Records, Minutes, Conclusions, Memoranda – CAB

    Foreign Office Records – FO

Published document collections

Blum, Robert M., and United States Congress Senate Committee on Foreign Relations. *The United States and Vietnam, 1944–1947: A Staff Study Based on the Pentagon*

Papers Prepared for the Use of the United States Senate Committee on Foreign Relations. U.S. Government Printing Office, 1972.

de Gaulle, Charles. *Le salut 1944–1946.* Paris: Pocket, 2010.

de Gaulle, Charles. *Lettres, notes et carnets 8 Mai 1945–18 Juin 1951.* Paris: Plon, 1983.

de Gaulle, Charles. *Lettres, notes et carnets. [5],.* Paris: Plon, 1983.

de Gaulle, Charles. *Lettres, notes et carnets. 1943–1945.* Paris: Plon, 1983.

de Gaulle, Charles. *Lettres, notes et carnets: Tome 2, 1942 – mai 1958.* Paris: R. Laffont, 2010.

Devillers, Philippe, ed. *Paris–Saigon–Hanoi: les archives de la guerre, 1944–1947.* [Paris]: Gallimard : Julliard, 1988.

'Foreign Relations of the United States.' http://uwdc.library.wisc.edu/collections/FRUS (accessed 14 May 2015).

Herring, George C. *The Secret Diplomacy of the Vietnam War: The Negotiating Volumes of the Pentagon Papers.* Austin: University of Texas Press, 1983.

Porter, Gareth, ed. *Vietnam: A History in Documents.* New York: New American Library, 1979.

Sen. Gravel, ed. *The Pentagon Papers: The Defense Department History of United States Decisionmaking on Vietnam. Vol. 1.* Boston: Beacon Press, 1971.

Williams, William Appleman, Thomas McCormick, Lloyd C. Gardner, and Walter LaFeber, eds. *America in Vietnam: A Documentary History.* Reissue edition. New York; London: W. W. Norton & Company, 1989.

Newspapers

L'Aube
L'Aurore
Le Figaro
Le Monde
L'Humanité
The New York Times
The Times
The Washington Post

Images

Figure 1: 1930s map of French Indochina from *Atlas des Colonies Françaises. Protectorats et Territoires sous mandat de la France.* Direction de G. Grandidier (Paris: Societé d'Editions Géographiques, Maritimes et Coloniales, 1933) reproduced in *La Culture du riz dans le delta du Tonkin*, Éditions de la Maison des sciences de l'homme, Prince of Songkla University, Paris 1995, Open Access Volume available at https://books.openedition.org/editionsmsh/docannexe/image/7980/img-1.jpg

Figure 2: Diagram summarizing the methodology of the analytics of this book. Diagram by Natalia de Orellana, 2017.

Figure 3: French diplomatic pathways 1945–48. Diagram by Natalia de Orellana, 2017.

Figure 4: D'Argenlieu at his desk in Saigon, undated. Archive Sainteny, Historical Archive of Sciences-Po, Paris.

Figure 5: Vietminh diplomatic pathways 1945–48. Diagram by Natalia de Orellana, 2017.

Figure 6: Ho, Sainteny, Leclerc and d'Argenlieu meet in 1946. Archive Sainteny, Historical Archive of Sciences-Po, Paris.

Figure 7: British diplomatic pathways 1945–48. Diagram by Natalia de Orellana, 2017.

Figure 8: US diplomatic pathways 1945–48. Diagram by Natalia de Orellana, 2017.

Figure 9: Representations in French diplomacy 1948–45. Diagram by Natalia de Orellana, 2017.

Figure 10: Representations in British diplomacy 1948–45. Diagram by Natalia de Orellana, 2017.

Figure 11: Representations in US diplomacy 1948–45. Diagram by Natalia de Orellana, 2017

Figure 12: Representations in Vietminh diplomacy 1948–45, Diagram by Natalia de Orellana, 2017.

Figure 13: Giap with Leclerc and Sainteny, late 1946. Archive Sainteny, Historical Archive of Sciences-Po, Paris.

Figure 14: Ba Đình Square on 2 September 1945. Archive Sainteny, Historical Archive of Sciences-Po, Paris.

Figure 15: Foreign Légionnaire in Vietnam, 1954. Wikimedia Commons, available at https://commons.wikimedia.org/wiki/Category:First_Indochina_War#/media/File:HD-SN-99-02041.JPEG

Books and articles

Adler-Nissen, Rebecca, and Vincent Pouliot. "Power in Practice: Negotiating the International Intervention in Libya." *European Journal of International Relations* 20, no. 4 (1 December 2014): 889–911.

Akita, Shigeru, Gerold Krozewski, and Shoichi Watanabe. *The Transformation of the International Order of Asia: Decolonization, the Cold War, and the Colombo Plan*. Abingdon: Routledge, 2014.

Alliance, PERTINAX North American Newspaper. "France's Joining Big Four Envisaged." *New York Times*, 21 March 1945.

"Annamese Accept Truce with French." *New York Times*, 3 October 1945.

"Annamese Fall Back Southwest of Saigon." *New York Times*, 29 October 1945.

"Annamite Revolt Spreads in Saigon." *New York Times*, 27 September 1945.

Argenlieu, Thierry d'. *Chronique d'Indochine: 1945–1947*. Paris: A. Michel, 1985.

Ashley, Richard K. "Living on Border Lines: Man, Poststructuralism, and War." In *International/Intertextual Relations: Postmodern Readings of World Politics*, edited by James Der Derian and Michael J. Shapiro, 259–321. Lexington, MA: Lexington Books, 1989.

Associated Press. "Communists Menace South Asia; Unified Blow at Resources Seen." *New York Times*, 27 June 1948.

Barthes, R. "S/Z." New York: Hill and Wang, 1974.

Bhabha, Homi. "Of Mimicry and Man: The Ambivalence of Colonial Discourse." *October* 28 (1 April 1984): 125–33. https://doi.org/10.2307/778467

Bhabha, Homi K. *The Location of Culture*. New York: Psychology Press, 1994.

Bradley, Mark Philip. *Imagining Vietnam and America: The Making of Postcolonial Vietnam, 1919–1950*. Chapel Hill, NC: University of North Carolina Press, 2000.

"British Aid French in Annam Uprising: Japanese Troops Are Said to Be Helping Allies Crush Revolt of Indo-China Nationalists." *New York Times*, 26 September 1945.

Busch, Peter. "Constructing Vietnam . . ." *Diplomatic History* 31, no. 1 (2007): 155–58.

Buttinger, Joseph. *The Smaller Dragon*. New York: Praeger, 1958.

Cassese, Antonio. *Self-Determination of Peoples: A Legal Reappraisal*. Cambridge: Cambridge University Press, 1995.

Césaire, Aimé, and André Breton. *Cahier d'un Retour Au Pays Natal*. Bordas Paris, France, 1947.

Chinh, Trừơnog. *The August Revolution*. Foreign Languages Publishing House, 1958.

Chinh, Trường, and Bernard B. Fall. *Primer for Revolt: The Communist Takeover in Viet-Nam*. 133. Cambridge: Cambridge University Press, 1963.

Cicero, Marcus Tullius. *De Inventione; De Optimo Genere Oratorum*. Cambridge, MA: Loeb, 1989.

"Colonies in Ferment." *New York Times*, 7 October 1945, sec. The Week In Review.

Conklin, Alice L. *In the Museum of Man: Race, Anthropology, and Empire in France, 1850–1950*. Ithaca, NY: Cornell University Press, 2013.

Connolly, W. E. "Identity and Difference in Global Politics." In *International/Intertextual Relations: Postmodern Readings of World Politics*, edited by James Der Derian and Michael J. Shapiro, 323–43. Lexington, MA: Lexington Books, 1989.

Connolly, W. E. *Identity/Difference: Democratic Negotiations of Political Paradox*. Minneapolis: University of Minnesota Press, 2002.

Connolly, W. E. *The Terms of Political Discourse*. Oxford: Blackwell, 1993.

Constantinou, C. M. *On the Way to Diplomacy*. Minneapolis: University of Minnesota Press, 1996.

Constantinou, C. M., O. P. Richmond, and A. Watson. *Cultures and Politics of Global Communication: Volume 34, Review of International Studies*. Cambridge: Cambridge University Press, 2008.

Cooke, Alistair. *A Generation on Trial: U.S.A. v. Alger Hiss.* Open Road Media, 2014.

Correspondent, IVAN KINGSLEY United Press. "INDO-CHINA RIOTS LAID TO VICHYITES: Disorders Said to Have Been Result of Arrests to Balk Independence Movement." *New York Times*, 4 January 1946.

Curtius, Ernst Robert. *European Literature and the Latin Middle Ages.* Princeton: Princeton University Press, 1953.

"Decline in Viet Minh influence", *The Times*, 11 March 1946.

Der Derian, J. *Antidiplomacy: Spies, Terror, Speed, and War.* Cambridge, MA: Blackwell, 1992.

Der Derian, *On Diplomacy: A Genealogy of Western Estrangement.* Oxford: Oxford University Press, 1987.

Der Derian, J., J., and Michael J. Shapiro, eds. *International/Intertextual Relations: Postmodern Readings of World Politics.* Lexington, MA: Lexington Books, 1989.

Derrida, J. *The Post Card: From Socrates to Freud and Beyond.* Chicago: University of Chicago Press, 1987.

Derrida, J. *Writing and Difference.* London: Routledge, 2001.

Derrida, Jacques. *La Verite En Peinture.* Paris: Editions Flammarion, 2010.

Devillers, Philippe. *End of a War: Indo-China, 1954.* New York: Praeger, 1969.

Devillers, Philippe. *Histoire Du Viêt-Nam de 1940 à 1952.* Paris: Editions du Seuil, 1952.

Du, Nguyen. *The Tale of Kieu.* Translated by Huynh. New edition. New Haven, CT: Yale University Press, 1987.

Fall, Bernard. *Street Without Joy: The French Debacle in Indochina.* Barnsley, UK: Pen and Sword, 2005.

Fall, Bernard B. *Hell in a Very Small Place: The Siege of Dien Bien Phu.* Second edition. New York, NY: Da Capo Press Inc, 2002.

Fall, Bernard B. *The Two Viet-Nams: A Political and Military Analysis.* New York: Frederick A. Praeger, 1967.

Fifield, Russell H. "The Thirty Years War in Indochina: A Conceptual Framework." *Asian Survey*, 1977, 857–79.

"Flare-up in Into-China: Nationalists Active Along Highway Northwest of Saigon." *New York Times*, 21 November 1945.

Foucault, Michel. *Archaeology of Knowledge.* London: Routledge, 2002.

Foucault, Michel. *Discipline and Punish – The Birth of The Prison.* Second Vintage Books edition. New York: Random House USA Inc, 1995.

Foucault, Michel. "Nietzsche, Genealogy, History." In *The Foucault Reader*, edited by Paul Rabinow. New York: Random House, 1984.

Foucault, Michel. "Nietzsche, Genealogy, History." In *Nietzsche*, edited by John Richardson and Brian Leiter, 139–64. Oxford: Oxford University Press, 2001.

Foucault, Michel. *Power/Knowledge: Selected Interviews and Other Writings, 1972–1977.* New York: Random House USA Inc, 1988.

Foucault, Michel. *Society Must be Defended.* London: Penguin, 2003.

Foucault, Michel. *The Archaeology of Knowledge.* London: Tavistock Publications, 1972.

Foucault, Michel. *The History of Sexuality Vol.1: The Will to Knowledge*. Translated by Robert Hurley. New edition. London: 1998.

Foucault, Michel. "The Order of Discourse." In *Language and Politics*, edited by Michael Shapiro. Oxford: Blackwell, 1984.

Foucault, Michel. *The Order of Things: An Archaeology of the Human Sciences*. London: Routledge, 2002.

"France in Indo-China." *New York Times*, 30 March 1947, sec. REVIEW OF THE WEEK EDITORIALS.

Franchini, Philippe. *Les Guerres d'Indochine: De La Bataille de Dien Bien Phu à La Chute de Saigon*. Vol. 2. Pygmalion/G. Watelet, 1988.

Franchini, Philippe. *Les Mensonges de La Guerre d'Indochine*. Éd. France loisirs, 2003.

Franchini, Philippe, ed. *Saigon: 1925–1945 : de la Belle Colonie à léclosion révolutionnaire, ou, la fin des dieux blancs*. Paris: Autrement, 1992.

"French Criticize Yalta Vote Plan." *New York Times*, 31 March 1945.

"Full-Scale War Predicted." *New York Times*, 5 January 1947.

Georges, Alfred. *Charles de Gaulle et la guerre d'Indochine*. Nouvelles Editions Latines, 1974.

"Georges Thierry D'argenlieu, 1038 Compagnons, Compagnons – Musée de l'Ordre de La Libération." http://www.ordredelaliberation.fr/fr/les-compagnons/946/georges-thierry-d-argenlieu (accessed 16 August 2016).

Gratien, Jean-Pierre. *Marius Moutet: Un socialiste à l'Outre-mer*. Editions L'Harmattan, 2006.

Greene, Graham. *The Quiet American*. London: Heineman, 1955.

Hanh, Nguyen Thi My. "Tributary Trade Activity in Diplomatic Relations between Vietnam & China in the Feudal Period." *Global Journal of Human-Social Science Research* 15, no. 7 (11 September 2015). http://socialscienceresearch.org/index.php/GJHSS/article/view/1521

Herring, George C. *America's Longest War : The United States and Vietnam, 1950–1975*. Fourth edition. Boston: McGraw-Hill, 2001.

Herring, George C. "The Truman Administration and the Restoration of French Sovereignty in Indochina." *Diplomatic History* 1, no. 2 (1977): 97–117.

Hess, Gary R. "Franklin Roosevelt and Indochina." *The Journal of American History* 59, no. 2 (September 1972): 353–68.

Hess, Gary R. "The First American Commitment in Indochina: The Acceptance of the 'Bao Dai Solution', 1950." *Diplomatic History* 2, no. 4 (1978): 331–50.

Hitchcock, William I. *France Restored: Cold War Diplomacy and the Quest for Leadership in Europe, 1944–1954*. Chapel Hill, NC: University of North Carolina Press, 1998.

"Ho Chi Minh Archive." https://www.marxists.org/reference/archive/ho-chi-minh/ (accessed 8 February 2016).

"Indo-Chinese Form New Rebel Faction." *New York Times*, 2 October 1945.

Jabri, V. "Michel Foucault's Analytics of War: The Social, the International, and the Racial." *International Political Sociology* 1, no. 1 (2007): 67–81.

Jabri, Vivienne. *Discourses on Violence: Conflict Analysis Reconsidered*. Manchester: Manchester University Press, 1996.

Jabri, Vivienne. *The Postcolonial Subject: Claiming Politics/Governing Others in Late Modernity*. Abingdon: Routledge, 2012.

Jackson, Robert. *The Malayan Emergency: The Commonwealth's Wars 1948–1966*. London: Routledge, Chapman & Hall, Incorporated, 1991.

Kerkvliet, Benedict J. *The Huk Rebellion: A Study of Peasant Revolt in the Philippines*. Lanham, MD: Rowman & Littlefield Publishers, 2002.

Kristeva, J. *Black Sun: Depression and Melancholia*. Reprint edition. New York, NY: Columbia University Press, 1992.

Kristeva, Julia. *Desire in Language: A Semiotic Approach to Literature and Art*. Edited by Leon S. Roudiez and Alice Jardine. Translated by Thomas Gora. New York: Columbia University Press, 1980.

LaFeber, Walter. "Roosevelt, Churchill, and Indochina: 1942–45." *The American Historical Review* 80, no. 5 (1975): 1277–95.

La Fontaine, Jean de. *Recueil 1*, Livre 5, Fable 5.

Lawrence, Mark Atwood. *Assuming the Burden: Europe and the American Commitment to War in Vietnam*. Berkeley: University of California Press, 2005.

Lawrence, Mark Atwood. "Transnational Coalition-Building and the Making of the Cold War in Indochina, 1947–1949." *Diplomatic History* 26, no. 3 (2002): 453–80.

"Malayan Police Hold 600 in Anti-Red Raids." *New York Times*, 22 June 1948.

Marr, David. *Vietnam: State, War, and Revolution*. Berkeley: University of California Press, 2013.

Marr, David G. *Vietnam 1945: The Quest for Power*. Berkeley: University of California Press, 1995.

Marvel, W. Macy. "Drift and Intrigue: United States Relations with the Viet-Minh, 1945." *Millennium: Journal of International Studies*, 1975, 10–27.

Minh, Ho Chi. *The Selected Works of Ho Chi Minh*. New York: Prism Key, 2011.

Morris, E. *The Fog of War: Eleven Lessons from the Life of Robert McNamara*. Documentary. Sony Pictures, 2003.

Mus, Paul. *Le Destin de l'Union Française de l'Indochine a l'Afrique*. Paris: Éditions du Seuil, 1954.

Mus, Paul. "The Role of the Village in Vietnamese Politics." *Pacific Affairs* 22, no. 3 (1949): 265–72.

Mus, Paul. *Viet-Nam: Sociologie d'une Guerre*. Paris: Seuil, 1952.

Navarre, Henri. *Agonie de l'Indochine: (1953–1954)*. Libr. Plon, 1956.

Neumann, I. B. "'A Speech That the Entire Ministry May Stand for,' or: Why Diplomats Never Produce Anything New." *International Political Sociology* 1, no. 2 (1 June 2007): 183–200.

Neumann, I. B. *At Home with the Diplomats: Inside a European Foreign Ministry*. Ithaca, NY: Cornell University Press, 2012.

Neumann, I. B. "Returning Practice to the Linguistic Turn: The Case of Diplomacy." *Millenium: Journal of International Studies* 31, no. 3 (2002): 627.

Nietzsche, Friedrich Wilhelm. "Genealogy of Morals." In *Basic Writings of Nietzsche*. New York: Modern Library, 2000.

Nietzsche, Friedrich Wilhelm. *Human, All Too Human: A Book for Free Spirits; Part I.* Translated by Alexander Harvey, 2011. http://www.gutenberg.org/ebooks/38145

Orellana, Pablo de. "Hand of the Prince: How Diplomacy Writes Subjects, Territory, Time and Conflict." King's College London, 2015. KCL Library.

Orellana, Pablo de. "Struggles over Identity in Diplomacy: 'Commie Terrorists' Contra 'Imperialists' in Western Sahara." *International Relations* 29, no. 4 (1 December 2015): 477–99.

Remme, Tilman. "Britain and Regional Cooperation in South-East Asia, 1945–1949." PhD, London School of Economics and Political Science (United Kingdom), 1990. http://etheses.lse.ac.uk/1138/

Romaniuk, Scott, Francis Grice, and Stewart Webb, eds. *The Palgrave Handbook of Global Counterterrorism Policy*. London: Palgrave Macmillan, 2016.

Roskolenko, Harry. "Communism in Vietnam: Recent Statements Queried, Role of French in That Country Criticized." *New York Times*, 7 July 1948, sec. BOOKS.

Said, E. W. *Culture and Imperialism*. New York: Vintage, 1993.

Said, Edward. *Reflections on Exile: And Other Literary and Cultural Essays*. London: Granta Books, 2012.

Said, Edward W. 'Arabesque.' *New Statesman and Society* 7 (1990).

Said, Edward W. *Orientalism*. London: Penguin, 2003.

Said, Edward W. "Representing the Colonized: Anthropology's Interlocutors." *Critical Inquiry* 15, no. 2 (1 January 1989): 205–25.

Salisbury, Harrison E. "Image and Reality in Indochina." *Foreign Aff.* 49 (1970): 381.

Sbrega, John J. "'First Catch Your Hare': Anglo-American Perspectives on Indochina during the Second World War." *Journal of Southeast Asian Studies* 14, no. 01 (1983): 63–78.

Sending, Ole Jacob, Vincent Pouliot, and Iver B. Neumann. "Future of Diplomacy, The." *International Journal* 66 (2011, 2010): 527.

Shapiro, M. J. *The Politics of Representation: Writing Practices in Biography, Photography, and Policy Analysis*. Madison, WI: University of Wisconsin Press, 1988.

Shapiro, Michael J. *Language and Politics*. New York, NY: New York University Press, 1984.

Shapiro, Michael J. "Literary Production as a Politicizing Practice." *Political Theory*, 1984, 387–422.

Shapiro, Michael J. *Reading the Postmodern Polity: Political Theory as Textual Practice*. Minneapolis: University of Minnesota Press, 1992.

Shapiro, Michael J. "Representing World Politics: The Sport/War Intertext." In *International/Intertextual Relations*, edited by James Der Derian and Michael J. Shapiro, 69–96. Lexington, MA: Lexington Books, 1989.

Shapiro, Michael J. "Strategic Discourse/Discursive Strategy: The Representation of 'Security Policy' in the Video Age." *International Studies Quarterly*, 1990, 327–40.

Shapiro, M. J., and H. R Alker. *Challenging Boundaries: Global Flows, Territorial Identities*. Minneapolis, MN: University of Minnesota Press, 1996.

Simms, Brendan. *Europe: The Struggle for Supremacy, from 1453 to the Present.* New York: Basic Books, 2013.

Siracusa, Joseph. "Lessons of Viet-Nam and the Future of American Foreign Policy." *Australian Journal of International Affairs* 30, no. 2 (1976): 227–37.

Siracusa, Joseph M. "The United States, Viet-Nam, and the Cold War: A Reappraisal." *Journal of Southeast Asian Studies* 5, no. 1 (1974): 82–101.

Spargo, Mary (*Post* Reporter) "Mere 14 Million Communists Are Altering Globe." *The Washington Post (1923–1954)*, 23 May 1948, sec. CURRENT EVENTS National and Foreign EDITORIALS Art Books.

Spector, R. "Allied Intelligence and Indochina, 1943–1945." *The Pacific Historical Review* 51, no. 1 (1982): 23–50.

"The War In Indo-China." *New York Times*, 23 June 1947.

TIMES, C. L. SULZBERGER Special to THE NEW YORK. "Indo-China Revolt Fateful to France: Other Empire Areas Watching Outcome of Dissidence in Troubled East Asia." *New York Times*, 25 December 1946.

TIMES, CHARLES E. EGAN By Wireless to THE NEW YORK. "Improved Empire Sought by French." *New York Times*, 4 July 1945.

TIMES, DANA ADAMS SCHMIDT By Wireless to THE NEW YORK. "Indo-China to Gain Limited Autonomy: De Gaulle Reveals Post-War Plan-Move Is Regarded as Anticipating Trusteeship." *New York Times*, 24 March 1945.

TIMES, HAROLD CALLENDER By Wireless to THE NEW YORK. "British Aid Is Seen for French Empire." *New York Times*, 19 August 1945.

TIMES, HAROLD CALLENDER Special to THE NEW YORK. "Blum Aims to End Viet Nam Revolts before Any Parley." *New York Times*, 27 December 1946.

TIMES, HAROLD CALLENDER Special to THE NEW YORK. "Colonial Problem Growing in France." *New York Times*, 20 December 1946.

TIMES, LANSING WARREN By Wireless to THE NEW YORK. "New Colony Plan Outlined in Paris: Change in Ministry's Name Symbolic of Program for Creating Empire Union." *New York Times*, 29 January 1946.

TIMES, ROBERT TRUMBULL Special to THE NEW YORK. "French Face All-out Colonial War: Indo-China Is Aflame With Many Incidents." *New York Times*, 29 December 1946, sec. The Week In Review.

TIMES, ROBERT TRUMBULL Special to THE NEW YORK. "Totalitarian Character of Ho's Regime Cited as Evidence – Japanese Are Said to Have Installed Viet Minh as 'Time Bomb.'" *New York Times*, 23 January 1947.

TIMES, Special to THE NEW YORK. "French to Discuss Indo-Chinese Reds." *New York Times*, 27 November 1946.

TIMES, Special to THE NEW YORK. "Government Takes Stern Steps To Stop Red Disorder in Malaya," 17 June 1948.

TIMES, W. H. LAWRENCE Special to THE NEW YORK. "U.S. Avoids Stand in Indies Dispute." *New York Times*, 14 November 1945.

Tizac, Andrée Françoise Caroline d' Ardenne de, Andrée Viollis, and André Malraux. *Indochine S.O.S.* Gallimard, 1935.

"To Win the Peace: Charter Takes Shape Foreign Ministers Leave Action Against Aggressors Question of Colonies." *New York Times*, 13 May 1945, sec. The Week In Review.

Tomaru, J. *The Postwar Rapprochement of Malaya and Japan 1945–61: The Roles of Britain and Japan in South-East Asia.* New York: Springer, 2000.

Tønnesson, S. "The Longest Wars: Indochina 1945–75." *Journal of Peace Research* 22, no. 1 (1985): 9–29.

Tønnesson, S. *Vietnam 1946: How the War Began.* Berkeley: University of California Press, 2010.

Tønnesson, Stein. *The Vietnamese Revolution of 1945: Roosevelt, Ho Chi Minh and de Gaulle in World at War.* London: PRIO Sage, 1991.

Tran, Nhung Tuyet, and Anthony Reid. *Viet Nam: Borderless Histories.* Madison, WI: University of Wisconsin Press, 2006.

"Transcript of Truman Doctrine Address to Congress (1947)." https://www. ourdocuments.gov/doc.php?doc=81&page=transcript (accessed 29 August 2016).

Trumbull, Robert. "Cominform Is in Sight for Southeastern Asia." *New York Times*, 18 July 1948, sec. Review of the Week editorials.

Turpin, Frédéric. *De Gaulle, Les Gaullistes et l'Indochine: 1940–1956.* Les Indes savantes, 2005.

United States Department of State. *Foreign Service List (Volume 1945).* Washington, DC: U.S. Government Printing Office, 1945.

Van Giau, Tran. "The Vietnamese Working Class," 1957.

Varga, Daniel. "Léon Pignon, l'homme-clé de la solution Bao Dai et de l'implication des États-Unis dans la Guerre d'Indochine," 2009. https://doi.org/10.3406/outre.2009.4426

Vu, Tuong. "'It's Time for the Indochinese Revolution to Show Its True Colours': The Radical Turn of Vietnamese Politics in 1948." *Journal of Southeast Asian Studies* 40, no. 03 (2009): 519–42.

Vu, Tuong. "Triumphs or Tragedies: A New Perspective on the Vietnamese Revolution." *Journal of Southeast Asian Studies* 45, no. 02 (2014): 236–57.

Vu, Tuong. *Vietnam's Communist Revolution: The Power and Limits of Ideology.* New York, NY: Cambridge University Press, 2016.

Whitmore, John K. "Literati Culture and Integration in Dai Viet, c. 1430–c. 1840." *Modern Asian Studies* 31, no. 3 (July 1997): 665–87. https://doi.org/10.1017/S0026749X00017108

Wodak, Ruth, and Michael Meyer, eds. *Methods for Critical Discourse Analysis.* Second edition. London: SAGE Publications Ltd, 2009.

Young, Marilyn B., and Robert Buzzanco. *A Companion to the Vietnam War.* Hoboken, NJ: John Wiley & Sons, 2008.

Index

Lightning Source UK Ltd.
Milton Keynes UK
UKHW021135080320
359953UK00006B/830

9 781784 538972